产学研合作创新组织模式比较研究

基于中国和奥地利的典型案例分析

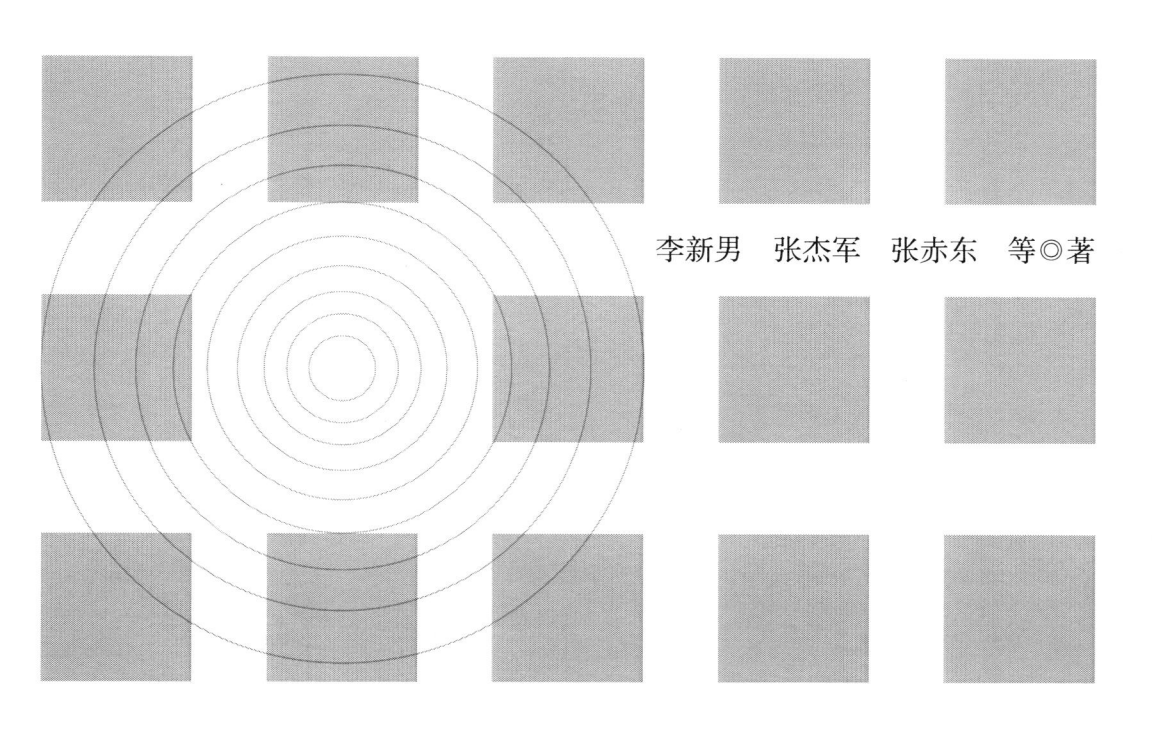

李新男　张杰军　张赤东　等◎著

知识产权出版社
Intellectual Property Publishing House
全国百佳图书出版单位

责任编辑：刘　爽　　　　　　责任校对：韩秀天
封面设计：杨晓霞　　　　　　责任出版：卢运霞

图书在版编目（CIP）数据

产学研合作创新组织模式比较研究：基于中国和奥地利的典型案例分析/李新男等著 . —北京：知识产权出版社，2014.1
　ISBN 978 - 7 - 80247 - 958 - 6

Ⅰ.①产… Ⅱ.①李… Ⅲ.①产学研一体化—对比研究—中国、奥地利　Ⅳ.①G640

中国版本图书馆 CIP 数据核字（2013）第 273153 号

产学研合作创新组织模式比较研究

李新男　张杰军　张赤东　等/著

出版发行：	知识产权出版社	邮　编：	100088
社　　址：	北京市海淀区马甸南村1号	邮　箱：	bjb@cnipr.com
网　　址：	http：//www.ipph.cn	传　真：	010－82005070/82000893
发行电话：	010－82000860 转 8101/8102	责编邮箱：	Liushuang@cnipr.com
责编电话：	010－82000860 转 8125	经　销：	新华书店及相关销售网点
印　　刷：	北京中献拓方科技发展有限公司	印　张：	16.25
开　　本：	787mm×1092mm　1/16	印　次：	2014 年 1 月第 1 次印刷
版　　次：	2014 年 1 月第 1 版	定　价：	45.00 元
字　　数：	356 千字		
ISBN 978－7－80247－958－6			

出版权专有　侵权必究
如有印装质量问题，本社负责调换。

本书在
中国科学技术部和奥地利联邦交通、创新与技术部资助合作研究项目
"中国和奥地利产学研合作组织模式比较研究"
报告基础上完成

前　　言

创新理论和实证研究都证明，科学界和产业界之间交互的知识流动对一国产业创新具有重要作用。国家创新系统（NIS）被定义为联合或单独致力于新技术开发和传播的不同研究机构集合，目的在于为政府部门在建立和执行影响创新过程的政策中提供框架。因此，这一系统是创造、储存、转移各种知识、能力以及定义新技术工艺的研究机构总和，并且这些机构之间彼此相关（Metcalfe，1995）。在国家创新系统中，企业与大学、科研院所之间创新网络的构建是至关重要的。

20 世纪 90 年代以来，促进产学研合作已经成为各国政府创新政策的核心内容之一。欧美国家的公共机构与私人机构合作（Public Private Partnerships，PPP）实践走在世界前列。政府通过为公私合作提供公共项目或服务，促进产业技术进步。奥地利政府在 1990 年推出了公私合作计划，其核心组成部分是卓越技术能力中心计划（COMET Programme）——通过项目支持产学研结合共建能力中心，并使其成为产学研联盟的实体化运作机构。这一措施成为欧盟公私合作实践的成功典范。为了充分发挥产学研各自的优势，加速科技成果转化，中国政府采取了一系列措施促进产学研结合，以强化产业技术创新活动。在中国科技部等多个部门的推动下，围绕重点产业技术创新的需要，产学研各方在自愿基础上组建了若干"产业技术创新战略联盟"。这已经成为中国政府推进产学研合作的一项重要政策措施。

作为产学研合作创新组织的长期、稳定形式，中国产业技术创新战略联盟和奥地利卓越技术能力中心既具有很多的相似性，又有一定的差异性。对二者的比较研究，可为双方政府进一步优化促进产学研合作政策提供重要的参考依据。因此，在中国科技部和奥地利联邦交通、创新与技术部的资助下，中国科学技术发展战略研究院（CASTED）和奥地利技术研究院（AIT）组成跨国研究团队，开展了对中国产业技术创新战略联盟和奥地利卓越技术能力中心的比较研究。

这次比较研究具有如下四个特征。

一是重调研。研究组对中国产业技术创新战略联盟和奥地利卓越技术能力中心进行了大量调研。书中内容基本都是第一手资料。调研分两个阶段开展：第一阶段是本国研究团队对本国联盟或卓越技术能力中心的调研，形成初步的调研报告；第二阶段是异地调研，双方分别派出调研组到对方国家进行实地调研，最后共同形成研究报告。

二是重比较。双方确立统一的分析框架，在充分讨论的基础上形成共识性的研究结论。在充分吸收创新研究理论与实证分析成果的基础上，基于产业技术创新战略联盟和卓越技术能力中心发展的实际情况，中奥双方课题组成员讨论设计比较研究和案例分析框架，指导案例调研，统领比较研究。在统一的分析框架下，两国课题组成员多次进行交流和讨论，对研究结论逐步达成共识。

三是重合作。研究是政府工作人员、研究者和产业技术创新战略联盟或卓越技术能力中心人员三方合作的研究成果。研究过程中，各方通力合作共同研究，从不同角度对研究提出分析建议。尤其是中国农业装备产业技术创新战略联盟、新一代煤（能源）化工产业技术创新战略联盟和钢铁可循环流程技术创新战略联盟等，从秘书长到工作人员都积极参与课题研究，并赴奥地利进行实地调研，为课题研究做出了卓有成效的工作。

四是重导向。比较研究具有十分明确的政策导向性。考察产业技术创新战略联盟或卓越技术能力中心发展的政策制度环境，将其与产业技术创新战略联盟或卓越技术能力中心的发展特征、趋势进行关联分析；考察政策制度的作用与影响，进而提出相关政策建议。

比较研究的成果是一项集体创造的成果。中国和奥地利产学研合作组织模式比较研究课题组的卓越努力得到了中国和奥地利政府的认可。作为中奥科技合作的这项重要成果在 2010 年上海世博会的奥地利科技周活动中进行了展示。并举行了大型国际学术研讨会。参加这个研究团队的人员包括：中方课题组成员李新男、姚为克、叶建忠、郭铁成、张杰军、苏靖、邢继俊、汤富强、赵慧君、张赤东、董桂兰、邸晓燕、马驰、赵捷、刘东、王庆元、吴芳、方宪法、韩伟、刘家强、杨骅、吴玲、岳文亮、阮军、周雪燕、吴海华、王金勇、马曙娜、李晓黎、王鄂生、郝建群等；奥方课题组成员 Inglof Schädler、Josef Fröhlich、Klaus Kubeczko、Thomas Scherngell、Manfred Horvat、Alexander Unkart、Rupert Pichler、Gottfried Göritzer、Richard Schanner、Reinhold Ebner、Gerald Schatz、Rudolf Scheidl、Werner Scherf、Simon Grasser、Otto Starzer、Theresia Vogel - Lahner 等。

在比较研究的过程中，中方李新男、张杰军、张赤东和奥方 Inglof Schädler、Josef Fröhlich、Thomas Scherngell 等全程参与组织与研究工作，包括课题立项、总体设计、制定研究框架、调研与研讨等，负责报告研究与撰写。中国农业装备产业技术创新战略联盟、新一代煤（能源）化工产业技术创新战略联盟和钢铁可循环流程技术创新战略联盟以及奥地利的 ACCM、MPPE、CTR 的主要负责人积极参与课题研讨和报告撰写，并提供了大量的素材和建议。在中奥双方研究与交流中，张杰军、张赤东、邸晓燕、董桂兰和 Josef Fröhlich、Thomas Scherngell 等承担了浩繁的中-英、德-英的互译工作。在此对每个研究人员的卓越工作表示感谢！

本书是在该项研究成果的基础上编写的。在完成比较研究后，李新男、张杰军和张赤东组织完成了"中国产业技术创新战略联盟跟踪调研"课题研究（2010～2011 年）；邸晓燕博士参与课题研究并在此基础上完成了"产业技术创新战略联盟的激励与规制政策研究"博士后的出站论文。这些后续工作不仅让我们对中国产学研合作创新理论与实践有了更多的了解和认识，更丰富了中国产业技术创新战略联盟案例分析，深化了相关产学研合作组织模式比较研究。在本书最后撰写过程中，李新男、张杰军和张赤东等对全书内容、结构进行了整体设计，对相关内容进行了筛选。最后，全书由李新男、张杰军和张赤东完成统稿工作。

在此，我们对奥地利联邦交通、创新和技术部部长 Doris BURES 女士、中国科学技术部曹建林副部长、科技部国际合作司靳晓明司长及中国驻奥地利使馆叶建忠参赞、李刚同志等对本项目工作的研究给予重要的支持和指导，深表谢意！

对在本书研究与撰写过程中，中国科技部和奥地利联邦交通、创新与技术部给予的资助，对中国科学技术发展战略研究院、奥地利技术研究院给予的大力支持，谨致谢意！

对参与本书研究的案例联盟以及半导体照明产业技术创新战略联盟、TD－SCDMA产业联盟、汽车轻量化技术创新战略联盟、长风开放标准平台软件联盟等参联盟给予的大力支持，也谨致谢意！

本研究由于受制于信息收集，尤其是奥地利方面信息的局限性，故在内容、观点等方面难免有不足和准确性不够的缺陷，恳请读者提出宝贵的批评意见和修改建议。

作者

2012 年 12 月

目 录

1 导言 ··· 1
  1.1 研究目的和意义 ··· 2
  1.2 实证框架 ·· 3

2 中国和奥地利支持产学研合作的政策措施 ······················ 7
  2.1 中国政府促进产学研合作的政策措施 ······················ 8
  2.2 奥地利产学研合作促进政策 ···································· 17

3 中国产业技术创新战略联盟案例 ······································ 23
  3.1 农业装备产业技术创新战略联盟 ···························· 24
  3.2 新一代煤（能源）化工产业技术创新战略联盟 ······ 37
  3.3 钢铁可循环流程技术创新战略联盟 ························ 48
  3.4 小结 ··· 53

4 奥地利能力中心案例 ·· 59
  4.1 奥地利机电一体化能力中心 ···································· 60
  4.2 材料、工艺和产品工程综合研究中心 ···················· 71
  4.3 卡琳西亚先进传感器技术研究中心 ························ 82
  4.4 小结 ··· 90

5 中奥案例比较分析 ·· 95
  5.1 共同点 ··· 96
  5.2 差异点 ··· 98
  5.3 小结 ··· 100

6 总结与展望 ··· 103

6.1 研究成果 ·· 104
6.2 对中方政策的结论分析 ·· 105
6.3 对奥方政策的结论分析 ·· 106
6.4 研究展望 ·· 107

参考文献 ·· 109

1

导 言

目前，人们普遍认为科学界和产业界之间的合作是提升企业、地区以及国家经济竞争力和创新能力的关键所在。各种创新经济学理论和实证分析著作都强调公众和私营部门之间知识流动和互动研究的重要作用（Schartinger 等人，2002）。创新方法系统中也体现出了这一点（Lundvall，1992），即强调创新体系中的所有参与部门，特别是公司、大学、研究机构以及技术创新政策之间有效衔接的重要性。这个系统性视角的特点是专注于创新体系中的机构（正式与非正式的）和主体网络，这在创新系统的不同层面上决定了创新与学习的方向和速度（Asheim and Gertler，2005；Edquist，2005；Malerba，2005）。

在此背景下，激励企业、大学和研究机构之间合作研究活动成了近期制订技术创新政策的基本要素。许多国家都确立了政策计划，以促进科学界与产业界的合作。早期著名的例子是日本 1976 年的超大规模集成电路（Very Large Scale）、1982 年发起的欧洲信息技术研究发展战略计划（ESPRIT）、1983～1988 年在英国启动的信息技术 Alvey 计划、1984 年开始的欧洲 RTD 框架计划、1986 年韩国的半导体研发部门计划、1987 年美国政府成立的半导体制造技术产业联盟（SEMATECH），以及根据尤里卡计划于 1988 年成立的欧洲联合硅次微米始创会（JESSI）、1991 年美国发起的先进技术计划以及英国的法拉第伙伴计划。

20 世纪 90 年代中期，奥地利政府建立了正式的政策计划支持各种形式的产学研合作——尤为著名的是奥地利能力中心计划（CCP），后来发展成卓越技术能力中心（COMET）。在过去的五年中，中国的科技政策不断完善产学研合作创新的政策措施，尤为突出的是在 2007 年后推出了一系列促进产业技术创新战略联盟（ITISA）的政策措施。

奥地利采用的政策措施是新的以项目为基础的支持行动，目标是鼓励自下而上的企业、大学和科研院所之间的合作。值得注意的是，在 OECD（2004）创新系统方法的背景中，奥地利的计划被称为具有革新性和影响力的激励科学界与工业界合作的政策措施。

中国的 ITISA 计划是开创产学研合作、构建创新全新模式的一项积极行动，力图在战略层面围绕产业技术创新链建立产学各方持续稳定的合作关系。与奥地利的计划不同的是，它清晰地聚焦于国家的战略需求，因此它与《国家中长期科学和技术发展规划纲要（2006～2020 年）》及该规划纲要中提出的 11 个重点领域密切相关。

1.1　研究目的和意义

该项目的目的是：基于公私合作伙伴关系的原则，探讨中国和奥地利的企业、大学和研究机构之间合作的组织模式。重点是关于中国和奥地利科学界与产业界合作的政策措施和组织模式的比较。在此之前,研究的目标是找出中奥科学界和工业界合作模式的共性与差异,从比较研究中得出政策启示。

该项目运用实证分析的案例研究。案例研究集中分析中奥产学研合作的具体案例,关注重点为合作的组织机制、治理结构和相应案例的法律框架(Scherngell etc,2010;张杰军等,2010)。中国的案例是中国科学技术部(MOST)指导建立的部分产业技术创新战略联盟(ITISA),包括农业装备产业技术创新战略联盟(TIPAAMI)、新一代煤(能源)化工产业技术创新战略联盟(ITISANCC)和钢铁可循环流程技术创新战略联盟(SARSPTI)。奥地利的案例包括奥地利机电一体化能力中心(ACCM),材料、加工、产品设计集成研究中心(MPPE),卡林西亚高级传感技术技能研究中心(CTR)。这些是奥地利联邦交通、创新和技术部(BMVIT)发起的卓越技术能力中心(COMET)项目的一部分,是目前奥地利最大的支持产学研合作的政策措施。

这一项目的重要性得到了最近集中研究科学界和产业界科学文献的重视。大量的理论和实证研究都表明,分析由公共政策计划形成的科学界与产业界合作的具体案例很重要,以便增强我们对科学界和产业界部门之间的合作研发机制的理解。因此,为促进科学界与产业界合作和相关政策的发展,选择中国 ITISA 案例和奥地利的 COMET 案例进行实证分析具有重大的科学与战略意义。

1.2 实证框架

我们所采用的分析框架,特别强调治理结构和责任、内部和外部关系以及知识创造和传播的过程。实证分析通过面对面访谈和收集分析被选中案例及其他机构提供的材料来进行。案例分析是中奥产学研合作组织模式比较研究的基础。

下面,简要介绍分析框架的主要组成部分。

(1) 目标及组织形式
- 项目的战略目标
  ——围绕战略目标集成资源
  ——衍生目标和该项目中应用的方法
- 选定案例的战略目标
- 选定案例的法律组织形式

(2) 治理结构和权责关系
- 治理结构和内部管理
- 合作各方之间可能妨碍交互、整合或转化的最严重问题
——利润、市场份额与学术卓越
——短期考虑与知识创造的长期积累
——排除竞争对手与知识公布
- 哪种治理结构和规则可以在联盟/中心中用来整合不同的个体？
- 不同层面上的合作组织
- 工作计划和任务/项目选择的组织
- 研发管理、控制和营销的特征
- 组织构架、权利和规则（例如知识产权问题）、行为准则、信息流动，这些特别有利于刺激新知识或最终创新的产生
- 部门、学科领域、规模或地区性的差异特征

(3) 内部成员及其与政府的关系
- 核心成员和发起者的确定
- 关系演进，它们之间的关系对联盟/中心发展的影响
- 相关政府部门的作用
- 联盟/中心的历史
——建立该中心/联盟过程中的关键事件（时间维度）
——事件演进过程中的障碍

(4) 知识产生与技术扩散
- 用于知识生产的共同资源
——人力资源
——机械，设备
——资金
- 合作成果的管理与扩散
——共同的产品
——共同的工艺
——共同的专利

——共同的研究成果

——联合组织的科学会议、研讨会等

——联合培养学生

——人力资源的交流和传播

(5) 法律和制度条件

- 不同领域（如社会、经济、科技等）的法律法规的相容性。奥地利的研究案例：

——大学组织法

——公共研究机构法

——就业法

——大学和研究机构融资规定

——欧盟竞争法

——税法

- 制度的作用和适用性评估

(6) 融资及资金管理

- 选定案例中融资和费用分担的不同模式
- 财政资源的管理和使用模式

2

中国和奥地利支持产学研合作的政策措施

本章将讨论中国和奥地利支持产学研合作的政策演变。产学研合作政策旨在解决科学界和产业界相互作用中创新体系的缺失环节。在介绍产业技术创新战略联盟（ITISA）之前，在 2.1 节中先分四个阶段详细介绍中国政府促进产学研合作政策的演变过程，并重点介绍近年来中国推动产学研合作最重要的举措——产业技术创新战略联盟的构建与发展。然后，在 2.2 节中讨论 20 世纪 90 年代以来奥地利支持科学界和产业界合作为目的的公私合作伙伴（PPP）计划的构建，介绍卓越技术能力中心（COMET）——奥地利最重要的支持科学界和产业界合作的项目的主要特征。

2.1 中国政府促进产学研合作的政策措施

产学研合作是技术创新体系的重要组成部分。促进产学研合作政策的演变体现了人们对技术创新体系认识的不断深入，特别是国家创新体系理论的发展。

近 30 年来，中国促进产学研合作政策是随着实践的不断深入而不断调整的。本节将促进产学研合作政策的演进情况分为两部分：首先简要回顾中国促进产学研合作的宏观政策，然后介绍专门针对产业技术创新战略联盟的政策。

2.1.1 促进产学研合作的宏观政策

（1）以改革推动产学研结合阶段（1985～1992 年）

1978 年，中国共产党十一届三中全会做出了实行经济体制改革的决定。与此相适应，科技体制也进行了改革。1985 年，以《中共中央关于科学技术体制改革的决定》为标志，我国科技体制改革进入新时期。该决定明确提出，要改革拨款制度，从资金供应上改变科研机构对行政部门的依附关系，使其主动为经济建设服务，转化科技成果；要开放技术市场，在政策和法律上承认技术成果也是商品，建立按照价值规律有偿转让的机制。国家先后颁布了《中华人民共和国专利法》、《中华人民共和国技术合同法》及相应的实施条例，为技术开发、技术转让、技术咨询、技术服务等各种技术交易制定了基本规则。改革科学研究的组织结构，改变研究机构与企业相分离，研究、设计、教育、生产脱节、军民分割、部门分割、地区分割的状况；大力加强企业的技术吸收与开发能力和技术成果转化为生产能力的中间环节，促进研究机构、设计机构、高等学校、企业之间的协作和联合，并使各方面的科学技术力量形成合理的纵深配置。

这一时期的产学研结合模式选择，特别强调应使科研机构进入企业或使两者实现紧密联合。1986年,《国务院关于进一步推进科技体制改革的若干规定》指出,以技术开发工作为主的大多数科研机构,特别是从事产品开发的科研机构,都应逐步进入企业、企业集团或与其实行紧密联合,研究开发经费应逐步依靠企业或企业集团从销售总额中提取。1988年,《国务院关于深化科技体制改革若干问题的决定》指出,科研机构可以和企业互相承包、租赁、参股、兼并,实行联合经营,或进入企业、企业集团,或发展成科研型企业等。

为了促进科技成果的转化,加强产学研结合,国家先后设立了一系列科技计划,着力解决国民经济和社会发展中的重大科技问题,加强科技成果向生产力转化的中间环节,促进科技成果尽快转化为生产力,使科技为经济建设服务。

(2) 探索市场经济体制下产学研结合新形式阶段(1992~1999年)

1992年,"十四大"明确提出把建立社会主义市场经济体制作为我国经济体制改革的目标。此后,对产学研结合的关注也从科技成果转化转向如何在市场经济体制下形成产学研有效结合机制。1992年,国家经贸委联合教育部、中科院共同实施了"产学研联合开发工程",是在国家层面上促进产学研结合的一大举措。

1992年国务院发布的《国家中长期科学技术发展纲领》提出,要通过多种方式推进企业之间,企业与研究开发机构、高等院校之间的横向联合,提倡以大中型企业为骨干,以优质名牌商品为龙头,通过科研和生产的联合,形成具备技术开发、生产、销售、服务功能的企业集团,特别要支持科技先导型或具有国际竞争力的企业集团。

1993年颁布的《中华人民共和国科学技术进步法》提出,应建立科学技术与经济有效结合的机制,国家鼓励企业建立和完善技术开发机构,鼓励企业与研究开发机构、高等院校联合和协作,增强研究开发、中间试验和工业性试验能力。国家鼓励和引导从事技术开发的研究开发机构单独或者与企业事业组织联合开发技术成果,实行技术、工业、贸易或者技术、农业、贸易一体化经营。这是我国第一次以法律形式提出鼓励产学研之间的联合和协作。

1994年,国家科委、国家体改委关于《适应社会主义市场经济发展深化科技体制改革实施要点》(国科发政字[1994]29号)提出继续鼓励研究开发机构以开发科技产业为目标,探索和实践技工贸、技农贸一体化经营。国家对这类机构在新产品、中试产品和技术性收入方面,实行扶植政策;支持科研机构与企业联合进行技术开发;支持有条件的科研机构直接进入大中型企业或企业集团,成为企业技术开发部或技术开发中心。同年，国家体改委、国家科技委和国家教委联合颁布了《关于高等学校发展科技产业的若干意见》，旨在规范和引导大学科技产业的发展走上健康有序的道路。

1995年，中共中央《关于加速科学技术进步的决定》中明确提出，要继续推动产、学、研结合，鼓励科研院所、高等学校的科技力量以多种形式进入企业或企业集团，参与企业的技术改造和技术开发。大中型企业要普遍建立健全技术开发机构，与科研院所、高等学校开展多种形式的合作，大力增强技术开发能力，逐步成为技术开发的主体。国务院《关于"九五"期间深化科学技术体制改革的决定》指出，"九五"期间，要初步建立起适应社会主义市场经济体制和科技自身发展规律的科技体制，形成科研、开发、生产、市场紧密结合的机制，建立以企业为主体、产学研相结合的技术开发体系和以科研机构、高等学校为主的科学研究体系以及社会化的科技服务体系，提高科技在国民经济中的贡献率。大中型企业和企业集团都应以市场为导向，逐步建立与科研机构、高等学校联合等多种形式的技术开发机构。

1996年我国颁布的《中华人民共和国促进科技成果转化法》（主席令第68号）提出，国家鼓励研究开发机构、高等院校等事业单位与生产企业相结合，联合实施科技成果转化。同时规定，国家财政用于科学技术、固定资产投资和技术改造的经费，应当有一定比例用于科技成果转化。国家鼓励设立科技成果转化基金或者风险基金，其资金来源由国家、地方、企业、事业单位以及其他组织或者个人提供，用于支持高投入、高风险、高产出的科技成果的转化，加速重大科技成果的产业化。

为了配合《中华人民共和国促进科技成果转化法》的实施，1999年国务院出台的《关于促进科技成果转化若干规定》提出：以高新技术成果向有限责任公司或非公司制企业出资入股的，高新技术成果的作价金额可达到公司或企业注册资本的35%（另有约定的除外）；科研机构、高等学校转化职务科技成果，应当依法对研究开发该项科技成果的职务科技成果完成人和为成果转化做出重要贡献的其他人员给予奖励。科研机构、高等学校的技术转让收入免征营业税。科研单位、高等学校服务于各业的技术成果转让、技术培训、技术咨询、技术承包所取得的技术性服务收入暂免征收所得税。

1999年，《科学技术部、财政部关于科技型中小企业技术创新基金的暂行规定》（办发[1999]47号）中，也明确了要优先支持产、学、研的联合创新，优先支持具有自主知识产权、高技术、高附加值、能大量吸纳就业、节能降耗、有利环境保护以及出口创汇的各类项目。

在这一阶段，由于中国确立了社会主义市场经济体制改革的目标，与之相适应的技术创新体系建设，推进产学研结合的政策都在探索之中。

(3) 探索新型产学研协作机制阶段（1999～2006年）

1999年，中共中央、国务院发布了《关于加强技术创新，发展高科技，实现产业化的决定》。该决定要求我国积极推进科技体制、教育体制和经济体制的配套改革，从根本上解决科技、教育与经济脱节的问题。同时提出，大中型企业要加强与高等学校、科研机构的联合协作。根据优势互补、利益共享的原则，建立双边、多边技术协作机制，通过相互兼职、培训等形式，加强不同单位科技人员的交流。企业研究开发经费要有一定比例用于产学研合作。明确提出支持发展高等学校科技园区，培育一批知识和智力密集、具有市场竞争优势的高新技术企业和企业集团，使产学研更加紧密地结合。

1999年，《中共中央关于国有企业改革和发展若干重大问题的决定》指出，要形成以企业为中心的技术创新体系，推进产学研结合，鼓励科研机构和大专院校的科研力量进入企业和企业集团，强化应用技术的开发和推广，增加中间试验投入，促进科技成果向现实生产力的转化。2000年国家经贸委发布《关于加速实施技术创新工程形成以企业为中心的技术创新体系的意见》（国经贸技术［2000］60号）提出要加强"产学研"联合机制建设，促进和鼓励大多数国有大型企业与高等院校、科研院所建立开放的、稳定的合作关系，通过成果转让、委托开发、联合开发、共建技术开发机构和科技型企业实体等，开展多种形式的产学研联合，逐步形成以企业为主体、高等院校和科研院所广泛参与、利益共享、风险共担的产学研联合机制。2002年，《国家产业技术政策》（国经贸技术［2002］444号）提出，要建立以企业为中心、风险共担的产学研结合机制。建立企业与大学、科研院所的产学研联合体，形成以市场为导向的研究开发体系和开放式的产学研合作机制。

2000年12月，科学技术部印发的《关于加强与科技有关的知识产权保护和管理工作的若干意见》（国科发政发［2000］569号）提出，要通过技术合同中知识产权归属与利益分享的合理约定，进一步加强产学研结合，提升科技成果转化能力和实际效果；要逐步调整科技成果的知识产权归属政策，除以保证重大国家利益、国家安全和社会公共利益为目的，并由科技计划项目主管部门与承担单位在合同中明确约定外，执行国家科技计划项目所形成科技成果的知识产权，可以由承担单位所有。2002年3月颁布的《关于国家科研计划项目研究成果知识产权管理的若干规定》（国办发［2002］30号）明确规定，科研项目研究成果及其形成的知识产权，除涉及国家安全、国家利益和重大社会公共利益的以外，国家授予科研项目承担单位享有所有权。国家根据需要保留无偿使用、开发、使之有效利用和获取收益的权利；同时，在特定情况下，政府可以行使介入权。

财政部、国家税务总局联合印发的《关于促进科技成果转化有关税收政策的通知》（财税字〔1999〕45号）规定，对于科研机构的技术转让收入继续免征营业税，对高等学校的技术转让收入自1999年5月1日起免征营业税；科研机构、高等学校服务于各业的技术成果转让、技术培训、技术咨询、技术服务、技术承包所取得的技术性服务收入暂免征收企业所得税；自1999年7月1日起，科研机构、高等学校转化职务科技成果以股份或出资比例等股权形式给予个人奖励，获奖人在取得股份、出资比例时，暂不缴纳个人所得税；取得按股份、出资比例分红或转让股权、出资比例所得时，应依法缴纳个人所得税。

国家级科技奖励制度也强调科技成果的应用，其中包含了促进产学研结合的内容。2003年修订的《国家科学技术奖励条例》规定，国家最高科学技术奖授予在当代科学技术前沿取得重大突破或者在科学技术发展中有卓越建树的，同时在科学技术创新、科学技术成果转化和高技术产业化中，创造巨大经济效益或者社会效益的科技工作者。国家科学技术进步奖授予在应用推广先进科学技术成果，完成重大科学技术工程、计划、项目等方面，做出突出贡献的公民、组织。

（4）产学研合作提升至国家战略高度的新阶段（2006年至今）

从2006年的全国科技大会到2012年的全国科技创新大会，产学研合作已经成为我国实施创新驱动发展战略的核心议题，是推进技术创新体系建设的重要核心内容。

2006年召开的全国科技大会提出要建设创新型国家。在大会上发布的《中共中央国务院关于实施科技规划纲要，增强自主创新能力的决定》提出，要建立以企业为主体、市场为导向、产学研相结合的技术创新体系；大力推进产学研相结合，鼓励和支持企业同科研院所、高等院校联合建立研究开发机构、产业技术联盟等技术创新组织。产学研结合作为技术创新体系的重要组成部分，被提到了前所未有的战略高度。《国家中长期科学和技术发展规划纲要（2006—2020年）》提出，只有产学研结合，才能更有效配置科技资源，激发科研机构的创新活力，并使企业获得持续创新的能力。必须在大幅度提高企业自身技术创新能力的同时，建立科研院所与高等院校积极围绕企业技术创新需求服务、产学研多种形式结合的新机制。该规划纲要建立了一系列促进产学研结合的优惠政策，包括税收激励、金融支持，鼓励产学研联合开展引进技术消化吸收再创新、依托转制院所和企业建设国家重点实验室等配套政策。这次全国科技大会标志着政府对产学研结合的政策推动进入了一个新时期。2006年，科技部、国资委和全国总工会三部委组织实施了以提高企业创新能力、推动产学研结合的"技术创新引导工程"。作为产学研结合的形式之一，产业技术创新战略联盟成为实施技术创新引导工程的重要载体。

"十二五"发展规划进一步强化了产学研合作在国家创新发展中的重要战略地位。《中华人民共和国国民经济和社会发展第十二个五年规划纲要》在"增强科技创新能力"中提出，要加快建立以企业为主体的技术创新体系，将联盟作为科技创新能力建设的重点。《国家"十二五"科学和技术发展规划》指出，在国家科技重大专项、科技支撑计划中，发挥产业技术创新战略联盟的作用，依托联盟突破一批关键共性技术；在国家创新体系建设中要深入实施国家技术创新工程，围绕重点产业、战略性新兴产业以及地方支柱产业和产业集群发展，推进产业技术创新战略联盟建设，构建产业技术创新链。此外，在国务院发布的《工业转型升级规划（2011－2015年）》，工业和信息化部发布的《高端装备制造业"十二五"发展规划》、《电子信息制造业"十二五"发展规划》等都将联盟作为推进产业技术创新的重要形式。

2012年在北京召开了规模空前的全国科技创新大会，中共中央、国务院发布《关于深化科技体制改革加快国家创新体系建设的意见》，就深化科技体制改革，加快国家创新体系建设的指导思想、主要原则和主要目标作出了全面部署。该意见中强调要强化企业技术创新主体地位，促进科技与经济紧密结合，其首要任务是建立企业主导产业技术研发创新的体制机制。该意见指出，加快建立企业为主体、市场为导向、产学研用紧密结合的技术创新体系，其中的一项重要举措是支持行业骨干企业与科研院所、高等学校联合组建技术研发平台和产业技术创新战略联盟，合作开展核心关键技术研发和相关基础研究，联合培养人才，共享科研成果。

为贯彻落实全国科技创新大会精神，2013年年初进一步发布了《国务院办公厅关于强化企业技术创新主体地位全面提升企业创新能力的意见》，其中提出以企业为主导发展产业技术创新战略联盟；支持行业骨干企业与科研院所、高等学校签订战略合作协议，建立联合开发、优势互补、成果共享、风险共担的产学研用合作机制，组建产业技术创新战略联盟；支持联盟按规定承担产业技术研发创新重大项目，制订技术标准，编制产业技术路线图，构建联盟技术研发、专利共享和成果转化推广的平台及机制；积极探索依托符合条件的联盟成员单位建设国家重点实验室；深入开展联盟试点，加强对联盟的分类指导和监督评估；围绕培育发展战略性新兴产业，结合实施国家科技重大专项，通过联盟研发重大创新产品，掌握核心关键技术，构建产业链；围绕改造提升传统产业，通过联盟开展共性技术攻关，解决制约产业升级的重大制造装备、关键零部件、基础原材料、基础工艺及高端分析检测仪器设备等难题；围绕发展现代服务业，通过联盟加强技术创新、商业模式创新和管理创新，培育现代服务业新业态。

2.1.2 推动产业技术创新战略联盟构建与发展的政策措施

支持产业技术创新战略联盟构建与发展的相关政策，从 2006 年至今，经历了大致四个步骤，同时随着联盟数量的增加、影响范围的扩大，支持方式也逐渐多样化。

（1）四家联盟试点的探索成立

2006 年，成立了由科技部、财政部、教育部、国家开发银行、全国总工会和国资委等六个部委组成的"推进产学研结合工作协调指导小组"。指导小组积极推动和鼓励产业技术创新战略联盟的构建和发展。政府推动产学研联盟构建的出发点是，以国家战略产业和区域支柱产业的技术创新需求为导向，以企业为主体，围绕产业技术创新链，运用市场机制集聚创新资源，实现企业、大学和科研机构等在战略层面的有效结合，共同突破产业发展的技术瓶颈。大学、科研机构或其他组织机构，以企业的发展需求和各方的共同利益为基础，以提升产业技术创新能力为目标，以具有法律约束力的契约为保障，形成联合开发、优势互补、利益共享、风险共担的技术创新合作组织。

2007 年 6 月 22 日，在上述六部委的大力推动下，农业装备产业技术创新战略联盟、新一代煤（能源）化工产业技术创新战略联盟、钢铁可循环流程技术创新战略联盟和煤炭开发利用技术创新战略联盟等四家产业技术创新战略联盟正式成立。这是继创新型企业建设工作开展后，实施"技术创新引导工程"的又一项重大举措。

（2）出台鼓励联盟构建的指导意见

2008 年，在总结上述四家产业技术创新战略联盟试点经验的基础上，科技部、财政部等六部委发布了《关于推动产业技术创新战略联盟构建的指导意见》，就产业技术创新战略联盟的意义、构建原则、构建条件、政府的推动作用等做出了界定，为构建产业技术创新战略联盟提供了政策方向。

该指导意见明确指出，产业技术创新战略联盟是指由企业、大学、科研机构或其他组织机构，以企业的发展需求和各方的共同利益为基础，以提升产业技术创新能力为目标，以具有法律约束力的契约为保障而形成的联合开发、优势互补、利益共享、风险共担的技术创新合作组织。推动产业技术创新战略联盟发展，有利于提高产学研结合的组织化程度，在战略层面建立持续稳定、有法律保障的合作关系；有利于整合产业技术创新资源，引导创新要素向优势企业集聚；有利于保障科研与生产紧密衔接，实现创新成果的快速产业化；有利于促进技术集成创新，推动产业结构优化升级。

该指导意见也指出，依据《中华人民共和国合同法》，构建联盟应具备以下基本条件：①要由企业、大学和科研机构等多个独立法人组成；②要有具有法律约束力的联盟协议，协议中有明确的技术创新目标，落实成员单位之间的任务分工；③要设立决策、咨询和执行等组织机构，建立有效的决策与执行机制，明确联盟对外承担责任的主体；④要健全经费管理制度；⑤要建立利益保障机制；⑥要建立开放发展机制。

对于联盟构建的行业领域的选择，优先鼓励在《规划纲要》提出的能源、水和矿产资源、环境、农业、制造业、交通运输业、信息产业及现代服务业、人口与健康、城镇化与城市发展、公共安全和国防等11个优先领域中组建联盟。同时还鼓励在新材料、新能源、信息产业、电动汽车、生物医药、节能环保和海洋等新兴产业上组建联盟。

（3）出台规范联盟发展的实施办法

2009年科技部发布了《关于推动产业技术创新战略联盟构建与发展的实施办法（试行）》，对联盟的构建、试点工作做出了明确规范，营造有利于联盟发展的政策环境，探索支持联盟构建和发展的有效措施。该实施办法指出，参加试点工作的联盟要积极探索建立产学研合作的信用机制、责任机制和利益机制，探索承担国家重大技术创新任务的组织模式和运行机制，探索整合资源构建产业技术创新平台、服务广大中小企业，探索率先落实国家自主创新政策，发挥行业技术创新的引领和带动作用，为更多联盟的建立和发展积累经验。

同年，经科技部等六部委的再次评审，在《关于选择一批产业技术创新战略联盟开展试点工作的通知》中正式公布了第一批产业技术创新战略联盟试点36家联盟名单。2010年6月，《关于选择部分产业技术创新战略联盟开展试点工作的通知》发布，又选择了20家符合条件的联盟开展试点工作，使试点联盟共增至56家。2012年4月，《关于发布2012年度产业技术创新战略联盟试点名单的通知》中再次发布新增的39家联盟试点名单❶，至此试

---

❶ 参见科技部网站（www.most.gov.cn）或中国产业技术创新战略联盟网（www.citisa.org）。

点联盟范围进一步扩大，联盟试点总数增加至 95 家。

至 2010 年 6 月，科技部、财政部等六部门已确定开展试点工作的这 56 家产业技术创新战略联盟是：

1. 钢铁可循环流程技术创新战略联盟
2. 新一代煤（能源）化工产业技术创新战略联盟
3. 煤炭开发利用技术创新战略联盟
4. 农业装备产业技术创新战略联盟
5. TD 产业技术创新战略联盟
6. 数控机床高速精密化技术创新战略联盟
7. 汽车轻量化技术创新战略联盟
8. 抗生素产业技术创新战略联盟
9. 维生素产业技术创新战略联盟
10. 半导体照明产业技术创新战略联盟
11. 长风开放标准平台软件联盟
12. 高效节能铝电解技术创新战略联盟
13. 大豆加工产业技术创新战略联盟
14. WAPI 产业技术创新战略联盟
15. 闪联产业技术创新战略联盟
16. 光纤接入（FTTx）产业技术创新战略联盟
17. 有色金属钨及硬质合金技术创新战略联盟
18. 化纤产业技术创新战略联盟
19. 存储产业技术创新战略联盟
20. 开源及基础软件通用技术创新战略联盟
21. 多晶硅产业技术创新战略联盟
22. 农药产业技术创新战略联盟
23. 染料产业技术创新战略联盟
24. 新一代纺织设备产业技术创新联盟
25. 太阳能光热产业技术创新战略联盟
26. 商用汽车与工程机械新能源动力系统产业技术创新战略联盟
27. 茶产业技术创新战略联盟
28. 杂交水稻产业技术创新战略联盟
29. 木竹产业技术创新战略联盟
30. 柑橘加工产业技术创新战略联盟
31. 油菜加工产业技术创新战略联盟
32. 缓控释肥产业技术创新战略联盟
33. 畜禽良种产业技术创新战略联盟
34. 饲料产业技术创新战略联盟
35. 肉类加工产业技术创新战略联盟
36. 乳业产业技术创新战略联盟
37. 长三角科学仪器产业技术创新战略联盟
38. 集成电路封测产业链技术创新战略联盟
39. 遥感数据处理与分析应用产业技术创新战略联盟
40. 小卫星遥感系统产业技术创新战略联盟
41. 航空遥感数据获取与服务技术创新战略联盟
42. 电子贸易产业技术创新战略联盟
43. 导航定位芯片与终端产业技术创新战略联盟
44. 地理信息系统产业技术创新战略联盟
45. 高值特种生物资源产业技术创新战略联盟
46. 有色金属工业环境保护产业技术创新战略联盟
47. 金属矿产资源综合与循环利用产业技术创新战略联盟
48. 传染病诊断试剂产业技术创新战略联盟
49. 医疗器械产业技术创新战略联盟
50. 尾矿综合利用产业技术创新战略联盟
51. 煤层气产业技术创新战略联盟
52. 冶金矿产资源高效开发利用产业技术创新战略联盟
53. 城市生物质燃气产业技术创新战略联盟
54. 再生资源产业技术创新战略联盟
55. 流感疫苗技术创新战略联盟
56. 食品安全检测试剂和装备产业技术创新战略联盟

（4）国家科技计划促进联盟发展的方式探索

2008年，科技部出台了《国家科技计划支持产业技术创新战略联盟暂行规定》，强调政府支持产业技术创新战略联盟发展，并为其营造良好的创新政策环境。对于试点联盟开展的符合国家战略目标、符合产业发展需求且具有较强的产业带动作用的技术创新活动，经科技部审核，在先行投入的基础上，国家科技计划将给予优先支持，为实现产业重大共性技术突破、促进产业结构优化升级、提升国家核心竞争力提供支撑。2010年，科技部协调有关部门，探索在"科技支撑计划"和"863计划"中以无偿资助、贷款贴息、后补助等方式支持联盟发展。

2012年6月，科技部发布了《进一步鼓励和引导民间资本进入科技创新领域意见》。该意见提出，鼓励更多的民营企业参与国家科技计划；支持有实力的民营企业联合高等院校、科研院所等组建产业技术创新战略联盟，组织实施产业带动力强、经济社会影响力大的国家重大科技攻关项目和科技成果产业化项目，依靠科技创新做大做强；经科技部审核的产业技术创新战略联盟，可作为项目组织单位参与国家科技计划项目的组织实施。

2.2 奥地利产学研合作促进政策

为了鼓励企业、大学和研究机构间的合作，奥地利在20世纪90年代采取了一系列政策措施，针对奥地利创新系统中存在的问题，采取新的基于计划的支持行为。

2.2.1 奥地利促进产学研合作的政策演进

奥地利技术政策在过去20年中不断扩充改进。政策性工具的多样性向创新流程的系统观转型，这普遍反映在20世纪90年代涌现的创新型系统中（包括但不仅限于Lundvall, 1922）。国家创新系统（NIS）被定义为联合或单独致力于新技术开发和传播的不同研究机构集合，目的在于为政府部门在建立和执行影响创新过程的政策中提供框架。因此，这一系统是创造、储存、转移各种知识、能力以及定义新技术的工艺的研究机构总和，并且这些机构之间彼此相关（Metcalfe, 1995）。基于这种技术背景，奥地利技术政策的中心开始转向这些创新系统中的彼此关联、互动和框架条件，标志就是建立起结构性并以项目为导向的资金。

这种背景下的关键要素就是企业、大学和研究机构之间的合作，在20世纪90年代中期，奥地利主要缺乏的就是这种合作。造成这些不足的主要原因不仅是供需不平衡，此外还受奥地利国内产业部门分类、缺乏临界物质和鼓励机制，以及学术界和产业界之间研究员流动性不强等因素的影响（Schibany，1998）。如上所述，COMET 是奥地利加强企业、大学和研究机构之间合作的一个代表性和突出性政策的体现。

2.2.2 自 1990 年确立的奥地利 PPP 计划

PPP 概念广泛应用于公共产品的提供，指的是公私合作提供公共项目或服务的制度安排。欧美国家和地区的 PPP 实践走在世界前列。奥地利的 PPP 主要集中在城市管理、经济与科技发展及文化教育等领域。1990 年奥地利在创新系统中推出了 PPP 计划，核心组成部分是 COMET 计划。它是奥地利在 20 世纪 90 年代推行的一项基于项目支持的、当前支持产学研合作政策力度最大的措施，目标针对奥地利创新系统中明显的薄弱环节，尤其是科学界与工业界关系方面存在的问题，辅之以公共研究机构（特别是大学）的管理体制改革。奥地利卓越技术能力中心计划是目前奥地利支持科学与工业合作的最重要的政策措施。

奥地利 COMET 计划由奥地利研究促进署（FFG）负责管理。FFG 是奥地利国家级的应用工业研究资助机构。COMET 计划是结构方案（Structural Programmes，SP）的一部分，其目标是创造一种使创新系统中的各个主体能够进行有效合作的环境。COMET 计划启动于 2006 年，由 1998~2007 年运行的奥地利能力中心计划演变而来，充分借鉴并吸取了卓越技术能力中心计划的经验和教训。COMET 计划将持续至 2017 年。

能力中心计划是奥地利政府促进产学研合作中最具代表性和最突出的一项计划。学术界和产业界的关系被认为是奥地利创新系统中最薄弱环节之一，主要反映在产业界通过研究合同对大学研究的资助水平低（1998 年大学经费总额中企业划拨部分所占比例：奥地利为 1.8%，欧盟为 6.4%），学术界和产业界没有战略性合作，以及产业部门对研发管理缺乏长远眼光等。

由于借鉴和吸取了奥地利能力中心计划的经验教训，COMET 计划特别强调实施高水平的前沿研究活动，建立良好的国际形象和国际显示度。COMET 计划的中短期战略目标是，在已经建立起来的若干能力中心的基础上，加强学术界和产业界的合作，大幅度整合中心内各个成员的能力，系统加强内容相关的协同配合。以往研究计划的有益成果和经验，特别是建立一种新的合作文化方面的经验，将在 COMET 计划中加以利用和强化。

同时，COMET 计划将在奥地利创新系统人力资源发展方面做出重要贡献，在研究和技术发展领域为研究人员提供具有吸引力的工作机会。COMET 计划的长期战略目标：在某些研究领域形成国际领先的优势，壮大并保证奥地利企业的技术领先地位，从长远的观点看，努力将奥地利建设成一个具有研究实力的国家。

为了在奥地利技术计划的政策组合中界定出 COMET，我们将简要介绍奥地利的政策性工具。首先我们要区分间接性（税收优惠）研发促进计划、直接性研发促进计划和公共研发资金（见联邦政府 2009）。由于 COMET 计划是奥地利直接研发促进计划的一项关键性举措，因此我们着重讨论直接性研发促进计划。直接性资金之所以不同是因为将收入作为补助金根据测评结果发放给申请人。直接资金从政府公共部门向测评优秀的申请人转移（见联邦政府 2009）。直接性研发促进计划方法的内在要求是抓住符合要求并紧扣主题和/或职能的重点。因此，有可能让那些公认的重大研发项目精确地向目标推进，或者可能通过专题项目促进科研机构基础研究与公司应用研究之间的合作（联邦政府 2009）。须注意的是，大学的基础基金应视为公共基金的一部分，而非直接性研发促进计划。

奥地利直接研发促进计划根据政策按一系列项目组织。这些项目划拨给各大奥地利管理机构及奥地利研究促进协会（FFG）、奥地利科学基金（FWF）、多普勒研究协会（CDG）以及奥地利商业服务机构（AWS）。根据基金总额占比，2007 年 FFG 管理了绝大部分的预算，约合 4 亿欧元（占奥地利直接研发基金的 62.5%，见联邦政府 2009）。FFG 关注应用产业研究用国内基金，管理商业和科学部门的研究项目、经济和研究机构的推动项目，以及学术界和产业界的合作网络。FWF 是奥地利基础研究基金组织，占直接性研发促进资金的 35%（2007）。CDG 主要赞助应用性研究，会员企业可直接获得新技术（占直接性研发促进资金的 1.5%）。AWS 是奥地利国家基金银行，广泛为企业型研发投资促进项目和服务提供贷款（约占直接性研发促进资金的 4%）。

COMET 计划由 FFG 管理，为不同项目提供各种赞助基金（见表 1）。COMET 计划是结构计划（SP）的一部分。该计划旨在创造一种让奥地利所有部门的创新系统高效合作的环境。此外，COMET 还支助区域性研发机构，从而使技术向中小企业转移，并同时培养研发人员。此外，配合 FFG 计划的还有为企业研发项目提供财务支助的通用计划（BP）、赞助奥地利企业参与跨界研究项目，与国际合作伙伴并轨的欧盟准备金（EIP）、关于奥地利研究局势战略优先并在与社会经济和技术需求相关且前景看好的领域推广研究活动的主题计划（TP），以及旨在推进奥地利宇航事业持续发展的奥地利太空应用计划

ASAP（ALR）。

表1　2008年FFG为有关项目提供的各种赞助基金统计

领域	计划	计划划分	项目	承担者	参与者	总成本	总资助额		现金价值	任务
ALR	ASAP		36	48	74	10,816		7,072	7,072	318
			36	48	74	10,816		7,072	7,072	318
BP	BASIS	一般资助	709	575	738	424,458	津贴	91,445	109,887	
							贷款	94,247		
							KKZ	2,866		
							折扣	540		
							州津贴	2,074		
							负债	40,127		
		总部设立	30	28	31	65,727	津贴	20,020	20,020	
		高技术创业	25	25	25	11,433	津贴	4,856	5,560	
							贷款	3,121		
			764	610	794	501,617		259,296	135,466	
	BRIDGE		96	216	255	30,218		17,767	17,767	
	EUROSTARS		8	11	11	6,309		3,378	3,378	
	创新代金卷		553	769	1,106	2,760		2,760	2,760	
			1,421	1,498	2,166	540,905		283,201	159,371	
EIP	对科学的采购融资	BWVIT份额	11	7	11	100		75	75	
		BMWF份额	205	83	205	1,516		1,141	1,141	
			216	90	216	1,616		1,216	1,216	
			216	90	216	1,616		1,216	1,216	
SP	AplusB									65
	brainpower austria									262
	CIR-CE		4	42	42	1,902		862	862	
	COIN	发展	13	36	43	7,523		4,330	4,330	
		合作与网络	13	69	73	5,208		3,125	3,125	
			26	103	116	12,731		7,455	7,455	
	COMET	K projects	7	68	73	27,153		8,728	8,728	25
		K1	11	387	413	187,747		57,241	57,241	
		K2	3	230	241	173,531		57,844	57,844	
		Phasing Out	4	35	35	4,025		1,367	1,367	
			25	645	762	392,456		125,180	125,180	25
	EraSME		6	6	6	2,946		1,429	1,429	
	FEMtech		11	11	11	584		324	324	57
	Forschung macht Schule		254	139	254	893		548	548	
	Josef Ressel Zentren		1	6	6	825		288	288	
	PUST	(FsA, Long Night)								298
	奥地利研究工作室		12	16	22	11,615		8,000	8,000	
	wfFORTE	wfFORTE/Laura Bass Centre								617
			339	878	1,219	123,951		144,085	144,085	1,323
TP	AT:net		54	85	85	21,785		5,143	5,143	100
	ENERGIEDERZUKUNFT		126	259	397	49,281		29,295	29,295	
	FIT-IT	ES	15	31	39	8,534		5,209	5,209	
		FIT-IT Initiatives	11	19	20	3,429		2,096	2,096	
		SemSys	13	26	35	3,889		2,923	2,923	
		SoC	7	14	23	10,988		5,943	5,943	
		Trust	7	13	16	4,672		2,948	2,948	
		Visual	12	22	27	3,735		2,623	2,623	
			65	114	160	35248		21743	21743	
	GEN-AU	ELSA	3	6	6	1,100		1,100	1,100	
		Pilots	5	5	5	503		435	435	
			8	11	11	1,603		1,535	1,535	
	IEA		24	10	25	1,822		1,822		81
	IV2S	A3	1	9	9	950		496	496	
		ISB	3	15	15	516		364	364	
		I2	3	7	7	879		430	430	
			7	31	31	2,346		1,290	1,290	

续表

领域	计划	计划划分	项目	承担着	参与者	总成本	总资助额	现金价值	任务
TP	IV2Splus	A3plus	18	50	66	11,010	5,388	5,388	165
		I2V	23	64	95	9,746	5,163	5,163	
		ways2go	32	67	105	5,892	4,528	4,528	
			73	166	266	26,648	15,079	15,079	165
	KIPAS	PL1—Networking	2	11	11	357	262	262	85
		PL2—Coop. R&D projects	3	12	12	2,085	892	892	
		PL4	7	17	18	1,191	1,111	1,111	
			12	37	41	3,632	2,265	2,265	85
	NANO	培养与教育深化举措							345
		NANO—Cluster	25	46	74	11,058	8,689	8,689	
		NANO Net	6	10	11	313	229	229	87
		支持测度项目	7	13	13	60	60	60	224
			38	66	98	11,431	8,978	8,978	657
	NAWI	Edz	10	24	26	1,862	1,105	1,105	194
		Fdz	32	78	88	7,564	4,710	4,710	
		Hdz	21	19	23	2,409	1,430	1,430	
			63	116	137	11,836	7,245	7,245	194
	Neue Energien 2020		31	80	84	12,782	5,713	5,713	
	TAKE OFF		32	64	78	16,797	9,161	9,161	65
			533	905	1,413	195,207	109,267	109,267	1,347
FFG			2,545	2,863	5,088	1,172,495	544,841	421,012	2,989

注：1. 资料摘自：联邦政府（2009）。
2. ALR 包括 ASAP、BP、EIP EU、SP、TP。

奥地利政府设定了严格的评审程序对能力中心进行评估。K1 和 K2 中心的评估主要有按照条件进行挑选的两个阶段（见表2）。第一阶段首先是对简短的研究建议进行内部和外部评审。外部评审由 FWF 和 CDG 共同负责，其中包含一个国际同行评审（peer-review）程序，目的在于测评学术界和产业界联合设计的研究项目、合作伙伴和合作质量以及国际曝光度（FFG2008b）。最后，评审团（第一轮评审团由 FFG 内部和外部评审专家

表2 COMET 计划能力中心评估程序

第一阶段	
奥地利科学基金会(FWF) 奥地利多普勒研究协会(CDG) 外部评审	奥地利研究促进署(FFG) 内部评审
委员会给出评审意见	
提交 K1/K2 中心详细申请	
第二阶段	
奥地利科学基金会(FWF) 奥地利多普勒研究协会(CDG) 外部评审	奥地利研究促进署(FFG) 内部评审
听证会	
评审专家组成员和相关主题领域专家	
委员会给出 K1/K2 中心资助建议	
联邦部长给出资助决议	

注：资料摘自 FFG（2008a）。

组成）根据内外部评审意见决定是否请项目申请团队根据内部和外部评审中提出的建议，并提交一份详尽的申请报告。决定可能有三种情况：通过申请，否决申请，或建议申请其他项目/中心的评估。通过申请，则进入第二阶段。申请人须提交说明目标、达标标准、财务预算明细以及人员配置的详细研究计划，再次进行内外部评审（第二轮评审团由 FFG 内部和外部评审专家组成）。外部评审由国际评审专家组负责给出评审标准以及详细的评审管理和财务预算（FFG2008b）。申请人、评审专家组成员和相关主题领域专家举行听证会，对申请进行评审，由第二轮评审团给出资助建议，或否决申请，或建议向其他渠道申请资助，最终由联邦部长决定是否进行资助。

在一期资助期间（为期 5 年），COMET 计划通过能力中心定期向研究促进署提交的汇报对中心进行评估，包括每半年提交一次报告以及其他正式或非正式的汇报。一期资助计划结束时，将对中心研究计划中目标的完成情况按照一定程序进行全面的评估。评估标准一般包括在经同行专家评审的国际刊物上发表论文数量、国际专利数量（包括申请的和授予的）、创新数量、战略研究项目所占份额、从其他科学基金获得资助情况、从外部研究项目中获得资助情况、从工业研究合同中获取经费的情况、论文数量和新的国际合作数量等。进一步的评估标准包括对附加性的评估，即对中心参与主体的创新行为所产生的影响进行评估，比如更高的研发费用投入，或者创造出一种新的合作文化等。附加性的评估主要通过对参与主体进行调查来实现。（更多信息见 FFG2008b）

总之，奥地利政府从 20 世纪 80 年代开始，就把"推动科学界与工业界的合作"作为提升国家经济活力和国际竞争力的重要战略措施，并通过各种形式鼓励产学研结合组建技术创新战略联盟；同时，积极推进公共科研机构和大学科研体制的改革，探索政府对技术创新战略联盟这类新型创新组织的管理模式；依据联盟创新目标任务的实现周期，按五年、七年、七年以上分别采取不同的支持方式。在实践中，由于**技术创新战略联盟是契约型的产学研合作组织，技术创新任务的落实需较长时间，要有常设机构和专职人员负责操作运行**。为此，奥地利政府把实施 COMET 计划（这是许多欧盟国家多年来支持产学研合作的一项重要举措）与推进联盟组织建设结合起来，支持联盟成员单位共同成立卓越技术能力中心，并**把这个能力中心作为联盟秘书处依托的运行管理中心和联盟的研发平台**。目前，奥地利国家层面建立的十多个技术创新战略联盟中都已建立了这样的中心。这些能力中心根据实际需要，有的按非营利机构管理，有的按股份制的合作研发组织管理，有的按公共研发机构管理，也有的注册成为股份公司，政府不作统一规定，一切以有利于技术创新联盟发展为前提。

3

中国产业技术创新战略联盟案例

本章按照共同的案例分析框架（见 1.2 节）分析三个中国产业技术创新战略联盟的组织模式，并总结三个联盟的共性特点。这三个案例是农业装备产业技术创新战略联盟（TIPAAMI）、新一代煤（能源）化工产业技术创新战略联盟（ITISANCC）和钢铁可循环流程技术创新战略联盟（SARSPTI）。

3.1 农业装备产业技术创新战略联盟

农业装备产业技术创新战略联盟（TIPAAMI）于 2007 年 6 月 10 日正式签约成立，由中国农业机械化科学研究院牵头组织中国一拖集团有限公司、山东时风（集团）有限责任公司、山东五征集团有限公司、福田雷沃国际重工股份有限公司、江苏常发实业集团有限公司、天津拖拉机制造有限公司、现代农装科技股份有限公司、中国农业大学、浙江大学、江苏大学、东北农业大学、黑龙江省农业机械工程科学研究院、山东省农业机械科学研究所、广东省农业机械研究所等共 15 家单位组成，涵盖了农业装备主要技术与关键产品领域。其中八家企业位列行业前 10 名，总资产占全行业规模以上企业的 33%，生产销售额占全行业规模以上企业的 44%，利税占全行业规模以上企业的 30%。联盟将探索建立以企业为主体、市场为导向、产学研结合的产业技术创新机制，集聚优势科技资源，致力于农业装备发展战略研究和共性、关键技术的联合研发，突破产业技术瓶颈，培育重大产品创制的产业集群主体，引领技术升级进步，扶持产业，支撑农业。

3.1.1 目标和组织形式

3.1.1.1 联盟的组建目标

联盟的近期目标：一是开展农业装备共性技术研究，包括农业装备数字化设计技术研究、可靠性技术研究和自动监测技术研究；二是开展重大产品关键技术研究和重大产品创制，包括适合我国农业特点的多功能作业关键设备、经济型农林动力机械、拖拉机配套作业机具等。经过 3~5 年的努力，形成行业共性技术创新体系的核心，开发出一批具有自主知识产权、对行业有重大影响的技术装备，使行业整体技术水平与国际先进水平的差距缩短 10 年。

联盟的中长期目标：①整合资源，建立产学研技术创新机制，构筑产业技术创新平台；②突破产业共性技术，解决行业发展中遇到的技术供给问题；③实现资源共享，面向行业促进技术扩散和转移。

3.1.1.2 联盟的组织形式

(1) 组织存在状态

① 联盟成员单位均签订联盟协议，经签署的协议每单位一份。联盟成员单位的权利和义务一致、平等，只对联盟协议上内容承担责任义务以及所形成的法律责任，各自经营活动独立，不受契约约束，对其他联盟成员的债权债务不负连带责任。

② 联盟是农业装备行业产学研合作进行技术创新的一种组织形式，不是实体，秘书处是其对外的代表。在联盟的运行中将会推进秘书处的专职化建设，在联盟理事长单位的支持下，做到了有专人从事相关工作。

(2) 法律地位与形式

联盟由积极投身于农业装备产业技术进步、从事相关技术与产品的研究、开发、生产、制造、服务的企业、科研单位和大专院校等相关机构自愿组成，它以契约为基础，仅仅是一个网络、一种平台。它没有独立的法人地位，在法律上既不是企业，也不是社团❶。秘书处是联盟对外的代表，目前秘书处依托于理事长单位组成，其人员、管理、财务属于理事长单位。

3.1.2 治理结构与权责关系

3.1.2.1 不同合作主体融合的阻碍

(1) 企业追求利润与学术界追求学术地位的矛盾

① 分歧的表现形式

利润最大化是企业永恒的目标。在合作中，企业更倾向于形成垄断或排他性的知识产权，形成独占市场的局面。因此在联盟项目执行中，企业要求参与研究人员对其合作研究项目的内容保密，并限制项目技术的扩散，包括以论文、专著等形式的知识成果特别是关键技术的展现。大学处于理论研究、新技术研究的前沿，其对新知识、新技术的追求源于大学的功能定位；而对于具体每个研究人员而言，获得新知识、新技术则有助于提升自身的学术地位和影响力。联盟作为一个技术创新平台，有助于大学获得经费资助，同时扩散其新技术、新知识，实现从技术到产品的延伸转化，从而对其知识、技术进行实践检验。然而，大学或科研机构所具有的对新知识、新技术扩散的动力和追求学

---

❶ 中国目前尚没有非营利机构法人，这与国外不同。

术研究价值的目标,如论文发表、著作出版等,与企业的排他性竞争目标产生矛盾。这种矛盾可能造成企业与高校、院所的合作难以深入和持久,往往导致企业委托给高校或院所研究的不是核心内容,因此,这样的一个合作过程对企业在关键、核心技术上的突破与进步并没有产生实质性影响。

② 分歧的焦点与程度

分歧的焦点在于研究成果、知识产权的权利分配问题。一方面,如果一项研究成果对于企业能够产生巨大的经济收益,研究人员应该得到该项研究成果的一定收益。对于企业,面对市场充满风险,研究成果的市场前景很难预测,研究成果的价值认同受市场风险的制约,研究投入有限,所以企业对于研究的支出是不够的。另一方面,从研究人员,特别是高校研究人员追求可以数量指标化的研究成果显示度,主要在于发表论文、出版著作来体现;而这在企业方面是不认同的。

从联盟的具体实践来看,现处于合作的早期,分歧产生的可能性虽然存在,但却还未表现出来。

(2) 企业短期利益与科研机构长期知识积累的矛盾

① 短期与长期利益的矛盾

基础技术、共性技术研究符合企业长期利益需要,但短期利益不明显,因此企业重视程度不够。在联盟中,一方面,企业很少乐于资助研究机构从事这些方面的技术研究,更多地是希望直接资助新产品、新工艺的开发研究;另一方面,科研机构在基础技术、共性技术研究方面研究的成果因为试验条件的限制不能较快地服务于产品研发,形成了"有技术、没产品"或者"有产品、低水平"的情况。

② 大学评价导向与企业需求的矛盾

对于大学研究者的评价更加注重于科研经费、高水平论文、著作、专利等,整体上表现出来的是大学对科研经费、论文、著作、专利等有更高的追求,因此没有成果产业与转化的压力。所以大学研究者更倾向于承担国家、部委的财政支持的科研项目,对企业委托研发并不热衷。长期而言,大学应把人才培养放在首位,重点是培养各种研究、产业所需的人才,并需要企业对生产实践的支持。

(3) 企业排他性竞争与合作的矛盾

① 联盟内企业市场份额与竞争状态

联盟有八家企业成员,均是行业重点企业,企业规模、产值、利润等占行业全部企业的30%以上。8家企业的主导领域和产品有所不同,企业有单一产品的市场优势,但每个企业整体上都没有形成强势地位,没有形成一家独大的局面。而且成员企业间存在同类型产品的竞争。

② 企业排他性竞争需要合作共赢

农业装备产业有其自身特点,单一企业很难获得绝对优势的地位,只能针对某一类型产品获取竞争优势。从整体上看,农业装备产业企业做大做强有三个途径:一是通过自身发展壮大,在市场竞争中赢得市场主导地位;二是兼并重组,将竞争者业务纳入到企业发展中;三是人才战略,通过优厚待遇吸纳竞争企业的骨干人员。

近年来,农业装备企业的兼并重组势头加快,大型跨国企业纷纷进入中国收购兼并国内企业,建立生产基地,抢占中国市场。国内大型企业也通过兼并重组等战略来进一步完善产业链,形成产业链的优势。从联盟自身而言,联盟成员中企业排除联盟竞争者的诉求并不明显,主要原因在于:一是企业竞争优势比较平均,二是企业的股权结构差异;三是不存在严重的技术壁垒问题。

3.1.2.2 治理结构

联盟的组织结构包括理事会、专家技术委员会、秘书处以及15家成员(理事)单位(图1)。

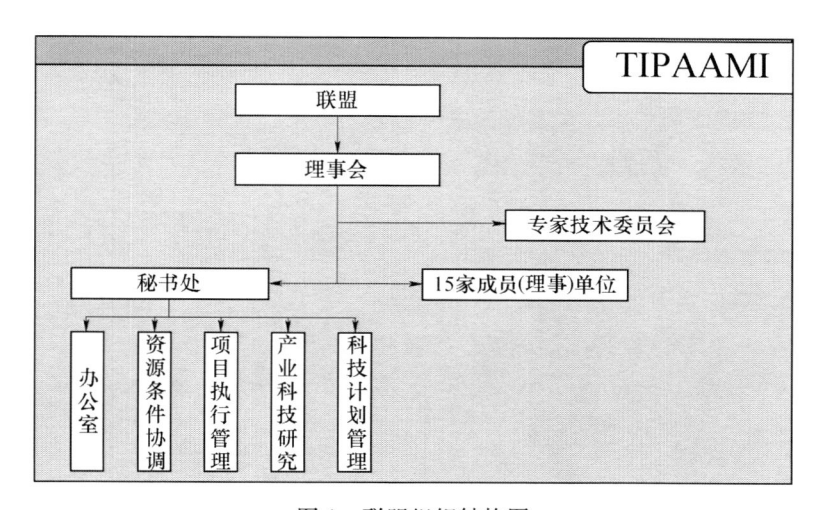

图 1　联盟组织结构图

资料来源:本部分图表资料如无单独注明,由农机联盟秘书处提供。

① 理事会

联盟理事会为联盟的最高权力机构,由联盟成员单位的法定代表人或其委派的代表组成，设理事长1名、副理事长3名和理事12名。理事会会议每六个月召开一次，必要时可增加、提前或延迟，由理事长负责召集、主持理事会会议。三分之二以上（含）理事出席方能召开，实行一人一票表决制，其审核事项须经全体理事三分之二以上（含）表决通过方能生效。

② 专家技术委员会

专家技术委员会为联盟理事会咨询机构，向理事会的决策提供咨询、建议意见，参加项目的立项、论证、评审、验收，提出建议、咨询意见等，由行业内、外知名的工程技术专家、企业家、经济专家、政策研究专家等组成，由理事会聘任，设主任1名、副主任3名、委员21名。专家技术委员会工作方式是专家技术委员会会议。根据需要定期与不定期召开，须有三分之二以上（含）委员出席，其审核事项须经到会委员三分之二以上（含）表决通过方能生效。

③ 秘书处

秘书处为联盟理事会常设的执行机构，直接受理事长领导，负责联盟日常事务和项目的协调、管理工作以及对外联络工作。秘书处设秘书长1名、副秘书长3名，下设办公室专职人员1人、资源条件协调专职人员1人、项目执行管理专职1人、产业技术战略研究专职人员2人、科技计划管理兼职1人。秘书处实行秘书长负责制。秘书长经理事会选举，由理事长聘任。秘书处工作人员由秘书长从理事长单位人员中聘任。

④ 成员单位

联盟有15家成员单位，每家成员单位均为理事单位。其中企业8家、大学4家、研究院所3家。成员单位通过协议约定、平等协商、公开信息等，形成权责平衡、公平参与、公开透明的责任关系。

3.1.2.3 联盟内部组织的具体管理方式

（1）围绕联盟运行的参与单位的资源投入

联盟主要以科技创新为推动因素，以科研项目为引导，参与单位投入的参与资源主要是科技相关资源，包括研发人员、实验仪器设备、配套资金等。

（2）围绕联盟运行的任务组织方式与构架

目前联盟的组织方式是项目组，由项目组组长负责，组长下设置管理小组（协调工作）和成员（各单位领导、专家）。

3.1.2.4 项目选择与主导

（1）如何确定项目

联盟理事会根据行业科技发展需求及联盟科技规划,提出拟定项目,经专家技术委员会指导,由理事长单位负责申报。国家科技计划项目及研发基金项目的申请与立项应满足符合国家产业政策、符合国家中长期科技发展规划纲要、面向行业科技发展需求以及符合联盟科技发展规划(2008—2015)的要求。项目立项过程见图2。

项目形成

国家科技计划项目	政府主管部门发布立项计划	联盟秘书处组织申报	政府主管部门组织可行性论证	立项
研发基金项目	联盟秘书处发布立项计划	成员单位组织申报	联盟专家技术委员会组织论证	立项
成员委托项目	成员单位技术需求	选择承担单位	立项	联盟秘书处备案

图2 项目立项过程示意图

项目评审重点关注:研究内容和目标,技术的先进性、创新性、新颖性,是否产学研结合组成优势研发团队,详尽的成果和知识产权约定等。

(2)谁来领导项目

项目由理事会领导、理事长单位负总责,秘书处负责日常管理等工作。具体项目的实施由联盟秘书处组织项目承担单位签订协议或合同。项目实行课题制,负责人按计划进度定期向理事会汇报。

技术委员会负责项目评估、监管。

承担的国家项目接受国家相关规定的监督、检查、评估、审计。

3.1.2.5 R&D项目的具体管理

(1)研发不同阶段的管理

制定联盟承担国家科技计划管理办法,按有关科技计划管理要求组织实施,进行监督管理。重点需要评估项目的实施:是否完成任务书规定的研究任务;取得成果的技术水平如何及其扩散程度;成果对本行业技术发展的贡献;是否完成专利、论文、标准、软件等目标;是否实现培养人才和形成创新团队目标等。

不同项目管理方式及联盟作用、不同项目实施方式和不同项目经费来源比例分别见表3~表5。

表3 不同项目管理方式及联盟作用

项目类别	任务管理	联盟作用
国家科技计划项目	政府科技主管部门与承担单位签订任务书	联盟秘书处组织实施、监督、检查、验收
研发基金项目	联盟秘书处与承担单位签订任务书	联盟秘书处立项、监督、检查、评估、审计、验收
成员委托项目	任务来源单位与承担单位签订委托合同	联盟秘书处备案、争议协理

表4 不同项目实施方式

项目类别	承担单位类别	承担单位数量	契约形式	成果表现
国家科技计划项目	成员单位、非成员单位	多单位承担	任务书	专利、论文、新产品、新装置、软件、标准等
研发基金项目	成员单位	多单位或单一单位承担	任务书	新技术、新装置、论文、标准等
成员委托项目	成员单位、非成员单位	多单位或单一单位承担	委托协议（合同）	产品或技术

表5 不同项目经费来源比例

项目类别	国家财政（%）	自筹经费（%）		
			企业单位	研究机构
国家科技计划项目	33~50	50~67	70~100	0~30
研发基金项目	33~50	50~67	70~100	0~30
成员委托项目	90~100（委托单位）	0~10	100	

注：数据由农机联盟秘书处提供。

（2）R&D成果与后期生产如何结合

联盟研发结合产业需求，基于企业产业发展的内在需求而确定的。研发成果形成后，按照联盟的知识产权约定和项目中关于成果的分配关系，在联盟内企业中优先进行转化。

3.1.2.6 权责关系与行为规则

（1）各主体的权责关系

各参加单位权责对等，协议约定。

成员的权利包括具有参与讨论和表决联盟发展的重大决策、决议和事项，对联盟提出建议、批评、监督，优先享有项目合作、权益分享、科技资源的获取权利，自由退出联盟等。义务包括拥护、遵守联盟协议，提供合作所需的必要条件和开放共享优势科技研发条件，推进成员单位间科研协作、信息共享，保护联盟知识产权及技术秘密等。

（2）参与各方基本的行为规则

参与各方应平等自愿、风险共担、利益共享。

（3）权责关系与行为规则对创新活动与信息流动的影响

对基础、共性技术研发活动具有很好的适应性，对涉及产业利益发展方面的适应上存在阻碍。

3.1.3 联盟内部及其与政府的关系

3.1.3.1 联盟的核心主体和发起者

理事长单位是联盟组建的主要倡导者，是联盟的核心主体。

3.1.3.2 参与主体之间关系的演化

（1）联盟发展中主体关系影响的确定

目前，在联盟内还不存在"领头大哥"。

（2）各方关系如何演变

基于共同利益需求，目前联盟主体间主要是合作研发关系。

（3）这种关系对联盟的影响

目前联盟成员之间合作是以企业或大学院所利益为纽带的关系，联盟发展没有稳定而牢靠的基础。

3.1.3.3 相关政府部门的作用

政府部门在联盟的形成中发挥了重要的指导和推动作用，同时也发挥了积极的主管职能。政府的理想角色是创新政策制定者、推动者。

3.1.3.4 联盟的历史

（1）历史形成过程

联盟形成的历史过程见图3。

联盟的成立依赖于长期以来理事长单位中国农业机械化科学研究院在行业方面的贡献和主导地位。中国农业机械化科学研究院作为我国农业装备行业具有五十多年发展历史的国家科研机构，从20世纪50年代建院开始就在推进农业机械化发展和农机技术进步方面发挥了主导作用，一直是行业先进技术的发源地和辐射源。改革开放以后，特别是科技体制改革以来，该院在摸索中寻找一条科技与产业良性循环发展的道路，创新能力、技术引领能力进一步巩固和加强。

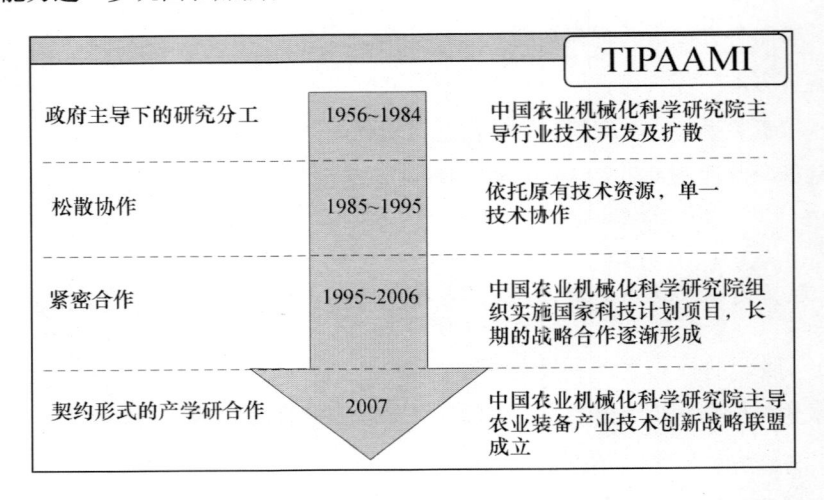

阶段	时间	说明
政府主导下的研究分工	1956~1984	中国农业机械化科学研究院主导行业技术开发及扩散
松散协作	1985~1995	依托原有技术资源，单一技术协作
紧密合作	1995~2006	中国农业机械化科学研究院组织实施国家科技计划项目，长期的战略合作逐渐形成
契约形式的产学研合作	2007	中国农业机械化科学研究院主导农业装备产业技术创新战略联盟成立

图3 联盟形成的历史过程

进入21世纪，国际科技进步和创新对农业装备产业提出了更高要求，自主创新、合作研发是农业装备产业技术进步的根本道路和服务中国农业和国民经济增长的重要动力，也促使农业装备产业技术不断发展、不断提升竞争力。农业装备产业技术创新战略联盟作为产学研合作的一种形式被农业装备产业中的骨干企业、科研院所、大学作为快速提升产业技术水平的一种科学的道路而采用。农业装备产业技术的发展进入从一家主导到一家引领，形成核心支撑与广泛参与的新的历史阶段。

（2）组建程序

联盟的组建经过前期调研、倡议、成立组建筹备领导小组、签订意向书、签订协议并宣告成立等阶段，具体组建程序见图4。

① 前期调研阶段，取得广泛共识。从我国发展现代农业和农村建设的战略任务出发，农业装备产业具备成立联盟的条件和相关政策环境，并得到了各级政府支持和企业的认可。

② 倡议阶段，完善筹备工作。由中国农业机械化科学研究院作为牵头单位，成立了联盟组建筹备领导小组，并起草了《农业装备产业技术创新战略联盟倡议书》。

③ 签订意向书阶段，确立联盟基本框架和机制。依照自愿原则，联盟首批发起单位由7家骨干企业（集团）、4所研发机构和4所综合性重点院校共15家单位自愿签订了

《农业装备产业技术创新战略联盟意向书》。由联盟领导小组组织完成了《"农业装备产业技术创新战略联盟"组建方案（草案）》，共商拟定签署了《农业装备产业技术创新战略联盟协议书》。

④ 协议签订，宣告成立，联盟进入实质运行阶段。2007 年 6 月 10 日，经过近 1 年时间的筹备，经科技部等有关部门认可，农业装备产业技术创新战略联盟作为首批四个联盟之一正式举办签约仪式宣告成立。

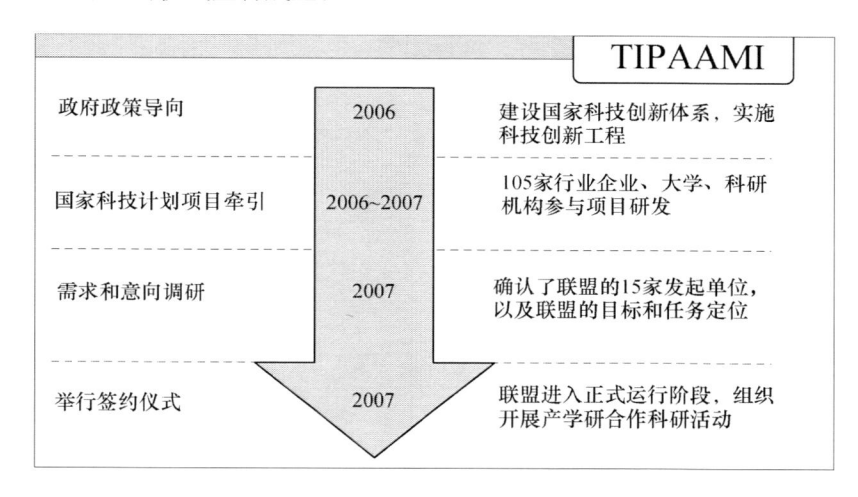

		TIPAAMI
政府政策导向	2006	建设国家科技创新体系，实施科技创新工程
国家科技计划项目牵引	2006~2007	105家行业企业、大学、科研机构参与项目研发
需求和意向调研	2007	确认了联盟的15家发起单位，以及联盟的目标和任务定位
举行签约仪式	2007	联盟进入正式运行阶段，组织开展产学研合作科研活动

图 4　联盟组建的程序

联盟的组建在政府部门、行业协会的支持下，在农业装备行业内取得了广泛共识，经政府有关部门认可，各方自愿以协议方式约定权利义务以及联盟运行保障，成为连接政府与产业、产业与科研的重要渠道。

（3）联盟建立过程中的重大事件

① 代表性事件

——以联盟成员单位为主体承担国家科技支撑计划重大项目"多功能农业装备与设施研制"。

——联盟成员单位共同签署联盟协议，联盟进入实质运行阶段。

——联盟召开"现代农业与食品制造装备技术发展战略研讨会"，为行业科技发展提供决策。

——联盟制定科技发展战略，规划联盟的科技发展目标、任务、重点等，为联盟今后的发展指明方向。

② 转折点

科技部首次以联盟为组织单位组织实施的国家科技支撑计划重点项目，对联盟发挥作用奠定基础。

（4）确定阻碍事件发展的因素

① 存在哪些阻碍因素

主要存在如下阻碍因素：联盟成员内企业单位之间的协调问题，理事长单位与联盟内大型企业之间的关系问题，联盟后续发展问题，联盟的组织运行与保障机制问题。

② 如何克服阻碍因素

遵循联盟协议，分工合作，发挥各自优势，确保成员单位的诉求充分表达，贡献与利益对等。

③ 预测与预防将来的阻碍因素

联盟法律地位、身份的明确化对联盟的定位、作用等有巨大影响。

3.1.4 知识创造和技术扩散

3.1.4.1 创造知识依靠的共同资源投入

（1）人力资源

① 产业界的人力资源投入基本可以确保联盟发展中科研项目所需的资源投入。

② 大学和科研院所的人力资源投入主要依靠相关院系或专业资源，大学层面的资源投入有限。

（2）机械与研究设备

① 生产与中试等投入的机械设备主要由企业投入。

② 科研仪器设备投入与共享主要依托大学、研究院所的国家级、省部级公共实验机构的仪器设备资源。

（3）资金

① 联盟研发基金首批募集 3000 万元，按照联盟成员单位的不同性质出资筹集，成员单位中企业每家 350 万元，院所每家 100 万元，大学不出资。

② 在外募集资金的渠道与方式上，资金筹措渠道包括争取的国拨科研经费、联盟成员自筹经费、行业或企业委托研发经费、捐赠资金和成果的部分技术转移收益。目前主要是政府以项目方式的投入。

3.1.4.2 合作成果的管理与扩散

(1) 联合研发的新产品

① 联盟内部如何分配合作成果

对于以国家财政资金为主而开发形成的知识产权,按国家科技计划管理办法的约定管理。

对于以自筹经费为主、利用联盟的共性平台技术深度开发的产品与工艺技术所形成的知识产权,按协议约定执行,一般归开发该技术的联盟成员单位所有。

② 利益分享机制的表达与实践

遵循"事先约定、优先共享、有偿转让、收益分享"原则和契约精神,约定利益分享机制。如有争议,通过联盟理事会会议解决。不同项目成果权利分享方式见表6。

表6 不同项目成果权利分享方式

项目类别	所有权	使用权	分享、转让方式	收益分享方式
国家科技计划项目	成果研发单位	成果研发单位	共同研发单位无偿使用,有偿转让其他单位	按不高于15%的比例提取纳入研发基金
研发基金项目	联盟	成果研发单位	成员单位无偿使用,有偿转让其他单位	100%纳入研发基金
成员委托项目	委托单位	委托单位	受托单位按约定使用,委托单位具有完全处置权	联盟不参与分享

(2) 联合专利的管理

① 知识产权无偿向联合开发成员单位辐射和推广,采取相对优惠的条件向联盟内未参与开发的其他单位有偿转让,采取有偿方式向联盟外的其他企业转让,所形成的收益中提取一部分纳入联盟开发基金。

② 国家引导支持所取得的知识产权按要求执行,以促进行业关键共性技术研发,提升行业技术水平,促进产业发展,保障现代农业和新农村建设,推动国民经济发展。

(3) 合作发表

① 署名权:遵循"谁开发,谁拥有,谁署名"的原则。

② 发表时机的协调:根据需要,由参与研究各方协商确定发表。

(4) 科学会议、研讨会等的共同组织

① 科学会议

主题选择：联盟根据行业科技规划或政府部门委托，组织召开此类会议，理事会确定会议承办单位。

成本分摊：由联盟理事会理事长单位承担费用，或由会议承办方承担费用。

② 研讨会

主题选择：根据联盟目标与任务以及行业科技发展规划等，由理事长单位提出，成员单位参加讨论，也邀请行业内其他单位参加讨论。

成本分摊：由联盟理事长单位承担有关会议组织费用。

(5) 联合培养人才

目前，联盟成员单位内企业、研究院所与大学联合培养人才方式主要是共同培养、委托培养两种方式。共同培养主要是研究院所与大学联合招生，大学主要负责课程教育，院所主要负责实践教育；委托培养主要是企业、院所委托大学培养骨干科技人才。

3.1.5 法律与制度环境

3.1.5.1 与现行法律和规则的兼容性

遵循相关的各项法律法规，如知识产权法、合同法、反垄断法及有关大学、公共研究机构的法律、国有资产管理法律法规等。

联盟最迫切关注的法律、法规与政策是部门与行业法规，希望能实现从下到上的制定流程。

3.1.5.2 法律和法规效力与适宜性的评估

(1) 法律与法规的影响

目前，部门规定方面主要是科技部发布关于成立联盟、支持联盟发展的有关规定。

(2) 对法律法规效力的评估

科技部部门规定都很有针对性和可操作性，对规范和支持联盟发展具有非常重要的作用。

(3) 联盟的建议

① 推进联盟的组织化，完善联盟的内部组织结构。

② 加大对联盟的运行支持。充分发挥联盟在产业技术创新中的作用还需政府财政政策的支持。

③ 对联盟的身份和地位作适当的安排。

3.1.6 资金筹集与管理

3.1.6.1 成本分摊模式

联盟管理与运行的基本经费来源渠道主要包括政府财政资助、成员单位分摊、单位或个人捐赠。目前，联盟的管理与运行费由理事长单位承担。从联盟的发展实践上看，成本分摊是一个必然的选择，联盟正在研究制定相应的制度及分摊规则。

3.1.6.2 财力资源的管理和使用方法

（1）财务管理遵循的规则：联盟指导、立项管理，谁出资、谁使用。

（2）具体实施细则

授权联盟秘书处所在法人单位设立专用账户或科目管理联盟经费。按联盟的项目计划任务书立项管理，专款专用，实行独立的财务预决算制度。建立严格的财务管理制度，保证会计体系合法、真实、准确、完整，严格执行国家规定的财务管理制度，接受经理事会确认的会计事务所审计并报理事会审查。资产来源属于国家拨款的必需接受国家有关规定的监督管理。社会捐赠、资助的，应当尊重捐赠、资助人的意愿，并将有关情况以适当方式向社会公开。通过联盟共性技术转化获得的成果转化收益，按协议约定分配。

（3）财务监督与控制

国家科研资金按国家有关管理办法执行；联盟成员投入资金、赞助资金按合同或协议约定要求执行有关监督管理机制。

3.2 新一代煤（能源）化工产业技术创新战略联盟

3.2.1 目标和组织形式

3.2.1.1 组建目标

（1）开发产业关键、共性技术。围绕《国家中长期科学和技术发展规划纲要（2006—2020年）》中确定的68项优先主题之一——"煤的清洁高效开发利用、液化及多联产"中的新一代煤（能源）化工产业技术的开发，面向产业需求，集中关注产业的关键技术、共性技术、市场热点技术的研发，并且要使技术迅速转化为生产力。

（2）建设产业技术创新资源的共享平台。通过整合和新建，形成面向联盟成员、面向行业、具有国内领先水平和国际先进水平的创新资源共享平台,提高创新资源的使用率,并努力确保不阻碍技术成果的推广。

(3) 构建完整的产业技术创新链。在联盟立足现有单元技术的基础上,注重系统集成,形成产业上、下游企业与公共研究机构间持续稳定的战略合作关系。

(4) 建立联盟的技术转移和扩散机制。建立和完善各种机制,加速创新成果在联盟内部和行业中的大规模商业化运用,促进科技成果的转移、推广和技术的集成与应用。

(5) 形成合理的人才交流与培养机制。通过联盟平台,推动联盟成员单位科技人才的联合培养和交流互动,使联盟成为培养高层次人才的重要基地。

3.2.1.2 组织形式

(1) 组建过程与程序

① 联盟牵头单位中国化学工程集团公司围绕组建目标,确定了选择具有成员单位资格的原则:创新需求符合国家产业政策;行业所需的共性和关键技术的拥有者或使用者;有一定的创新基础;能够有助于建立产业技术创新链条。

② 向符合条件的成员单位发送邀请函,共同商讨联盟组建方案和联盟协议。

③ 签订联盟协议,宣告联盟正式成立。

联盟实行开放机制,将不断吸收新的创新资源,吸收能对联盟发展有利的具有技术、资金等方面优势的单位。

(2) 组织存在状态

采取虚实结合的组织形式。联盟现由科研院所、企业等14家煤化工行业的重要单位组成。通过理事会和专家委员会会议研究、决定重大事项,通过秘书处常设机构和专职人员处理日常工作。

(3) 法律地位与形式

联盟是非法人契约型组织。

3.2.2 治理结构与权责关系

在产学研结合的机制中,大学和科研院所通过提供原始技术,获得验证平台,与企业进一步深入研究,提高研发应用能力;培养研究生,发表学术论文,有利于通过学校内部的管理考核;从技术转让中获得收益,研发新技术。企业通过提供前沿市场需求、应用场所、转化桥梁和关键设备,获得并应用先进技术,提高在市场中的竞争力,得到预期收益。有可能获得有关部门的资金资助。基于以上需求,各方主体才能有机结合,共同发展。

3.2.2.1 不同合作主体融合的阻碍

(1) 企业追求利润与学术界追求学术地位的矛盾

企业的目标是赚取尽可能多的利润,而学术界的目标是在国内外发表尽可能多的论文;企业追求减少成本,经济可行的技术方案,而学术界追求大量申报专利,不注重技术的应用成本。企业与学术界评价标准和评价体系的差异,严重阻碍了合作产出成果的效率和质量。

(2) 企业短期利益与科研机构长期知识积累的矛盾

煤化工产业的开发研究需要企业前期大规模的投入,风险较大,而产业的关键、共性技术需要科研机构长期知识积累和反复试验论证。二者时间与收益的差异会阻碍部分产业技术的合作开发。

(3) 企业排除竞争者与公共科研机构追求知识扩散的矛盾

联盟内的企业属于上下游关系,一般不存在竞争关系,其希望公共科研机构将技术成果纳入联盟平台,优先掌握技术成果,获得使用优惠。公共科研机构则希望扩大技术转让范围,多方对比选择,获得更多收益,同时扩大技术的影响力。技术成果扩散的差异对二者紧密合作有一定影响。

3.2.2.2 治理结构

根据联盟协议,联盟理事会是联盟的领导和协调机构。理事会下设秘书处,受理事会领导,是联盟的日常服务机构,负责日常事务和项目的协调、管理工作。专家委员会是联盟的技术咨询机构。

该联盟组织结构图如图 5 所示:

理事会由成员单位各选派 1 名代表组成,设理事长 1 名。目前,理事会由 15 名成员组成。其职责

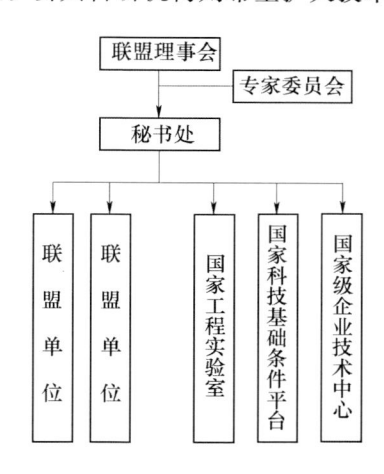

图 5 联盟组织结构

为批准管理制度;批准成员单位的加入;审查和批准技术开发计划;决定项目立项、实施方案、预算、资金计划、验收等事项;决定经费的筹措、使用事项;决定技术成果的推广及收益分配方案;其他重大问题决策。

专家委员会由各联盟成员单位委派一至两名专家，并外聘国内外在行业内有着重要影响力的知名专家、学者组成。现联盟有22名专家，设名誉主任1名，主任1名，副主任1名。其职责是为理事会的决策提供咨询、建议意见；提出技术发展方向与重点工作方向，指导秘书处制定技术发展计划；参加项目的论证、评审、实施、招标、检查、验收，提出建议、咨询意见；其他重大决策咨询。

秘书处由各成员单位主管科研（技术开发）部门的一名负责人组成，秘书处依托单位可增派一人。秘书处设秘书长一人，由秘书处依托单位派出。秘书处实行专职化，现有专职化工作人员4名。秘书处下设项目管理部、财务和资金管理部、法律事务部、市场推广部、基地管理部及信息中心六个部门。秘书处职责为：组织制订管理制度；组织制定技术发展计划，拟定具体的开发项目；组织联盟有关成员签订具体的项目协议；对项目协议的执行情况进行全程监控和协调，组织对项目成果的验收；对项目的立项、知识产权归属、成果推广等事项进行管理；负责日常工作。

3.2.2.3 联盟内部组织的具体管理方式

（1）围绕联盟运行的参与单位的资源投入

中国化学工程集团公司作为理事长单位负责日常联络与组织工作，委派秘书处专职人员。联盟中的企业提供共用办公经费、研发经费；科研院所提供科研队伍、实验仪器设备等。

（2）围绕联盟运行的任务组织方式与架构

联盟采取项目组织方式是实行项目总负责人制。总负责人组织制定项目总体计划、经费安排，组织、协调项目组内各参与方的工作，定期向秘书处报告工作进展情况。理事长单位授权秘书处对项目的实施情况进行检查，每年将完成情况进行汇总并向理事会报告。

3.2.2.4 项目选择与主导

（1）如何确定项目

秘书处在专家委员会提出的联盟技术发展方向与重点工作方向的指导下，制定技术发展计划，并按照计划拟定具体的开发项目，报理事会批准。理事会可授权秘书处按市场方式组织招标确定项目承担方，也可根据专家委员会的评审意见确定项目主要承担方，其他有意愿的成员可以不同方式加入。另外，有关成员可自愿结合提出项目申请，由秘书处提出意见，经专家委员会评审，并报理事会批准确定项目。目前联盟正在实施的中试、工业示范（试验）项目有 4 个，其中 3 个来源于技术发展计划，1 个来源于成员单位自愿结合提出的项目申请。

（2）谁来领导项目

项目由理事会领导，理事长单位总负责。秘书处组织有关承担单位在联盟协议框架下签署具体的项目协议，明晰责、权、利关系。项目组接受秘书处的管理、协调和监督。

3.2.2.5　R&D 项目的具体管理

（1）研发不同阶段的管理

在项目实施过程中，联盟实行重要节点控制管理，见图 6。

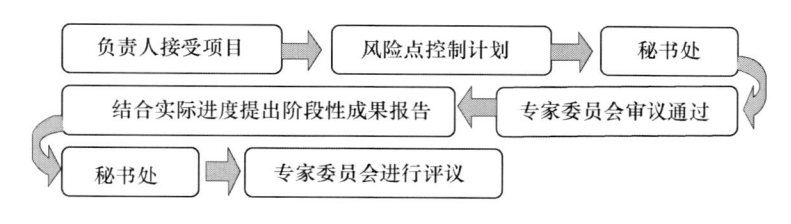

图 6　项目实施节点控制示意图

在联盟协议和项目协议的双重约束下，保证了项目各执行单位享有产业技术创新链中各种资源，获得外部创新资源，提升自身创新能力，并且从创新成果使用和推广中受益。在重要节点管理的严格控制下，保证了项目实时有序地按照协议进行，确保了项目质量。

（2）R&D 成果与后期生产如何结合

联盟研发的技术符合产业需求，具有普遍推广性。经工业试验成功后可在联盟内外推广扩散。

3.2.2.6　权责关系与行为规则

（1）各主体的权责关系

根据联盟协议，各成员的权责对等。每个项目有具体项目协议约定各主体的权责关系。各成员的基本权利义务如下：

各成员的权利包括自愿加入或退出联盟；选派代表担任联盟理事；通过联盟参与政府项目和联盟项目的开发；参与政府项目时，可获得联盟配套资金、国家政策以及资金的扶持；参与联盟项目时，可获得联盟配套资金的扶持；对联盟技术成果的使用享有优先权和优惠权。

各成员的义务包括遵守本协议的规定和联盟管理制度的规定；不得设置障碍影响联盟技术成果的转移和推广；保护联盟知识产权不受侵犯；保守联盟技术秘密；承担相应的技术开发任务，提供相应的资源支持，为参与各方密切合作、共同发展贡献力量。

（2）参与各方基本的行为规则

根据联盟协议，参与各方应密切合作，风险共担、利益共享。

（3）权责关系与行为规则对创新活动与信息流动的影响

根据联盟协议和具体项目协议，各成员单位之间相互合作、相互交流，共建研发支撑平台。

3.2.3 联盟内部及其与政府的关系

3.2.3.1 核心主体和发起者

联盟由在煤化工领域具有重要影响力的规划单位、科研院所、生产企业、工程公司和设备制造企业等14家单位组成，构成了完整的产业链。中国化学工程集团公司牵头组建，以其强大的工程化、系统集成能力起到了核心作用。

3.2.3.2 参与主体之间关系的演化

（1）联盟发展中主体关系影响的确定

各成员单位对关键、共性技术的共同需求。

（2）各方关系如何演变

科研院所各具有不同的技术优势，企业之间是上下游合作关系，科研院所与企业合作研发，因此各成员单位的竞争不明显，关系没有明显变化。

（3）这种关系对联盟的影响

各成员单位对有前景的行业关键技术研发合作的积极性较高，但在具体项目合作中有时很难协调利益各方的分享比例。

3.2.3.3 相关政府部门的作用

政府对联盟的成立起到了积极的推动作用；为联盟发展提供政策支持，发挥引导、协调作用；同时将部分研发项目列入国家科技计划中，并给予了一定的资金资助。

3.2.3.4 联盟的历史

（1）联盟建立过程中的重大事件

① 在科技部等六部门的推动下，通过签署战略联盟协议，"新一代煤（能源）化工产

业技术创新战略联盟"正式成立。

② 在对产业情况调研分析的基础上,针对制约产业发展的突出问题,根据现有能力,联盟统筹规划了"第二代煤气化"、"褐煤洁净高效利用"、"合成气制醇醚"、"甲醇深加工"、"碳二产品"五个创新领域。

③ 联盟作为组织单位,理事长单位作为责任主体实施国家科技支撑计划"煤制烯烃"重点项目,并获得政府资助资金1213万元,占项目总投资的6.7%。

④ "流化床甲醇制丙烯(FMTP)工业技术开发"获得重大突破,经中国石油和化学工业协会组织的鉴定委员会鉴定,主要技术指标和总体技术处于国际领先水平。

⑤ 政府有关部门与理事长单位签署《联盟秘书处专职化建设工作委托协议书》。理事长单位应研究完善联盟管理制度,创新工作机制,探索建立适应联盟不断发展的秘书处专职化模式。政府有关部门资助工作经费30万元。

(2) 确定阻碍事件发展的因素

① 存在哪些阻碍因素

a. 法律地位问题。联盟的非法人性质决定了其不能承担责任,不能作为实体承担项目委托开发中的风险,因而由理事长单位承担。这导致了联盟权利与义务的不对等,使其不能发挥真正的管理作用。

b. 考核机制问题。联盟的专职化人员仍属于原有单位,因此只能按所在单位规定进行考核,但又存在不能充分研究联盟发展中问题的缺陷。

② 如何克服阻碍因素

确立联盟的实体地位,完善组织、考核等各项机制。

③ 预测与预防将来的阻碍因素

持续发展问题。联盟的目标就是开发产业关键、共性技术,项目是其重要的抓手与依托。如不能持续开发新技术就很难使联盟持续稳定发展。

3.2.4 知识创造和技术扩散

3.2.4.1 创造知识依靠的共同资源投入

(1) 人力资源

各参与企业均应指派相应的专职管理人员,在具体的项目中依据项目合同分派研发人员和技术人员。各大学和科研院所由参与的院系或研究部门直接指派研究人员参与项目。企业与科研院所的人员在研发项目的全过程进行交流合作。

联盟现有的人力资源和实验平台见表7。

（2）机械与研究设备

由参与研发的科研院所提供实验室、研究中心等的仪器设备。企业提供中试、工业试验等的机械设备。

（3）资金

① 项目经费以成员单位投入为主，以联盟配套资金、社会募集、银行贷款、争取政府配套资金支持为辅。大学、科研院所不出资。

② 技术开发准备金来源于联盟从每一次技术成果的使用许可或转让收益中提取一定比例资金以及接受联盟成员和其他单位的捐赠。技术开发准备金用于具体项目的配套扶持、相关开发人员的奖励等支出。

表7 联盟现有资源

人力资源	实验平台
中国工程院院士4名	国家重点实验室3个
长江学者4名	国家技术推广中心2个
"973首席科学家"5名	国家技术转移中心2个
国家设计大师4名	国家工程研究中心1个
国家煤化工领导小组顾问组成员1名	省、部级重点实验室8个
	国家级企业技术中心2个
	省级企业技术中心9个

3.2.4.2 合作成果的管理与扩散

在联盟协议和《联盟知识产权管理办法》中约定知识产权的保护措施，从专利的申请、技术的保密到对联盟成员违反协议造成知识产权流失的惩罚和赔偿均作出了原则规定。在各具体开发项目合同中进一步细化知识产权的权属和使用，以确保知识产权保护的规定具有可操作性。

（1）联合研发的新产品

联盟研发的成果主要形成新技术、新工艺、专利、论文和专著，不形成新产品。

（2）联合专利的管理

① 国家资助资金研究开发形成的知识产权，按国家相关管理办法规定管理。

② 联盟自筹经费研发形成的知识产权归项目各合作单位享有；项目研发单位原有

的技术权属不变，研发形成的新成果，各项目执行单位按合同确定权属和比例获得收益。

③ 由两家以上（含两家）联盟成员合作开发完成的技术成果，须经合作各方一致同意才能申请专利。合作各方共同申请专利前，应签署《共同申请专利和确认专利权益协议》，明确申请专利费用、专利年费分担、排名顺序等内容。若一方书面确认放弃专利申请权的，其他方可申请专利。其专利申请费及年费由申请方承担。在专利申请获得批准后，放弃专利申请权的一方有权无偿使用该专利技术。

④ 联盟内部实行优惠、优先、有偿使用技术成果；联盟对外推广时按当时的市场定价，不得设置障碍；成员单位有阻碍技术对外推广情况时，联盟将依照相关规定执行有关部门的强制许可。

⑤ 联盟提取一定比例的成果有偿费用作为联盟技术开发准备金；项目合作单位按贡献大小（技术和资金投入）确定收益分享比例。

(3) 联合产生的工艺或技术管理

联盟成员均负有保护知识产权及技术秘密的义务。在具体项目启动之前，项目涉及各方应签订技术保密协议或条款，技术保密协议或条款不得与协议中的有关规定相矛盾。在具体项目的开发过程中，对于符合技术秘密保护条件的技术（含申请专利前的技术），合作各方均应提出，经共同认定后成为合作各方的技术秘密进行保护。

(4) 合作发表

联盟研发所产生的有关著作权属于研发各方共有，其排名顺序按合作各方的实际投入及贡献程度事先商定。

(5) 科学会议、研讨会等的共同组织

① 科学会议

联盟根据有关部门的委托组织召开会议，由理事长单位承办。

② 研讨会

根据联盟目标与技术发展计划，由理事长单位组织，邀请相关技术领域的单位和个人参加，与成员单位进行交流研讨。

(6) 联合培养人才

通过召开各种会议，促进企业与科研院所人才交流，培养复合型人才。大学可将研发项目作为实践基地，与企业共同培养骨干科技人才。

3.2.5 法律与制度环境

3.2.5.1 与现行法律和规则的兼容性

总体上与现行法规兼容，符合《中华人民共和国合同法》和《中华人民共和国反垄断法》等有关法律的规定。

3.2.5.2 法律和法规效力与适宜性的评估

(1) 法律与法规的影响

目前，规范联盟的主要是科技部发布的有关规定，其中明确了联盟的成立条件、责任人以及支持联盟发展的相关规定。这些规定引导了联盟发展，确立了项目实施中的责任人。

(2) 对法律法规效力的评估

科技部的有关规定对联盟发展具有直接规范性和引导作用。但支持联盟发展的有关规定与现行科技创新管理体制不一致，导致在实际操作中仍然依照原有体制的规定，降低了有关支持联盟规定的力度。

(3) 联盟的建议

建议在国家创新体系中明确联盟地位；在制定行业相关政策时充分听取联盟的意见；营造促进合作创新的政策环境，为企业间竞争前的技术创新合作提供合理的支持。

3.2.6 资金筹集与管理

3.2.6.1 成本分享模式

联盟经费包括共用办公费、项目经费、技术开发准备金等。

共用办公费经理事会研究确定每年承担的具体数额，均由联盟成员中的企业承担。

项目经费以成员投入为主，以联盟配套资金、社会募集、银行贷款、争取政府配套资金支持为辅。目前，联盟自筹了近7亿资金实施4个项目，其中一个项目得到了国家资助资金共1213万元，现尚未拨付❶。

技术开发准备金是从每一次技术成果的使用许可或转让收益中提取一定比例资金，

---

❶ 为2008年12月进行实地调研时联盟秘书处负责人的回复。由于政府工作流程问题，当时联盟获得的政府资助资金尚未到位。

以及接受联盟成员和其他单位的捐赠组成。

3.2.6.2 财力资源的管理和使用方法

（1）财务管理遵循的规则

根据联盟协议，联盟制定了《财务管理办法》《共用办公费用预算管理》等资金管理办法。有关政府资助项目资金依据政府有关资金管理办法。

（2）具体实施细则

联盟实行独立的财务预决算制度，设立独立账户，专款专用，由专人管理，集中管理联盟各项经费。

（3）财务监督与控制

① 具体管理措施

联盟研发项目要充分利用现有资源（如实验设备、实验室、中试装置及现有公用工程等），减少投资；项目经费按重要节点，分阶段评估、分阶段拨付；在划拨政府资助项目资金时，合作各方自筹资金必须到位，并且预留5％作为项目保证金；理事长单位可以委托理事会认可的社会中介机构对项目进行监督、检查和评估。

② 经费管理流程

经费管理流程见图7。

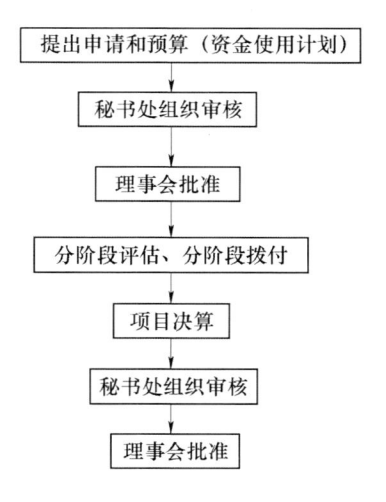

```
提出申请和预算（资金使用计划）
          ↓
     秘书处组织审核
          ↓
       理事会批准
          ↓
  分阶段评估、分阶段拨付
          ↓
        项目决算
          ↓
     秘书处组织审核
          ↓
       理事会批准
```

图 7　经费管理流程

3.3 钢铁可循环流程技术创新战略联盟

3.3.1 目标和组织形式

3.3.1.1 组建目标

在 WTO 条约框架下,本战略联盟将持续承担行业关键技术、共性技术及重大前沿技术的开发。

- 以钢铁行业共性、关键技术开发为重点,大力提高钢铁产业自主创新能力,解决行业在资源、能源、环境的瓶颈问题,开发新一代钢铁可循环流程重大技术和若干项具有自主知识产权、对行业有重大影响的共性技术,保证钢铁行业持续健康跨越发展。
- 促进钢铁工业重点企业、科研院所、大专院校的科技资源共享,形成建立在产业技术创新价值链基础之上的合作机制,建立以企业为主体、市场化的多元化投融资机制和促进成果转化的有效机制。
- 探索提升钢铁行业自主创新能力的有效方式。

3.3.1.2 组织形式

(1) 组建过程与程序

中国钢研科技集团、宝钢、鞍钢、武钢、首钢、唐钢、济钢七家大型钢铁集团,以及北京科技大学、东北大学、上海大学三家钢铁行业主力大学联合商定成立新型产学研合作组织——钢铁可循环流程技术创新战略联盟,于 2007 年 6 月正式签约成立。

(2) 组织存在状态

采取虚拟与实体结合的组织形式。战略联盟由理事会、专家技术委员会和秘书处以及常设办公室等组成,接受中国钢铁工业协会的领导。

(3) 法律地位与形式

联盟是一个非法人契约型组织。

3.3.2 治理结构与权责关系

3.3.2.1 不同合作主体融合的阻碍

(1) 企业追求利润与学术界追求学术地位的矛盾

企业在高强度的竞争中追求利润,因此倾向于对于终端产品和工艺开发,以及降低成本的渐进性创新；中国钢研科技集团更加重视行业共性技术的研发；大学追求研究水平的先进性和在国际上的影响。这三方的发展目标存在一定的分歧。

（2）企业短期利益与科研机构长期知识积累的矛盾

二者之间存在一些矛盾，但不明显。

3.3.2.2 治理结构

以战略联盟协议为准则，明确各成员的责、权、利。在发起单位自愿结合的基础上，制订并签署联盟协议，成立在契约约束基础上、长期合作的战略联盟。

理事会主要职责是，根据专家技术委员会的建议，决定联盟技术发展方向与重点工作任务，协调资金筹措、使用、成果转化及收益分配方案等联盟重大决策事宜。理事会每年定期召开，商议有关事宜和做出有关决策。联盟理事会由联盟成员单位主要领导组成，设理事长一名，由理事会理事选举产生。

专家委员会主要职责是，负责制定联盟的技术发展方向与重点项目，对项目进行论证、监督、评审；根据行业技术发展趋势，制定项目滚动计划。技术委员会委员由钢铁行业专家领导18~20人组成，由理事会聘任。

联盟秘书处主要职责是，在理事会的领导下，负责联盟日常事务和项目的协调、管理工作。联盟秘书处设秘书长一名，副秘书长五名，联络员十名。目前有专职人员三名，由理事会聘任。联盟秘书处办公地点设在中国钢研科技集团公司。

通过联合共建实验室、工程研究中心、合资创建技术公司等方式推动股权式联盟实体的发展，并积极促进联盟成员科技资源的开放共享，形成行业技术创新的平台。

联盟吸纳具备独立法人资格、从事钢铁工艺流程技术及产品研发、制造和服务的企事业单位成为联盟成员，享受联盟成员权利，承担联盟成员义务。各联盟成员是独立的法人实体，联盟与联盟成员之间不形成债权债务关系。

联盟成员为各理事会成员，初始联盟理事会成员由联盟十家发起人组成。承认本协议的非联盟成员，经理事会成员提名，提出申请，由理事会决议通过后，可成为联盟理事会成员。

3.3.2.3 联盟内部组织的具体管理方式

（1）围绕联盟运行的参与单位的资源投入

日常的联络工作与组织工作主要由钢铁总院负责，秘书处的相关人员除各单位指派人员外，其他专职人员由钢铁总院负责。

(2) 围绕联盟运行的任务组织方式与构架

目前主要采用项目组的方式。实行项目总负责人制,项目总负责人把握整体方向,组织专家制定总体内容、计划,经费安排,协调各参加单位的研发工作,定期向专家委员会和理事会汇报。

3.3.2.4 项目选择与主导

联盟的项目确立是经联盟专家技术委员会论证后,由理事会讨论通过。

3.3.2.5 R&D项目的具体管理

(1) 研发不同阶段的管理

由项目负责人负责管理,并接受专家委员会的监督和评审,接受中国钢铁工业协会的监督检查。

(2) R&D成果与后期生产如何结合

新一代可循环钢铁生产流程主要针对我国当前钢铁工业的能耗高、污染大的弊端,研发成果将是今后中国绿色钢铁生产的一个突破,具有普遍的推广意义。但在后期生产上还没有具体的实践。

3.3.2.6 权责关系与行为规则

联盟采用共同研发、成果共享机制。

3.3.3 联盟内部及其与政府的关系

3.3.3.1 核心主体和发起者

联盟中目前没有"领头大哥",中国钢研科技集团仅起到"桥"的作用。

3.3.3.2 参与主体之间关系的演化

目前中国的钢铁产业处于完全的市场竞争状态,钢铁产业集中度很低,联盟中的七家企业的总产量也仅占全国总产量的24%左右,企业之间竞争很激烈。因而,为了降低环境污染、降低能耗,在相关协会和部门的协调组织下,联盟企业在产品层面竞争激烈,但在政府导向的"节能减排、保护环境"共性技术方面开展研发合作。

这种市场的竞争关系影响了联盟的合作,经常导致合作项目久谈不决。

3.3.3.3 相关政府部门的作用

相关政府部门发挥了积极的裁判员的作用,为联盟的发展提供了一定的支撑辅助条件。

同时联盟积极接受国家有关部门的指导，争取国家项目支持。

此外，联盟还接受钢铁工业协会的指导，积极承担钢铁工业协会组织的项目。

3.3.4 知识创造和技术扩散

3.3.4.1 创造知识倚靠的共同资源投入

（1）人力资源

各方都须投入一定的人力资源。在研发阶段主要由中国钢研科技集团和相关大学投入人力资源；在试验发展阶段以企业投入人员为主。

（2）机械与研究设备

相关企业投入一定的设备进行中间试验。

（3）资金

资金上，采取国家项目资金资助与联盟自筹资金相结合的办法。

3.3.4.2 合作成果的管理与扩散

联盟成员单位就联盟内共同开发技术的知识产权签署相关协议。该协议将约定联盟内所产生的知识产权的归属问题、推广应用的利益分配方案及后续进入联盟的成员单位或退出联盟的原成员单位在知识产权共享方面应遵循的基本原则，以避免联盟的知识产权和联盟成员单位已有技术的知识产权受到侵权。

（1）联合研发的新产品

联合研发形成的新技术成果产业化中，强化利益激励与风险共担的关联机制，对勇于承担开发风险和试验使用新技术的受用企业，优先获得创新技术的知识产权。

（2）联合专利的管理

在联盟项目启动前，由各承担单位与项目组织单位共同签署知识产权协议。事先约定所产生的知识产权归属问题及推广应用时的利益分配原则；参与国家项目的各承担单位须对知识产权的共享原则做出承诺。

在完成技术成果后，须合作各方一致同意，才能申请专利。合作各方共同申请专利前，应签署《共同申请专利和确认专利权益的协议》，明确申请专利的费用以及专利年费分担内容，申请人排名按约定的单位排名执行；一方书面确认放弃专利申请权的，其他方可申请专利，其申请费及专利年费由申请方承担。

对于已形成的专利技术，在向该技术受用方实际应用转移时，由专利权所有方与受用方共同协商专利技术转移的相关问题。

联盟各方均有保护联盟知识产权及技术秘密的义务。联盟项目启动之前需签订技术保密协议,技术保密不得与联盟协议中相关规定矛盾。

当联盟内某一成员单位主动退出联盟时,该退出单位将自动放弃与联盟的缔约关系,也不再享受其在联盟内对归属联盟的知识产权的共享条件。

(3) 联合产生的工艺或技术

对于以国拨经费资助研究开发的低污染、高效化生产、节能、降耗等共性平台技术,须无偿向联盟内成员单位辐射和推广。向联盟外辐射和推广时将采取有偿转移方式。

对于利用联盟共性平台技术深度开发的有特色的产品技术及工艺技术,所形成的知识产权在向其他企业辐射和推广时,将采取有偿转移方式,不能作为"排他"技术由承担单位所垄断。

联盟项目产生的专利、技术秘密以及非专利技术成果向联盟外许可或转让须经理事会审议,以书面形式执行。其所获收益,各方按实际投入及贡献大小商定分配的比例。

联盟项目承担各方可以在本单位和拥有 50% 以上股份的企业中无偿地使用本项目生的专利、技术秘密以及非专利技术成果,合作开发方均有在本单位的使用权,该使用权指将本项目开发的技术成果或产品应用于本单位的生产、工艺和设备中使用。

关于知识产权管理相关条款的修改,由联盟成员提出并经联盟理事会讨论通过方可生效。

(4) 合作发表

联盟研究项目所产生的与科学、技术成果有关的著作权属于项目责任方和合作方共同所有,其排名顺序按责任方和合作方的实际投入及具体贡献程度商定。

(5) 科学会议、研讨会等的共同组织

联盟将根据发展需要举办相关的科学会议和研讨会。

(6) 联合培养人才

联盟聚集 14 家单位,拥有近 800 人的研发队伍。

为调动科技人员的积极性,创新技术的受用方要提取一定比例的成果转化奖励基金或集资建立该基金,对有突出贡献的科技人员进行奖励。

3.3.5 法律与制度环境

总体上与现行法规兼容,符合《中华人民共和国反垄断法》的规定;但在联盟资金管理等方面有个别点不相适应。

3.3.6 资金筹集与管理

3.3.6.1 成本分享模式

联盟经费包括日常办公费用、项目经费等。其中,办公室的场地由钢研总院负责,办公室成员中各人员的劳务费用由各自单位负责。

经费来源主要有国家项目经费、联盟成员自筹经费。

3.3.6.2 财力资源的管理和使用方法

（1）财务管理遵循的规则

根据国家有关规定,项目经费实行课题制管理,根据合同使用。

（2）具体实施、财务监督与控制

项目承担任务的联盟单位按照课题任务书实行全面预算、过程控制和全成本核算。联盟经费委托秘书处依托单位设立专门账户,单独核算管理。根据项目合同相关规定进行资金调配,实行预决算制度,专款专用。每年以财务报告形式报理事会审查,并接受第三方审计。项目的验收将根据国家的有关管理办法或合同约定的方式进行及时验收。

通过共性技术的转化和实施,可提取一部分成果转化收入资助会员单位,以竞标的形式,开展行业共性技术的创新。提取比例及具体执行方案由联盟理事会另行商讨制定。

3.4 小结

3.4.1 联盟的基本特征

从上述三个案例分析可见,中国产业技术创新战略联盟是产学研合作创新组织的一种新的形式,其核心是政府引导、产学研结合、契约关系。

（1）从要素组成上看,一是联盟有明确的技术开发方向和技术产出目标,符合国家战略目标或区域重点产业发展的需求;二是签订联盟契约,对参加联盟的具有独立法人地位的产学研各方主体进行法律约束;三是盟员单位要有共同投入,利益共享、风险共担。

（2）从组织形态上看,联盟是在政府的引导下,充分运用市场机制,以影响产业或企业长远发展的共性技术创新需求和重要标准等为纽带,通过各种技术创新要素的优化组合，建立的一种长期、稳定、制度化的产学研利益共同体。

（3）从运行机制上看，联盟本身一般不具有独立的法人地位，是通过契约明晰盟员单位的责权利关系，确立投入、决策、风险承担、利益分配、知识产权归属等机制，保障联盟正常运作。

（4）从主要任务上看，一是实施技术合作，联手突破和发展产业核心技术；二是形成公共技术支撑平台，实现创新资源的有效分工和合理衔接，提高技术创新资源的利用效率，实行知识产权分享，形成产业技术标准；三是实施技术转移，加速创新成果的大规模商业化运用，直接推动产业核心竞争力的提升；四是联合培养人才，推动人员交流互动，增强产业的持续创新能力。

（5）从联盟组建的方式上，一种方式是先由项目再组建联盟，就是依托已立项的国家重大科研项目为牵引和载体，构建联盟；另外一种是先建联盟再支持项目，就是依据产业发展战略需求组建联盟，再通过国家重大科研项目支持联盟的发展。

3.4.2 三个联盟的相似点与差异点

从中国的农业装备产业技术创新战略联盟、新一代煤（能源）化工产业技术创新战略联盟、钢铁可循环流程技术创新战略联盟的具体实践分析可知，虽然都是在政府的引导下成立的产业技术创新战略联盟，在组织形式、目标定位、治理结构等方面具有普遍的相似性，但由于所处行业特征、参与主体等方面的不同，联盟之间也有一定的差别，表现出不同特点。

（1）在组建目标与组织形态方面，三个联盟都具有共同的目标是：一是开发产业共性和关键技术；二是要构建创新平台和产业技术创新链，形成产业技术价值链；三是要推进技术转移和扩散，培养行业技术人才。但它们的目标也有不同之处。由于农业装备产业存在弱、小、散的问题以及产品结构性矛盾问题，以及产业技术直接面向产品终端用户的特点，农业装备联盟的技术导向是产品性技术，提出要创制重大产品，以提升产业技术和产品结构层次。而新一代煤（能源）化工产业技术创新战略联盟、钢铁可循环流程技术创新战略联盟的技术导向是面向中间生产制造商，不是面向终端用户，因此以服务性技术开发为主。

三个联盟的组织形态相似，均是契约形式下的非实体组织，将过去松散的合作以契约形式确定下来，形成制度化、规范化的组织形态，成为一种开放合作与交流的平台。

这种组织形态下的产学研组织，同时具有散、合的特点，既能充分发挥共同研发的优势，又能充分调动参与各方的积极性和资源，同时对组织的管理和运行也提出很高的要求。

（2）在权责关系上具有突出的共同点，即形成合理、运行有效的治理结构以及合理确立参与主体的责任、权益与行为规则是联盟运行和管理中的关键。在中国的这三个产业技术创新战略联盟实践中，有基于联盟的契约型组织形态，以及政府主导和企业为主、研究机构与大学参与的组织分工形式，其治理结构实质是形成一种以议事为导向的决策层和执行层分开的治理机制，三个联盟在这方面具有高度的一致性。决策层方面设置理事会和专家技术委员会，理事会由成员单位各推选代表组成联盟理事会，由理事会根据成员单位对联盟的贡献程度推选其代表作为理事会的负责人；专家技术委员会由理事会从联盟从事技术领域专家中遴选，其中包含一部分成员单位选出的代表，非成员单位中的代表也占有一部分的比例。执行层方面主要是联盟秘书处，秘书处设置由联盟理事会决定，根据理事会决议形成执行责任，负责联盟的日常运行和管理，秘书长是秘书处对外代表，也是联盟实际的对外代表，理论上，秘书处可与理事长单位分开，但实践中，秘书处均依托于理事长单位设置，以确保秘书处工作及人、财、物的保障。联盟的产业技术创新研发的主体是成员单位，成员单位对技术创新研发有很大的自主性，由于联盟的松散的组织形态和不能影响成员单位自身决策，秘书处仅能依据形成的契约才能履行有限的权责。

不同性质参与主体的发展责任各不相同。企业成员其责任是利用其资金、市场优势支持研发，包括直接委托大学、科研机构研发或向大学、科研机构购买技术成果等形式，以推进企业产品技术的升级，进而促进产业技术进步；研究机构成员可利用其应用研发的条件、人才优势，为企业产品技术的突破提供技术支撑，同时获取进一步研究所需的资金和条件支持；而大学成员因国家对大学定位着重于人才培养、理论研究，不直接进入技术竞争领域参与市场竞争，其责任是为技术创新提供理论支持和通过科研项目培养可与企业、科研机构对接的创新人才，并获取科研经费，以提高论文产出的水平。

（3）与政府的关系基本相似。政府的公共管理和公共服务职能决定了政府对联盟的支持，联盟的目标定位和价值观是政府支持联盟的必要条件，没有政府的支持，联盟目标实现和价值定位就有障碍。一方面，推进技术进步、促进产业发展是政府促进经济发展、提高国民收入的政策举措，通过推动构建联盟这种产学研合作创新组织推进政府目标的实现。另一方面，联盟的目标定位和价值观——实现资源的最大化利用、开展产业技术创新、促进产业技术进步，也符合政府发展战略方向，契合政府的政策举措。正是依赖政府的支持，联盟才得到发展，而成为政府推进产业技术创新战略联盟建设的实践和典范。

（4）技术成果的应用和扩散原则相似。以协议的方式确立知识产权、技术扩散等方面的各方权利和义务，是三个联盟合作研发中的关键性要素。其合理的、科学的权责机制是联盟健康持续运行的重要保障。联盟致力于并支持和鼓励先进技术和成果的应用和扩散，以促进产业技术创新与进步。中国的三个产业技术创新战略联盟在这方面基本相同：知识产权约定方面均遵循"事先约定、分类管理、优先共享、有偿转让、收益分享"的基本原则，就是以协议的方式约定不同合作形式下双方或多方的知识产权权利和义务，在保证参与各方利益诉求得到满足的前提下，可以以有偿转让、有偿共享的方式对外发挥作用，实现知识产权的收益最大化，形成的收益按照贡献大小及投入多少等在参与形成知识产权的主体和联盟研发基金之间分配；技术和成果扩散方面遵循的基本原则是"谁开发、谁拥有、合作共享、对内优惠、辐射行业"，在明晰所有权、使用权、收益权的前提下，联盟形成的技术成果应根据不同来源形式确定不同的扩散、转让条件向行业内企业扩散或转让，形成的收益因成果来源性质、权属和参与主体的贡献、投入等不同确定收益分享机制。

三个联盟权责关系形成的复杂性有一定的差别。农业装备产业技术创新战略联盟形成的技术成果可直接进入终端市场的竞争，企业成员单位之间因市场竞争的需要对技术成果的扩散较为谨慎，其谨慎表现在对成果权属和收益分享的确定上，其权责关系的调节和平衡至关重要。新一代煤（能源）化工产业技术创新战略联盟、钢铁可循环流程技术创新战略联盟技术成果不直接进入终端市场的竞争，联盟技术成果应用于企业的生产制造过程所形成的技术和产品才是竞争市场中的产品，因此，其企业成员单位之间的竞争的重点问题是联盟技术成果的权属，相对而言，企业成员更愿意投入到联盟的共同研发中，以确保技术成果的权属有其一部分，这种权责关系更多地表现为投入多少等可以量化的指标，技术成果权责关系较为简单。

（5）非独立法律主体地位相同。从法律主体的角度，联盟是产学研合作组织的一种新形式，是不同民事主体间以订立合同或协议的方式确立的一种合作框架，是民事关系，不是一个作为组织存在的实体，参与主体不能独立作为法律主体参与经济活动，不直接承担法律责任，这就避免了法律法规对实体组织的法律主体确认问题。当前，法律定义的主体只有自然人和法人，中国的三个联盟均不是独立的实体组织，不是法人，不能作为法律主体承担责任，现行的法律框架下，政府部门对联盟的支持必须依托于联盟中某一法律主体，主要是联盟理事长单位。

（6）经费筹集和管理方式相似。目前，联盟的主要经费分为日常运行费、科研项目费。日常运行费来自成员单位的缴纳，主要是理事长单位提供；科研项目费主要来自政府财政科研经费、联盟研发基金（或技术储备资金）。联盟研发基金或者技术储备资金主要来源于成员单位投入、科技成果的收益。管理方面，对不同来源和用途的资金实施不同的管理，日常运行费纳入到秘书处所在的单位（一般是理事长单位）单独设账管理，独立核算，秘书长对经费管理使用负责；财政科研经费以项目形式，按相关财政管理制度和规定管理使用，财政部门、科技部门按分工实施监督，项目承担单位及其法定代表人、项目责任人对经费管理使用负责，一般也要求单独设账，独立核算；研发基金管理由联盟理事会经成员单位同意制定相应的管理使用规定，一般是委托秘书处所在的单位（如理事长单位）单独设账管理，独立核算，以项目形式使用；项目承担单位及其法定代表人、项目责任人对经费管理使用负责，联盟理事会、秘书处行使监督管理职能。总体上，联盟的经费筹集和管理是遵循"联盟指导、立项管理，谁出资、谁使用"的普遍性原则，优化成员单位之间的科研合作的资金流，提高资金产出效益，核心是体现权利和义务的平等，以及研发风险共担、收益共享。

4

奥地利能力中心案例

COMET 计划是奥地利联邦政府近年来支持产学研合作的一个重要政策措施，也是其支持联盟持续发展的重要举措。奥地利政府将卓越技术能力中心计划与支持联盟长期发展紧密结合起来，作为推进联盟实体化的一个重要载体。比较研究中所选择的三个奥地利卓越技术能力中心是奥地利机电一体化能力中心（ACCM）、材料工艺和产品工程综合研究中心（MPPE）和卡琳西亚先进传感器技术研究中心（CTR）。

4.1 奥地利机电一体化能力中心

奥地利机电一体化能力中心（ACCM，下文简称"机电一体化中心"）是奥地利最大的产学研联合研发中心（K2－中心）之一。机电一体化的跨学科研究把产品设计和生产过程等不同研究领域的要素结合起来，尤其是机械工程学的精确度、电子控制、信息学和系统思维。机电一体化中心重点关注的内容包括计算和实验过程仿真、机械系统和模型控制、复杂环境下的数据控制、机电整合设计和驱动系统、传感器和信号，以及不同工业领域的无线电通信和微波技术（FFG 2008a）。这些领域的研究将会实现传感器网络的数据高速传送和高集成磁力轴承系统的问世。

4.1.1 目标和组织形式

4.1.1.1 战略目标

目前，机电一体化中心是欧洲机电一体化领域的领先研究机构之一。该中心的科学目标是在未来十年内成为机电一体化研究领域的全球领先者。要实现这个全面的战略目标需要实现以下分目标：

——把国家在机电一体化领域的现有能力整合到一起。

——与产业界和科学界的主要国际组织连成网络，密切合作，建立和深入发展这些网络很有必要。

——建立科学和产业密切合作的新文化，包括将优化的技术诀窍转让给企业。

——结合企业的战略利益调整机电一体化中心的研究。

——积累机电一体化领域的创新趋势。

——从区域政策的角度，机电一体化中心的战略目标是成为区域和整个奥地利经济中 R&D 的主要参与者，从而增强奥地利的国际吸引力和竞争力。

——通过吸引高级研究人员和发展高水平共性战略研究项目来优化机电一体化的人

才资源。

——通过机电一体化中心和合作伙伴的教育设施，加强培养机电一体化专业工程师。

——从商业管理的角度，机电一体化中心的短期目标是平衡预算，使其维持在奥地利 COMET 计划预先的资助金额之内。该组织模式致力于机电一体化中心的长期巩固和继续发展。

4.1.1.2　法律组织形式

机电一体化能力中心采用了股份有限公司的组织形式，是一个非营利性质的有限责任公司。这是因为公司最适宜于管理参与合作伙伴之间的资金流，并为机电一体化中心的工作流程以及股东和合作伙伴之间的关系提供适当的法律基础。机电一体化中心的权利和义务与任何其他股份有限公司相同。它的三个股东分别是林茨机电一体化中心股份有限公司、Vatron 股份有限公司和约翰开普勒林茨大学（JKU）。林茨机电一体化中心（LCM）股份有限公司曾是 COMET 先前项目——奥地利能力中心项目（2.1.2 部分）的竞争力强化中心。Vatron 是当地机电一体化领域的主要公司，归奥地利钢铁联合公司和西门子所有。约翰开普勒林茨大学是上奥地利州最大的大学，尤其重视工程和技术。

4.1.2　治理结构和权责关系

关于机电一体化中心内部组织和内部治理结构的介绍，主要包括参与的合作伙伴的权利（比如知识产权）和行为准则，着重强调 R&D 管理的分析、优先发展主题的详细说明和机电一体化中心不同层次的组织合作。

4.1.2.1　不同合作主体融合的阻碍

阻碍不同主体之间合理性融合的问题在很大程度上与产业和科学合作伙伴加入机电一体化中心的不同动机有关。基本上，企业和研究机构参与机电一体化中心的动机截然不同，这是由这两种个体潜在的不同合理性导致的。

企业加入机电一体化中心的动机是想利用先进中心集中的高水平的能力。因此，加入机电一体化中心项目的公司期望能得到专门技术问题一体化的解决方案。公司期望能够实现合作研发和知识创造，在一个专业的平台内生产所需的知识，比通过市场中众多不同的供应商获得的方式更廉价，同时也更有效率。除去效率，企业能够通过参与机电一体化中心的 R&D 活动得到 COMET 基金提供的额外资助。此外，参与的企业能够把已整理过的，甚至隐性知识整合到自己的知识库中。值得强调的是基础研究和应用研究之间的关系使机电一体化中心对企业具有很大的吸引力。企业合作伙伴从基础研究开始，进行具体创新，产生新产品或新工艺。这在很大程度上是由于机电一体化中心的基础研究成果能够被机电一体化中心的股东转化成创新产品。在该中心组织中，它的研究人员是由林茨机电一体化中心股份有限公司、Vatron 股份有限公司和约翰开普勒林茨大学雇佣的。因此，固定的员工使得组织内部相互之间的了解增强。

  由于他们特定的合理性，大学和企业的动机并不相同。大学关心的是提高他们与其他大学相关的指标等级。因此，他们对发表文章和提高学术声誉，包括国际影响力感兴趣。与大学相反，企业作为公共产品的生产者，并不想把创造的知识公开发表。在机电一体化中心的案例中，大学能够为研究培训人员争取到额外的资助，尤其是在国际产业和研究人员的网络内更容易完成由基金支持的硕博士论文。由此可能会产生高质量的论文，从而成为高品质的出版物。这对大学来说很有吸引力。同样有吸引力的还有，大学能够与新的国际合作伙伴取得联系。这是因为，网络化对于运用其他基金资源的联合研究项目的未来应用至关重要。

4.1.2.2 治理结构和整合不同合理性的规则

  作为有限责任公司，机电一体化中心有自己的义务。依据所有权，三个股东是机电一体化中心的最高和最终决策者。股东提名机电一体化中心的中心管理层。中心管理层对机电一体化中心战略目标的实现负责，共同管理六个研究领域（计算和实验过程建模与仿真、力学和模型控制、信息和控制、机器和零部件的机电一体化设计、传感器和信号、无线电技术）和机电一体化中心的核心功能（控制、校正等）。目前，中心管理层由林茨机电一体化中心股份有限公司和 Vatron 股份有限公司由各一名人员组成，对机电一体化中心负总责，包括下列特殊任务（ACCM，2008）。

——领导机电一体化中心和对外代表机电一体化中心。

——维护与资助机构以及研发机构之间的关系。

——根据与合伙人创建的项目时间表遵守期限、质量和成本要求。

——法律、人事、财务和项目进度控制事宜。

——投资和管理事宜。

——保证对研究项目制定计划，并按时间表执行。根据 COMET 计划要求，研究项目应与合伙人共同确定。

——预算、成本和财务规划，以及人事管理规划。

——项目执行纲要和规则。

——与领域协调员商定合伙人提出的新项目提议,同时考虑科技顾问委员会的意见。

六个研究领域都通过由股东提名的部门经理(部门协调员)进行协调。每个部门都有主要研究人员、高级研究人员和中级研究人员。主要研究人员通常都是大学终身教授。

机电一体化中心管理层由监事会监督,其中心组织模型见图8。监事会由每个股东派出的两名代表组成。根据奥地利公司法条款完成合法定义的任务,监事会应对机电一体化中心长期科技和经济发展作出贡献。监事会成员应就监事会谈判内容和以监事会成员名义获得的商务信息严格向外界保密。监事会成员的任期结束时,该保密义务仍有效。中心管理层应按要求和定期向监事会汇报业务状况和机电一体化中心公司情况。此外,对于重要事务,以及中心管理层未采纳科技顾问委员会的建议时,中心管理层应向监事会理事长作出书面或口头汇报。中心管理层欲向股东大会呈报的所有事宜,皆须首先在监事会中予以处理。监事会作出的决议与科技顾问委员会的建议有冲突时,须2/3多数投票通过(ACCM,2008)。

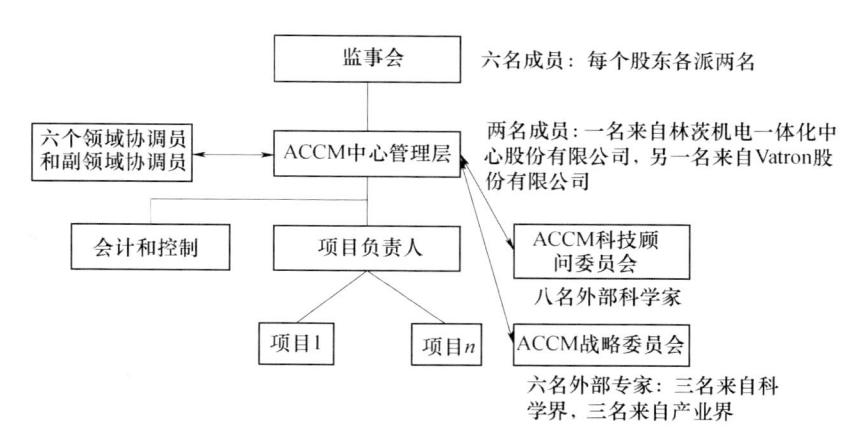

图8 机电一体化中心的组织模型

科技顾问委员会是机电一体化中心另一个重要的顾问机构。该委员会由六名外部专家组成,产业界和科学界各三名,讨论机电一体化中心的战略目标和预算问题。主要任务是为机电一体化中心中心管理层提供科技咨询服务和支撑,以期达到评估标准。该委员会的组成应体现科技和工业经验方面的平衡:委员会成员不得同时为机电一体化中心公司合伙人或资助合伙人,并应具备经认可的高级科技或普通科技整合资格。成员最好在研究项目评估方面或在大型研究项目工业实践方面经验丰富。委员会成员应保证到位,且兼有其他能力。科技顾问机构不附属于机电一体化中心中心管理层（ACCM，2008）。

关于机电一体化中心参与合作伙伴不同合理性整合的问题，一个重要的举措就是在机电一体化中心所有重要的部门中，比如科技顾问委员会，平均分配来自科学界和产业界的成员。在这种环境下，透明度非常重要。但是必须注意到，企业、大学和研究机构之间由于不同合理性而产生的障碍在应用阶段被基本消除。应用阶段对于整合不同合理性至关重要，它对合作伙伴之间信任和共同语言的培养起关键作用。在机电一体化中心的应用阶段，工作团队集中工作三年。因此，协作良好的团队，尤其包括那些核心人员，在2008年机电一体化中心开始之前已经形成。总而言之，由于各种各样的联合项目和核心合作伙伴之间关系的发展，合作氛围在过去这些年已经形成。

4.1.2.3　不同层次的合作组织

在机电一体化中心内，不同合作级别之间（即研究人员、项目主管、主要研究人员、高级研究人员、中级研究人员、区域经理及中心管理层）的相互关系在申请阶段已经计划好。完整的研究项目是在多公司项目和战略项目的基础上组织的。多公司项目包括不同的产业项目和额外的战略研究部分或基础研究部分。战略项目与机电一体化中心总体的战略研究定位紧密相连，比多公司项目能产生更多的通用知识。项目主管对项目目标的实现负责。因此，它成了项目合作伙伴之间进行合作的接口。在六个研究领域，部门协调员负责确保该领域的战略目标能够通过潜在的战略项目或多公司项目实现。部门协调员要在例会上向机电一体化中心的中心管理层汇报进展情况，执行机电一体化中心组织矩阵机构下各研究领域中的科研任务。机电一体化中心的中心管理层负责任命部门协调员及其助理，推荐各领域的主要研究人员和项目主管（项目主管不是主要研究人员）。部门协调员及其助理构成统一平台，向中心管理层提出科技事宜方面的建议，特别是与研究计划有关的事宜。部门协调员将和相关主要研究人员和项目主管共同制定措施，以实现各自领域的目标，并与中心管理层进行协调。

4.1.2.4　实施计划的组织、任务或项目的选择

机电一体化中心的基本实施计划和优先选择主题最初在项目建议书里概述。核心合作伙伴对选择优先项目起关键作用。最初，机电一体化中心申请了7100万欧元的经费。批准的2008—2012的预算是5700万欧元。因此，在接到获得资助的通知之后，考虑所有项目需要的资源，通过与合作伙伴的两轮讨论，确立一个具体的实施计划来进行优先主题的进一步设置（一些最初的规划项目不得不从基本实施计划中去掉）。2008—2012年的

详细实施计划已经制定,包括所有计划项目的清单、人员、工作流程、机器、设备、场所等都作了安排。项目开始之后,既定的主题方向是约定不可改变的。但是,在复杂的R&D活动过程中,改变经常是必须的。因此,部门协调员和/或科技顾问委员会能建议新的优先主题和项目。部门协调员在例会上向中心管理层提出他(或她)的建议。如果这个建议被认为是有意义的,科技顾问委员会就会关注。然后,科技顾问委员会就会向中心管理层提出建议。中心管理层拥有最终决定权,并汇报给监事会。

4.1.2.5 R&D管理:控制和营销

如上所述,机电一体化中心有两类项目,即多公司项目和战略项目。R&D管理包括项目控制和项目成果的营销,比如通过发表文章。每个项目的组织都要有清晰的项目计划,包括资源、重要节点、预算等。产品结构管理是机电一体化中心的关键管理手段,比如资源规划和项目成果营销。在机电一体化中心的产品型谱中,每个研究项目都被分配到一个研究领域和专门的产业分支中,即机电一体化中心研究领域在项目应用和产业分支联系的基础上产生潜在的客户。表8描述了机电一体化中心产品结构的概貌。

表8 机电一体化中心的产品结构管理

	按科学学科组织的项目							公司伙伴需要一个广阔的机电一体化联合体(平台)				
							产业分支/应用					
	机械系统构建者							部件供应者(子系统)				
ACCM领域	炼钢	工具机器与生产厂	塑料加工	内燃机	农业机械	纺织机械	移动设备	综合测量与传感器系统	液压驱动及传动系统	电力驱动器	自动化软硬件	通信应用的集成电路
计算与实验过程模型与仿真	■	■										
机械学与控制模型	■				■							
信息与控制												
机电一体化设计	■									■		
传感器和信号	■											
无线技术	■											

4.1.2.6 权利和义务、行为准则和信息流

机电一体化中心参与合作伙伴的权利和义务在联盟协议和项目具体合作合同中有明确规定。联盟协议规定了总体的责任,比如合作伙伴的加入和退出;合作伙伴的取消期是6个月,必须在年底才能取消。对于合作伙伴来说,协议签订之后权利和规则都具有强制性。也就是说,以协议为准,他们必须提供约定的资源,比如以现金、人员或基础

设施的形式。

一个关键问题就是知识产权的管理。机电一体化中心协议定义了为 K2 基金项目的机电一体化中心研究结果授权的一般框架。相关权利的精确定义应在项目具体合同中予以确立，项目具体合同应按照机电一体化中心协议（ACCM，2008）的一般原则订立。除了知识产权，项目具体合同还应包括项目层次上的现金流和基础设施规定。知识产权法规至关重要，尤其是在整合合作伙伴不同合理性的背景下。机电一体化中心的产权法规致力于平衡所有合作伙伴间的利益，确保尽可能多地将研究成果付诸实践。

机电一体化中心的方法总结如下：多公司项目的案例包括了工业项目和基础研究的部分，公司具体的成果由各自的公司拥有，即公司合作伙伴必须在项目开始之前确定具体的主题领域，因为该公司要提出产权要求。主题领域的定义在项目合作伙伴间的双边会议上进行协商，在项目具体合同中进行规定。主题领域按产品、服务领域、客户、合作伙伴竞争对手依次定义。合作活动应列出主题领域，确保紧扣主题和项目结果的既定用途（ACCM，2008）。

机电一体化中心协议对多公司项目的合作公司一方作如下规定：

——不同成果由各自合作伙伴拥有。

——不同合作伙伴在其规定的活动领域享受专属使用权。

——有专利成果的，不同专利由相关合作伙伴申请并拥有。合作合同中应作出相关规定。发明人拥有非竞争性使用权。

机电一体化中心协议对多公司项目的基础研究一方作如下规定：

——基础研究成果由机电一体化中心拥有。

——项目合作伙伴对基础研究成果作出贡献的，无论是直接参与研究，还是委托代理，均享有非独占性使用权。

——若项目合作伙伴许可第三方将基础研究成果用于合同目的之外的用途，机电一体化中心将按相应的比例获取因授权许可使用所带来的净利润（扣除相应费用的利润）。

——由于项目之间相似性、成果性质以及合作伙伴的不同，各公司享受权利与研究成果的相关性也不同。

——研究成果涉及专利的，应在向专利署申请审理专利后一个月内通知所有项目合作伙伴。

——战略项目的成果由机电一体化中心拥有。对战略成果的产出作出贡献的每个项目合作伙伴均有权免费使用成果，但该使用权是非独占性的。与非机电一体化中心合作伙伴的公司相比，合作伙伴有权提前三月获悉专利申请，并拥有优先购买权。

关于出版规则，战略项目产生的成果不受任何出版限制。在多企业项目的案例中，计划的文章发表必须在所有合作伙伴都参加的例会上讨论。通常，如果有一个项目合作伙伴反对发表计划，必须找到合适的解决办法。这可能会导致变通的出版方式，但只包括初步或概念上的成果。机电一体化中心对出版所作的正式规定如下（ACCM，2008）：

——协议合作伙伴根据 K2 计划目标约定，合作伙伴应加快获得发表配额。

——研究项目的研发成果未经相关项目合作伙伴同意不得发表。

——若有发表意图，机电一体化中心或参与项目的合作伙伴应先征得受发表内容影响的合作伙伴的同意。受发表影响的项目合作伙伴若无重大理由不得拒绝同意发表。若发表提议被拒，应于四周内书面陈述理由。若四周内未对发表提议作出反应，视为默认。

——与战略研究项目相关的出版物不受此限。

4.1.3　中心内部及其与政府的关系

4.1.3.1　核心合作伙伴与发起人

机电一体化中心有三个股东和 42 家企业合作伙伴，包括中小企业（SMEs）和 36 家科学合作伙伴组成。核心主角是三个股东。约翰开普勒林茨大学是核心科学合作伙伴，包括 14 家研究所。科学领域其他的核心合作伙伴还有维也纳技术大学和坦佩雷大学（芬兰）。核心企业合作伙伴，除了林茨机电一体化中心股份有限公司和 Vatron 股份有限公司，还有奥地利钢铁联合公司、西门子、IHTech Sondermaschinenbau und Instandhaltung 股份有限公司、Salvagnini Maschinenbau 股份有限公司和卢森宝亚国际有限公司。这些公司集中在工业工程和电子行业。

4.1.3.2　关系的发展

机电一体化中心的股东得益于长期建立的合作氛围。机电一体化领域在过去几年已经被上奥地利州确定为优先发展主题。约翰开普勒林茨大学于 1990 年建立了机电系，是世界上最早开展机电一体化研究生项目的大学。在 20 世纪 90 年代，约翰开普勒林茨大学和地方企业（奥地利钢铁联合公司、Vatron 股份有限公司）在机电一体化方面通过小型项目或人员流动建立了合作关系。

4.1.3.3　相关政府部门的作用

上奥地利州的一些区域技术政策加强了该领域中核心主角之间的关系。在这种背景下，机电一体化中心与地区政府之间建立了良好的关系。相关政府部门的作用主要受机电一体化中心与FFG之间相互关系的影响。FFG代表运输创新技术部（BMVIT）和经济事务与劳动部（BMWA）。这种关系一方面关注选择过程（即事前评估），另一方面关注机电一体化中心持续的监督和评估过程（详细的评估过程见第二部分）。

4.1.3.4 中心或联盟的历史

在20世纪90年代建立的关系基础上，上奥地利州在COMET的前期项目中建立了机电一体化领域的两个能力中心。工业技术机电一体化能力中心（IKMA）创建于1999年，竞争力强化中心林茨机电一体化能力中心创建于2001年。根据访谈调研，两个能力中心促进了合作氛围的形成，使当地机电一体化领域的能力得到显著提高。在上奥地利州机电一体化引进和奥地利议会2001年研究技术发展高级战略（RFTE）的基础上，林茨机电一体化中心、Vatron股份有限公司、工业技术机电一体化能力中心和约翰开普勒林茨大学开始了进一步发展上奥地利州机电一体化的最初构想，包括在林茨（上奥地利州）建立机电一体化高级研发中心的战略文件。FFG在2006年发布了COMET的新项目，两家核心合作伙伴决定申请建立一个K2高级研发中心。紧跟COMET项目的竞争性招标，根据事前评估，机电一体化中心被选中，并于2008年开始运作。

林茨机电一体化中心成功案例

林茨机电一体化中心（LCM）成立于2001年，是COMET早期在奥地利创办的17个K字头中心之一。如今它已发展为一家独立有限公司，以及ACCM K2中心的三大股东之一。该中心是研究员和政府部门公认的奥地利国内在应用机电研究领域的领先机构。LCM现已成功开展该领域内150多个合作研发项目。其服务范围沿着整条创新链围绕合作展开——从概念设计到成品，包括七大能力（机电设计、过程模拟、电气驱动、液压驱动、情报分析和故障诊断、多体&多领域动态和结构控制，以及感应器和通讯）。

LCM的顺利发展表现在其为学术界作出的巨大贡献：出版了500种出版物，发表了100篇硕士论文。LCM是上奥地利州机电领域的主要合作平台，汇集了众多大学、企业和研究机构的研究员。它对上奥地利州的机构合作文化作出了突出贡献。LCM的突出表现受到一系列创新奖励，比如2009年最佳企业，2008年MEC奖，2007年跨界奖，2005、2003、2002年上奥地利州创新奖，2003年Trauner奖以及2002年Peqasus银奖。

4.1.4 知识创造和技术扩散

4.1.4.1 知识创造的联合资源

机电一体化中心知识创造最重要的投入是机电一体化中心项目研究人员投入的知识。表9展示的是机电一体化中心在2008年的人力资源的概况。在机电一体化中心工作的研究人员并不是机电一体化中心雇佣的。绝大多数研究人员受雇于三大股东，其他研究人员来自参与的合作伙伴。机电一体化中心强调研究人员的工程和机电一体化背景。目前，来自不同合作伙伴的大约200名研究人员在机电一体化中心的联合项目中工作。

机电一体化中心的研究项目要求有相当规模的基础设施，包括场所、实验室、机器和设备。项目中需要和利用的基础设施不属于机电一体化中心。通常来说，所用的基础设施在联营协议和项目具体合同中加以规定。在第一个五年资助期间，机电一体化中心得到COMET项目的财政资助是5700万欧元。每年的项目预算大约是1200万欧元。

4.1.4.2 合作成果的管理和扩散

合作成果的管理和扩散在联营协议和项目具体合同中都有规定，比如知识产权和发表文章的规定。管理合作成果的重要工具是产品型谱。机电一体化中心的期望成果在项目建议书中提出。至于

表9 2008年机电一体化中心的人力资源统计

ACCM项目工作人员类别	人数
总数	152
科研人员	133
全职	60
主要研究人员	17
高级研究员	37
中级研究员	71
技术人员	5
行政（管理，控制等）	14
青年科学家	—
实习生	—
博士生和硕士研究生	7

表10 2008～2012年机电一体化中心的产出要求

1. 研究成果	
在科技期刊上发表的论文（篇）	625*
专利和许可证	40
2. 研究项目	
战略项目的份额	20%
3. 额外项目	
企业合作伙伴研究强度的增加	15%
4. 人力资源	
高级培训（人）	27
博士论文（毕业的）（篇）	75
硕士论文（毕业的）（篇）	175
5. 网络（个）	
企业	40
研究机构	40
国际合作伙伴	32
国内合作伙伴	48
6. 成本和预算/万欧元	
从第三方获得资金	200

注：其中235计划成为科学企业合作发表文章，必须说明ACCM对创新产出的数量没有具体的要求。但是，在协议中，90%的企业合作伙伴期望参加ACCM能开发新产品。

其他的案例，机电一体化中心创造的知识通过不同的出版模式和区域及国家创新体系中的专利扩散。表 10 概述了机电一体化中心的产出要求，表 11 总结了机电一体化中心在 2008 年的成果。

表 11　2008 年机电一体化中心的知识成果

1. 研究成果	
发表文章（篇）	159
专利申请（个）	2
专利批准	—
参加会议	22
2. 教育	
博士论文（毕业的）（篇）	—
博士论文（尚未毕业）（篇）	3
硕士论文（毕业的）（篇）	—
硕士论文（尚未毕业）（篇）	14

注：注意创新并没有列在这里，因为创新并没有正式的包含在 ACCM 的目标标准中。ACCM 视创新为新商品。但是，ACCM 是一个非营利性质的研究机构。

4.1.5　法律和制度环境

4.1.5.1　与不同领域现行法律和法规的兼容性

大体上，目前的制度环境没有对机电一体化中心的成立和顺利运行形成明显障碍。但是，至于税收条例，并没有明确说明机电一体化中心能在何种程度上利用奥地利税法中所谓的"Forschungs-freibetrag"❶，允许创新企业扣除基本的 R&D 支出后再减免 25% 的税收，因为在机电一体化中心的案例中很难区分产业合同研究和基础的 R&D。因此，在这种背景下一个更加精确的法规会更加有益。

奥地利就业法与机电一体化中心的模式兼容，并为管理机电一体化中心项目工作人员提供了合理的框架。每个研究人员对机电一体化中心项目的贡献都有明确规定。比如，一个受雇于大学的研究人员可能把他 30% 的工作时间投入到机电一体化中心的项目上，其他的工作时间为大学服务。在这个例子中，这名研究人员 30% 的薪水由机电一体化中心 COMET 基金支付。机电一体化中心作为有限责任公司，有资格得到国家科学和研究促进项目的资助（比如奥地利科学基金会对基础研究提供资助，奥地利科学促进会对应用研究提供资助）。此外，机电一体化中心也可以向欧共体研究技术开发和示范第七框架计划（FP7）提交项目建议。

4.1.5.2　制度环境的效果评估

从机电一体化中心管理的角度来看，制度环境为机电一体化中心能力中心的成立提

---

❶ 德文。中文大意为：针对某一特定对象的 R&D 活动的津贴补助。

供了适宜的环境。尤其是国家和地区利益的相互影响得到平衡,在成立的过程中并没有产生棘手的障碍。目前的法律法规,比如大学法、就业法和税法,并没有对机电一体化中心能力中心的成立造成明显的或排他性的条文,而是相互兼容。

4.1.6 融资和资金管理

4.1.6.1 融资模式和成本分摊

现在机电一体化中心的预算几乎100%来自于COMET基金,五年5700万欧元。其中,50%(2850万欧元)来自于国家基金(30%)、州基金(20%)。总基金中5%由大学提供。后者是通过实物捐赠的形式来提供的,包括人力资本和实物资本,比如设备使用和材料供应。剩下的45%预算来自参与的企业,然而企业贡献的65%是以现金方式提供,35%则以实物捐赠的方式。

4.1.6.2 财力资源的管理方式和利用

机电一体化中心运用任何有限责任公司都有的强制手段来管理资金资源,就像机电一体化中心的中心管理层一样,尤其在控制和会计方面。机电一体化中心的管理层解决预算事务,股东大会和监事会对预算事务进行控制(见4.1.2)。财力资源只可用于完成机电一体化中心的研究项目。

4.2 材料、工艺和产品工程综合研究中心

材料、工艺和产品工程综合研究中心(MPPE,下文简称材料综合中心)是一个集中研究材料、工艺和产品工程的卓越技术能力中心计划K2中心。材料综合中心是一个合资研究机构——莱奥本材料中心科技股份有限公司(MCL)的主要组成部分,是MCL领导下的非营利性合资机构。该中心重点强调材料开发、材料加工、加工技术和材料的创新应用。材料科学,包括材料的加工处理和工程设计,是一个跨学科研究领域,重点研究材料的微观结构及其宏观特性之间的相互关系。因而,材料综合中心提供各种不同材料测试的可能结果,以对产业界提供支持,并且与来自科学和产业界的合作伙伴密切合作,实施众多的研发项目。

4.2.1 目标和组织形式

4.2.1.1 战略目标

材料综合中心旨在在材料科学与产品工程领域开展国际性高层次的基础和应用研究。在此背景下，总体战略目标是把材料综合中心建设成为拥有国际地位的材料和材料技术先进中心，专门从事有关材料开发、加工、制造和应用的复杂、多学科研发中心。此外，材料综合中心意在达成以下战略目标：

——将先进中心建设成为学术和产业界在材料科学领域进行有效合作的战略平台，以创造这一技术领域的产学研结合联合体。

——材料综合中心将提高研发能力，提升合作伙伴的知识生产与创新能力。

——促进材料科学新的研发人员和专家的教育和培训。

——材料综合中心旨在促进和巩固自身在该领域的地区性和全国性的同行中占有一席之地。

——长期的经济战略目标是巩固材料综合中心独立研究机构的地位。在COMET计划资助结束后，其经费一部分来自其他资金，一部分由产业合同研究和产品开发提供。

从 MCL 股东这个角度来看，他们大多是当地公共研究机构，战略目标是把 Leoben 周边区域打造成著名的国际性材料科学与产品工程设计中心。

4.2.1.2 法律组织形式

材料综合中心（K2中心）是一个 MCL 领导下的非营利性合资机构。值得注意的是，材料综合中心得到的 COMET 计划的经费是 MCL 预算的主要部分（最高达到92%）。MCL 和任何有限责任公司一样，用相同的强制性要素和权利作为管理手段。采用这种组织形式是为了确保 MCL 和 FFG 之间，以及 MCL 和合作伙伴之间的资金交易转移进行得简单、透明和规范。另外，有限责任公司的组织形式提供适当的法律平台来控制材料综合中心的战略定位，提供一个稳定的法律保障，并为股东提供适当的管理手段。MCL 的股东有莱奥本大学（the University of Leoben）、约安尼姆研究股份有限公司、莱奥本市、奥地利科学院、维也纳科技大学和格拉茨科技大学。

材料综合中心的组织模型见图9。

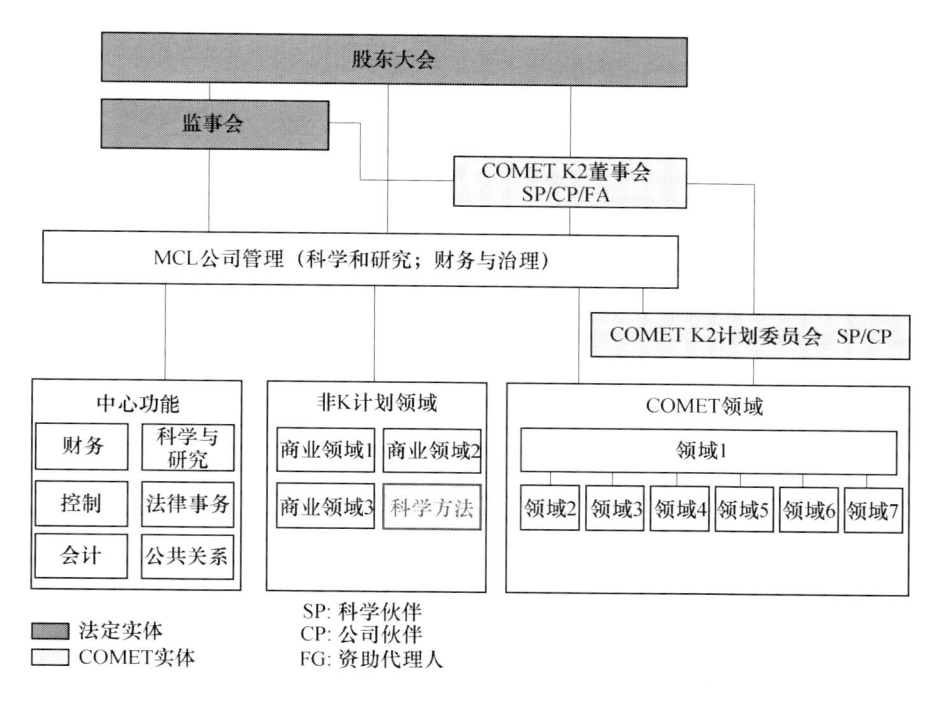

图 9 材料综合中心的组织模型

4.2.2 治理结构和权责关系

4.2.2.1 不同合作主体融合的阻碍

像机电一体化中心案例一样，阻碍不同合理性整合的问题在很大程度上与激励企业和科研院所参与材料综合中心的动机有关。公司的动机是为了有机会参与高水平、综合性和高度集中的研究活动。公司可以通过材料综合中心联系高等院校，例如在寻找一个非常具体的专业领域的高素质研发人员的情况下，就可以发挥材料综合中心的作用。因此，建立关系网络是公司参与材料综合中心最重要工作之一。公司合作伙伴有机会接触到该技术领域的核心人员，不仅仅是通过正式途径，而且还包括非正式方式。此外，他们有机会筛选新主题领域，了解新技术的发展，并且他们因为材料综合中心实施战略研究项目而有机会接触相应的战略研究领域❶。由此，参与的公司可通过与材料综合中心合

---

❶ COMET 计划的战略研究项目与中心的全局战略研究方向密切相关，与多组织项目相比可以产生更多的通用知识。

作伙伴的互动来刺激新知识库的激活，并通过这种方式将新知识整合到自己的知识库。

除了建立关系网络和筛选新主题领域，企业参与材料综合中心计划的一个关键动机是为了降低成本、减少产品研发以及技术创新的风险。这通过以下三种机制实现：第一，通过与不同的科学和产业合作伙伴的网络合作可以降低成本；第二，需要由公司合伙人实施的研发项目，由公共基金负担了部分经费；第三，中长期非核心但与研发计划存在潜在联系的研发活动可以由材料综合中心合作者承担。

大学参与材料综合中心的动机是多种多样的：第一，被选择的大学主要致力于提高大学自身的科学技术基础知识、研究问题的方法以及科学基础结构。一些大学特别提倡获得更深层次的方法论知识。第二，在其他情形下，高校的动机在于通过材料综合中心这个平台有可能计划并完成与高素质国际合作伙伴进行战略研究的目标。通过这种途径，一些正在参与的大学渴望提高他们科学产出的质量。第三，有些大学，参与的关键性因素是可以有机会与国际合作伙伴建立关系网络，这可能会带来有额外资助的联合研究项目。第四，被选定的高等院校强调培养国际水平研究人员和其他博士申请者的可能性，特别是在创作博士论文的情形下。这些论文由材料综合中心提供财政资金。论文通常可以出版，这是高等院校重要的绩效评价标准。

4.2.2.2 治理结构和整合不同主体的规则

在 MCL 领导下材料综合中心的企业组织模式，即集团领导，负责材料综合中心的组织和战略发展。MCL 是一家非盈利性有限责任公司，包括一个 COMET 领域——针对 COMET 计划内的活动和一个非 K 领域——针对 COMET 计划外的活动。COMET 领域让单个伙伴小组有机会通过 COMET 董事会和 MCL 公司 COMET 计划委员会参与决策制定。MCL 股东在董事会上要执行股东的权利和义务，特别是在管理者的提名和任命方面。股东大会履行奥地利法律对有限责任公司规定的任务。董事会主席为维也纳大学的一个教授，不是由各合作伙伴中推举出来。COMET 计划相关其他责权包括任命监事会成员和确认监事会议事规则（见 MPPE 2008）。

监事会和股东大会控制材料综合中心的管理部门，它负责材料综合中心战略目标的实现和材料综合中心研究计划的执行。材料综合中心管理部门领导公司三个重大的部分：中心职能（包括融资、技术管理、控制、法律部门、会计和公共关系）、COMET 研究部分和非 COMET 研究部分。管理部门执行下列任务（MPPE，2008）：

——执行研究计划，包括开发团队技能，激发项目和战略规划。

——保证所需的项目组合。

——项目预评估。

——根据报告规则向资助代理机构报告。

——COMET董事会和COMET计划委员会的组织支撑，如会议召开、资料派发和会议记录等。

——申请后续资助期限。

在COMET计划下，监事会执行下列任务（MPPE，2008）：

——审查材料综合中心战略规划和概念、年度研究计划、年度评估、年度账目、管理报告和组合应用，并向股东大会汇报审查结果。

——批准COMET董事会的议事规则。

——任命和罢免COMET董事会主席。

——根据材料综合中心公司合伙人的推荐，任命和罢免董事会和计划委员会中的公司代表。

——根据材料综合中心公司科研机构的推荐，任命和罢免董事会和计划委员会中的科研机构代表。

——施第里尔省政府有权指派两名成员到监事会中。

COMET研究部分分为九个研究领域（材料综合研究、工艺和产品工程、多尺度材料设计、高精度的材料加工和制造、损坏机制、进化和造型设计、高级工艺工具技术、轻量级耐疲劳设计、功能特性元件的设计和可靠性），每一个部分由一个领域管理者领导。非COMET研究部门的研究资金（大约占MCL预算总额的8%）由其他来源提供，包括三个商业单位。

材料综合中心治理结构的其他重要组成部分是COMET的K2董事会和K2计划委员会。在材料综合中心中，K2董事会是最重要的决策主体，执行下列主要任务：

——根据MCL管理部门的建议向监理会提出战略事宜方面的建议。

——对COMET下的多组织项目和战略项目细化框架条件。

——根据合伙人提议推荐计划委员会成员为监理会候选人。

——根据MCL管理部门的提议向监理会推荐COMET研究计划。

——根据管理部门的提议和计划委员会的推荐，对COMET项目作出决策。

——根据COMET项目报告监督可研究目标成就。

COMET董事会由公司合伙人和科研机构各一半人数组成，国际伙伴也应占有席位。FFG代表在COMET董事会中无投票权。

K2计划委员会支持材料综合中心管理中有关研究项目的问题，并且还担当咨询委员会的角色。它由材料综合中心的七个研究领域代表组成，并且对新项目或是主题的优先权提供建议。计划委员会的任务包括评估项目建议书、向董事会提供建议、参与研究计划深入探讨。该计划委员会由公司伙伴和研发机构各占一半人数组成，以确保专有技术的平衡。由此，材料综合中心治理结构与机电一体化中心治理结构有着显著的区别。

4.2.2.3　不同级别的合作组织

材料综合中心不同级别人员（研究人员、项目负责人、关键研究人员、领域管理者和一般管理人员）的合作关系在材料综合中心建议书中有详细说明。完整的材料综合中心研究计划在项目的基础上组建。项目可分为战略项目、多公司项目和单一公司项目。战略项目是从材料综合中心基本战略定位考虑制定的更广泛和更强调基础研究导向的项目，而多公司或单一公司项目通常涉及具体的应用。项目组长负责操作执行。因此，需要组织来自材料综合中心不同参与者的项目成员进行合作。项目的成绩和科学产出由领域经理和所谓的各个领域重点研究人员进行评估。全局研究计划层面上的管理和组织合作则交给材料综合中心管理部门。

4.2.2.4　实施计划的组织，任务或项目的选择

在材料综合中心中，战略实施计划和优先研究主题的选择在第一资助期（2008—2012年）项目建议书中进行描述，已经有了项目层次（包括战略项目和多公司项目）。这包括人事分配以及项目所需的基础设施（如机器、设备、实验室等）。材料综合中心的具体主题领域和任务在申请阶段也被确定下来。材料综合中心成立后，任务及新优先主题的选择可以由计划委员会提出建议，即领域管理者或领域成员可以在这个平台上提出新的优先主题。计划委员会决定是否将新建议提交到战略委员会，由战略委员会决定通过或否决建议领域。该评估是建立在新建议的科学先进性及与材料综合中心战略方向的相关性基础之上的。

4.2.2.5　研发管理：控制和营销

项目组长负责项目管理。材料综合中心管理中心负责总体计划管理。每个项目都是通过一个明确的工程计划进行组织，包括资源、重要节点、预算，等等。研究人员在某一项目上的工作时间自动实时记录。时间计划和预算问题由材料综合中心的财务控制部

门进行监管。项目成果和新产品及工艺的营销通过通讯和出版物来完成。它是由材料综合中心公共关系部门管理的。

4.2.2.6 权利和义务、行为准则和信息流

第一,材料综合中心通过 MCL 与 FFG 之间的合同协定进行系统管理。它说明了 FFG 向 MCL 提供的资金流,以及 MCL 需提供的产品和服务。第二,在材料综合中心建立之前由所有合作伙伴签订的联盟合同是规范合作伙伴权利和行为的主要文件,诸如欧盟对于资助或合伙人进入和退出制定的条例、对于不同类型项目制定的通用知识产权规则以及对于出版物制定的规则,通过取消期制度注销合作伙伴关系等。第三,项目具体合同规范具体项目的合作,包括被认为是最重要部分的知识产权法规。

相对于机电一体化中心而言,战略项目和多公司项目知识产权法规有所区别。材料综合中心协议定义了一般条款,更多特殊条款将在项目特定合同中定义。战略项目结果通用规定如下(MPPE,2008):

——参与战略项目的所有合伙人皆可使用研发成果。

——若战略项目产生可获得工业产权的发明,应遵守本协议中与名称、使用和开发权相关的条款。

——若获得了工业产权,参与战略研究项目的合伙人(以项目合同为基础)应有权获得项目合同项下业务领域方面的付费非专营许可证。该许可证的期限为无限期,并无区域限制,可独家转让给附属企业。

——若 MCL 或参与的科研机构放弃申请或持有工业产权,其他参与本项目的科研机构和公司合伙人应有权获得项目合同项下活动领域的该等产权,并支付一定金额费用。

单公司和多公司项目结果的主要规定如下(MPPE,2008):

——参与战略项目的所有合伙人皆可使用研发成果。

——若单公司或多公司项目产生可获得工业产权的发明时,合伙人应在项目合同中预先商定使用和开发权的类型和程度以及申请方式。

——由单公司或多公司项目产生的工业产权,MCL 和参与项目的研发机构有权获得项目合同规定的公司合伙人业务领域以外的非专营可转让许可证,以及项目合同规定的公司合伙人活动领域以外的非专营不可转让许可证。

——若公司合作伙伴、科研机构或 MCL 放弃其工业产权,该工业产权应无偿提供给参与发明的合伙人。若该合伙人也放弃,则该工业产权应转让给参与项目的其他合伙人。

材料综合中心在战略项目中比在多公司项目中对知识产权占有更高的份额。然而，在战略项目中产生的知识必须通过许可提供给材料综合中心所有的合作伙伴。在多公司项目中，知识产权通常根据其在项目具体的合作合同中说明优先主题，在项目参与者之间进行分配。

出版物的规则如下。在多公司项目中，可能的出版物需要通过咨询所有参与项目的合作伙伴后进行协调。每个项目伙伴必须对出版计划提供一个正式批准。当秘密被泄露或所有权受到侵犯时，项目伙伴可以反对一个出版物。那么，出版物的内容需要被重新考虑或延迟出版。一般来说，材料综合中心的多公司项目应该促进所有参与合作伙伴的联合出版。项目合作伙伴可以在一年内禁止在项目过程中完成的硕士和博士论文的出版。

4.2.3　中心内部及其与政府的关系

4.2.3.1　核心主体和发起者

约 30 个企业和 20 个研究机构参加了材料综合中心。在科学界方面，莱奥本大学是材料综合中心的核心合作伙伴（参加了 6 个不同的部门），这也与它的历史及其在莱奥本（施蒂里亚省）城市中心的位置有关。核心的产业合作伙伴是 Böhler Uddeholm 和 Voest Alpine——奥地利两家规模最大的钢铁生产企业。这些核心的合作伙伴给材料综合中心联盟带来了一些小型和中型的公司。

4.2.3.2　参与主体之间关系的演化

莱奥本大学通过合同研究，特别是劳动力流动，与材料综合中心的核心产业合作伙伴建立长期合作关系。这种合作关系最早可以追溯至 1840 年。地方产业对维持莱奥本大学在此地区的发展中发挥了重要作用。因此，莱奥本大学和当地产业之间的关系有着悠久的传统。在决定申请一个奥地利能力中心项目（COMET 联合 K-plus 中心项目）的过程中，股东之间关系有了进一步发展，故材料综合中心可以理解为是一个由核心伙伴所建立的这个 K-Plus 中心的后续。

4.2.3.3　相关政府部门的作用

作为项目的所有者——交通、创新与技术部及经济事务、家庭和青年部❶的代表，

---

❶ 现经济事务与劳工部的前身。

FFG 在 COMET 计划的管理中扮演着代理者的重要角色。FFG 负责对材料综合中心进行事前和事后评估。此外，地方和区域政府在建立中心的过程中扮演了至关重要的角色。一些地区的政策措施，表明了材料综合中心作为最重要的创新者和区域经济发展推动者的重要地位。对于所有的 COMET 中心而言，在地区中的角色是其声誉的一个重要方面。

4.2.3.4 联盟的历史

为了鼓励莱奥本科学与产业界在材料科学领域的合作，MCL 于 1999 年正式成立。在 K－Plus 计划得到良好的事前评估后，MCL 被改造成一个股份有限公司。K－Plus 中心事后评估鼓励核心伙伴继续合作，并在后续的 COMET 计划中申请 K2 中心。对 MCL 已有资源和合作者，以及合作者之间已经建立的协作文化的评估，是这个决策的基础。这同样受到当地和地区政府机构的大力支持。

MCL 的成功历程

MCL 是 COMET 计划下的一个 K－Plus 中心，即奥地利性能计划中心。奥地利决策者普遍认为，MCL K－Plus 中心特别注重开发全新建模和模拟技术，对加强在材料学领域的技术竞争优势作出了重要贡献。一方面表现为对科学界的贡献，新推出 700 种出版物和硕博论文；另一方面，MCL 研究成果促进了参与公司引进大量产品和工艺创新，特别是在材料加工和材料工程方面。

MCL 成功完成的项目，其总费用为 3300 万欧元。MCL K－Plus 中心特别注重进一步维持和开发奥地利，特别是莱奥本附近的材料领域方面的公司、大学和研究机构之间的合作性文化，从而为成功申请 K2－中心 MPPE 打下了基础。

4.2.4 知识创造和技术扩散

这部分对材料综合中心知识生产过程的投入进行了全面的概述，介绍了有关具体成果目标和目标标准的部分数字。

4.2.4.1 知识创造的联合资源

与机电一体化中心和卡琳西亚中心类似，材料综合中心人力资本和研究者的知识是知识创造最重要的投入。表 12 概述了 2008 年材料综合中心的人力资源概况。材料综合中心科研人员的学科背景侧重于工程和机电工程。目前，材料综合中心约有 125 名员工，其中科研人员约 90 人，行政人员 35 人。

材料综合中心的总部设在莱奥本市。基础设施包括一幢有很多实验室的办公楼。项目所需的其他设施（如机器设备）通常根据项目具体合同的规定进行租赁。COMET 计划在第一个五年期内对材料综合中心的资助约为 5300 万欧元。

4.2.4.2 合作成果的管理与扩散

材料综合中心合作成果的管理和扩散在联盟协议和具体的项目合同中都有规定。项目提案中概述了材料综合中心期望产生的成果，FFG 将在五年之后评价其成果。由材料综合中心产生的知识可以通过研究人员在材料综合中心和合作伙伴之间的流动进行充分地扩散。表 13 概述了 2008—2012 年材料综合中心期望的成果，而表 14 总结了 2008 年材料综合中心的成果。

表 12　2008 年材料综合中心的人力资源统计

MPPE 员工	
总数	89
科研人员	74
全职工作人员	53
核心研究人员	5
高级科学家	10
一般科学家	57
技术人员	8
行政人员（管理和控制等）	7
青年科学家	
实习生	—
硕士和博士研究生	27

表 13　2008～2012 年 MPPE 期望产出值

1. 研究成果	
科学期刊出版物（件）	195
专利和许可证（件）	3
2. 研究项目	
战略项目分享	21.7%
3. 额外成果	
企业合作者研发强度增长比例	15%
4. 人力资源（名）	
核心研究人员	35
高级培训	105
博士研究生（已毕业）	76
硕士研究生（已毕业）	65
5. 成本和预算	
日常开支的份额	12.5%
获得第三方资金（百万欧元）	7

表 14　2008 年材料综合中心成果

1. 出版物	
科学期刊（期）	28
会议文献（件）	30
书籍	0
其他出版物（件）	5
2. 专利	
申请数（个）	0
授权数（个）	0
3. 社会活动	
展览	0
科学专题会和研讨会/次	1
4. 教育与培训	
高级培训（期）	33
博士论文（篇）	42
硕士论文（篇）	11

4.2.5 法律和制度环境

4.2.5.1 与不同领域现行法律和法规的兼容性

根据材料综合中心管理情况,目前的体制环境与材料综合中心的建立和管理相符合,材料综合中心的目标符合奥地利就业法律框架。材料综合中心员工根据奥地利就业法的相关规定受聘于MCL。奥地利就业法为大学的研究人员无薪休假提供了一个合理的框架,即他们在资助期或具体项目期内受雇于MCL,但有权再回到大学。税法与材料综合中心的规定兼容,但缺少提供具体的激励措施。

4.2.5.2 制度环境效果评估

制度环境为材料综合中心的建立提供了合适的环境。特别是奥地利就业法提供了一种合适的法律框架,允许材料综合中心与合作者间的研究人员进行流动。

其他积极或消极的影响目前尚不显著。

4.2.6 融资和资金管理

4.2.6.1 融资模式和成本分摊

MCL的总预算资金大约为5750万欧元,其中92%(约5300万欧元)来自COMET第一期5300万欧元的资助。MCL预算的8%来自其他外部资金,如欧盟项目和国家项目(Bridge Programme),以及产业合同研究和实验室服务的收入。

5300万欧元的COMET基金中公共资源占50%,包括国家资金(30%)和省级资金(20%)。其余的45%由来自企业合作伙伴的资源所组成,以及以现金方式提供的参与其中的大学的贡献占5%(这不包括在公共基金内)。大约66%的企业资源以现金方式提供,其他的则以实物方式提供,包括人员和有形资本,如设备和材料。大学的资源则全部为实物形式。在材料综合中心案例中,一个值得注意的现象是,一些企业100%提供现金,而另一些企业100%贡献实物。当然,如按照COMET确立的规则,所有合伙公司的捐赠最多可以有50%以实物的形式提供。

4.2.6.2 财政资源的管理和利用方式

与任一有限责任公司相同,材料综合中心使用强制管理要素来管理资金,特别是控制与会计。预算环节由材料综合中心管理部门执行,并由股东大会与监事会控制。资金主要用于完成材料综合中心的研究项目。

4.3 卡琳西亚先进传感器技术研究中心

以产业为导向的卡琳西亚卓越技术能力中心（CTR，下文简写为卡琳西亚中心）坐落于卡琳西亚州的菲拉赫市，致力于智能先进传感器技术的研究工作。该中心以公共股份有限公司的形式组建而成，是奥地利在智能传感器领域最大的非大学类科研机构，由奥地利 COMET 计划提供部分资金资助。该中心的研究项目可分为三大块：光学系统技术、声表面波传感系统技术及光学微系统技术。

4.3.1 目标和组织形式

4.3.1.1 战略目标

卡琳西亚中心是 COMET 计划中的一个 K1 中心。由于卡琳西亚中心既是一个接受 COMET 计划资助的中心，又是一个可以接受研究合同和其他非 COMET 计划的资助资源的非大学类研究中心，所以卡琳西亚中心可以确定不同的战略目标。

从股东的角度来看，卡琳西亚中心的战略定位主要是区域性的。即股东们的目标是把卡琳西亚中心建成地区创新的领头羊，联合当地企业和科研机构的研究力量，从而为当地经济发展尤其是对中小型企业发展带来积极的影响。此外，通过不同的形式与公众活动，卡琳西亚中心要致力于提高公众对研发活动在以知识为基础的区域性经济实体和社会实体中具有重要作用的认识。

作为一个先进技术能力中心计划资助的 K1 中心，卡琳西亚中心有如下战略目标：

——在国际层次上，实现智能传感器领域以产业导向的合作研发取得突破。

——在奥地利的智能传感器领域，建立学科和产业联合的卡琳西亚中心核心机制。

——在国际最高科学水平层次上，促进创新技术发展。

——发表高质量的期刊论文、合著文章、学位论文，保证科学产出的卓越性。

——长远上，卡琳西亚中心将致力于成为一个不依赖卓越技术能力中心计划资助也能独立生存的能力中心。

——从企业管理的角度来看，卡琳西亚中心的短期目标是实现研究中心的开支与前期投入资金（如奥地利卓越技术能力中心计划和其他资金来源）的平衡，长期目标则是努力实现稳步的增长。

4.3.1.2 法律组成形式

参与主体可以为中心自主选择法律组建形式。按照奥地利和国际的立法，卡琳西亚中心是以公共股份有限公司❶的形式组建而成。因为卡琳西亚中心的股东（如卡琳西亚开发署、奥地利产业联合会卡琳西亚分会、菲拉赫市政府、德国弗劳恩霍夫协会有限公司）具有排他性，采用这种公司形式可以避免政治上的影响和控制。通过利用股份有限公司的通常性和强制性管理手段，尤其是监事会（见本章4.3.2），可以把政治上的影响最小化。

卡琳西亚中心的内部组织结构见图10。

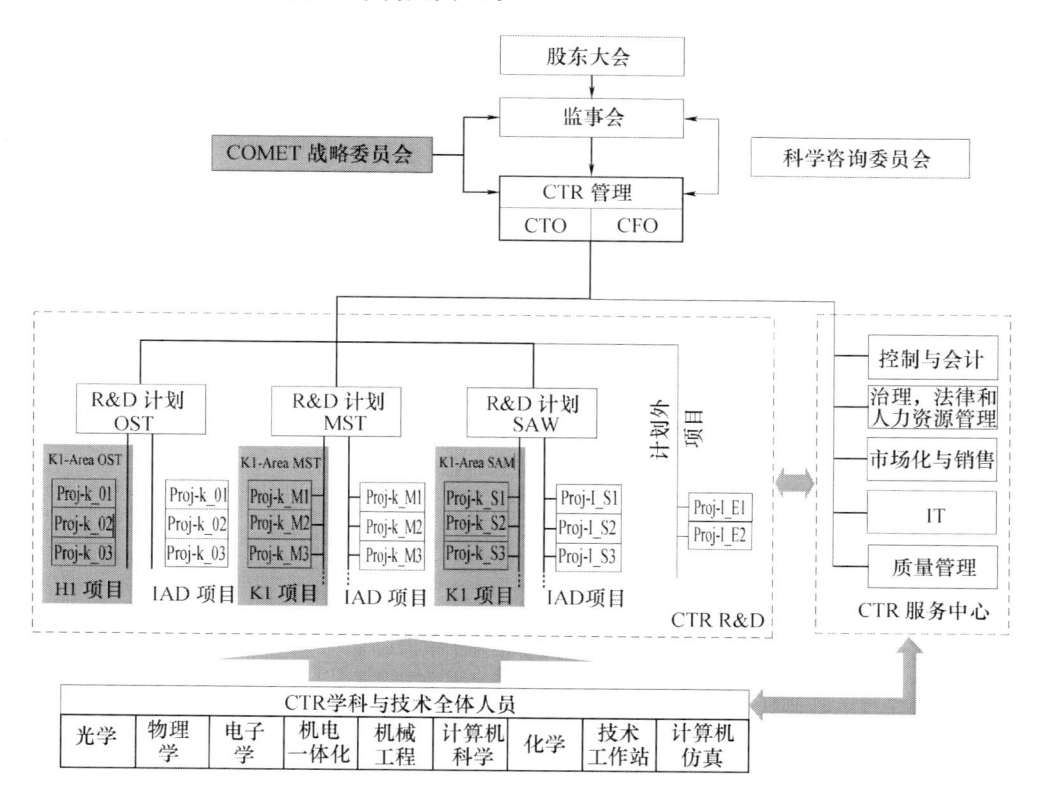

图10 卡琳西亚中心的内部组织结构

---

❶ 公开股份有限公司（Public Limited Company，PLC），指公司股份或公司债可以对外公开招募的股份有限公司（limited liability company），一般而言对于股东股权的转移均不限制，但是公司股东人数，必须至少在7名以上——译注。

4.3.2 治理结构和权责关系

4.3.2.1 不同合作主体融合的阻碍

在卡琳西亚中心内,企业和高校各自加入中心的动机与另外两个案例中观察到的情况大致相同。首先,加入卡琳西亚中心的企业能够有机会在不同的传感器技术领域接触到企业外的高水平技术,并运用这些外部技术来完成特定研究项目。有时,尤其是规模较小的参与企业,它们的研究项目会涉及非常专业和狭窄的研究领域。这样,企业通过把外部的知识整合到企业内知识体系中,从而在实际应用中实现真正的创新。其次,企业加入卡琳西亚中心后可以为已制定的长期研发计划争取到额外的资金,即相对于独自R&D或通过市场获取的途径,企业通过卡琳西亚中心的内部合作可以降低研发活动成本。此外,企业还能享受到卡琳西亚中心内部关系网络带来的其他各种好处。

公共科研机构参与卡琳西亚中心的主要动机是要加入到这个合作关系网络中。参与卡琳西亚中心的公共科研机构,对与其他致力于相近研究领域的公共科研机构和公司取得联系表示出极大的兴趣。取得这种联系的一个好处是,能为将来运用非COMET计划资金进行合作项目研究提供了可能性。在这个意义上,公共科研机构正有意识地把握机会来缩小基础性研究和应用性研究之间的距离。

如同其他案例一样,高校和企业参与者之间的主要区别在于它们不同的战略目标。企业关注的主要是在完成前需要保密的具体的创新;而高校关注的是学术公开和较高的学术声誉,包括在国际上的显示度。所以,中心的目标和活动要很慎重地加以安排以便在产业主体和科研机构主体之间取得一种平衡,从而创造出双赢的局面。

4.3.2.2 治理结构和不同主体合作规则

作为公共股份有限公司,卡琳西亚中心的各必要组成部分都具有上市公司的结构特点。股东对卡琳西亚中心有最高和最终的决定权。在年度股东大会上,卡琳西亚中心的总体战略得以制定和监管。股东大会提名监事会的成员。监事会一年召开四次会议,根据卡琳西亚中心管理层的报告来审视卡琳西亚中心战略目标是否得以实现。卡琳西亚中心管理层(包括首席执行官和首席财政官)负责执行卡琳西亚中心的战略目标和研究计划。他们管理卡琳西亚中心三个研究领域(光学系统技术、声表面波传感系统技术及光学微系统技术)和综合事务(控制和会计、依法行政和人力资源管理、市场营销和销售、信息技术和质量管理)。

各研究领域由领域主管领导负责特定领域研究计划的执行和研究项目的分派。每个领域有一个研究带头人，负责协助领域主管管理提出新的研究项目。卡琳西亚中心管理层和监事会有COMET计划的特别战略理事会和科学顾问理事会支持。科学顾问理事会由来自产业和学科的数位专家、一位监事会成员以及数位奥地利研究促进署（FFG）的官员组成。科学顾问理事会把握卡琳西亚中心的科研方向，并为监事会和卡琳西亚中心管理层提供建议。

对于融合不同参与主体的理性诉求，战略理事会具有十分重要的作用。它专门致力于在科学参与者与公共科研机构的战略决策之间取得平衡。然而，需要注意的是，须在应用阶段尽力地去除出于不同理性诉求而导致在企业、高校和研究机构之间存在的壁垒。应用阶段对于融合不同主体的理性诉求至关重要，同时它还能在参与者之间形成信任和共同语言。

4.3.2.3 不同层次上的合作组织

卡琳西亚中心在不同层次人员（研究人员、项目负责人、研究带头人、领域主管、研究中心管理层）的合作关系在应用阶段中已计划好的。完整的研究项目是在计划的基础上组织的。在应用阶段中的具体研究项目是确定的，包括各种资源和人员配置。项目负责人负责实现该项目的目标。而研究带头人负责监管一个研究领域的所有项目，并对领域主管进行汇报。领域主管向研究中心的管理层汇报各项目的进展情况，同时也和研究带头人一起对更改研究主题或新的研究主题提出建议。

4.3.2.4 实施计划的组织、任务或项目的选择

卡琳西亚中心的实际运作计划在项目计划书中已得以确定。计划书在课题层面上详细地阐述了研究计划，如对于任务和项目的选择已由参与各方在实施层面上进行讨论。卡琳西亚中心建成以后，新的优先主题或研究项目，以及新的研究伙伴能够通过研究领域主管和研究带头人共同向上推荐到研究中心管理层。然后，由监事会作出最终决定。同时，战略理事会和科学顾问理事会也能推举新的研究项目、新的优先主题或新的研究伙伴。卡琳西亚中心管理战略项目、多公司项目以及单公司项目。战略项目的主题研究方向比较宽泛，但也明确地以强化卡琳西亚中心的核心知识基础为目标。大体上，战略项目几乎涉及所有研究中心的参与主体。多公司项目较为明确，涉及两个以上的参与主体。而单公司项目最为明晰，参与主体只有一个，这样的研究项目占到研究中心所有研究项目的14%。

在项目计划书中，卡琳西亚中心研究计划的第一个项目周期（前四年）已被详细地制定出来。对于第二个项目周期（三年）的研究计划，则需要递交另外制定的项目计划书。项目的实施方案包括项目必要的人员配置、基础设施准备、原材料以及时间进度表。实施方案（包括人员配置和资金投入）的短期监管由卡琳西亚中心管理层来按年执行，监事会负责审查。

4.3.2.5 研发的管理：控制与营销

卡琳西亚中心的所有项目都按标准化程序管理，即所有项目的管理方式相同。每个项目都有明确的项目计划，包括各种资源、重要事件、预算等。项目开始后，每个研究人员的工作量、所需的各种资源等都有明确的安排。每个月，卡琳西亚中心管理层对项目的内容和预算进行控制检查。项目组合管理的方法在卡琳西亚中心管理层配置资源时十分重要。

4.3.2.6 权责关系、行为准则和信息交流

卡琳西亚中心的计划方案，包括针对每个参与主体的投资意向书和书面委托书，是联盟协议规范化的基础。在签署这些协议书后，参与主体的权责关系得以确定。即他们必须提供在协议中许诺的各种资源，如现金、人员或基础设施等。同时，协议书中也将参与主体的准入和退出机制规范化。联盟协议至关重要，且由于不同参与主体的价值取向迥异而很难达成。卡琳西亚中心这个案例中共同协议的达成即较艰难。此外，项目的特别条款规定了在特定项目中某个参与主体与研究中心之间的现金流方式。

核心条款涉及知识产权（IPR）和出版法规。卡琳西亚中心的 IPR 与机电一体化中心和材料综合中心案例中的情况类似。知识产权的规范如下：在多公司项目中，参与主体必须阐明他是在哪个特定的领域支持研发。能划归于这个特定领域里的项目产出，就由该参与主体独享。不能划归于任何一个先前阐明的特定领域的项目产出，就归卡琳西亚中心拥有。但是，卡琳西亚中心项目的所有参与主体都能够通过授权获取该知识。某个参与主体合作前就拥有且又对于项目有帮助的知识产权，其所有权仍由该参与主体独有。就战略项目而言，产生出的知识由卡琳西亚中心所独有，但所有参与企业都可以通过授权获取该知识。总的来说，企业对于卡琳西亚中心的知识产权条款表示满意，因为他们通常更优先关注于自身特定研究领域。对于单公司项目，产出成果由参与方独享。

至于项目公开出版的规定，联盟中每个想公开出版项目成果或项目初期结果的参与主体，都必须把计划公开出版的内容告知项目负责人，再由项目负责人告知卡琳西亚中

心的所有参与主体。四周内参与主体可以出具一份详细的说明来反对公开出版（如新知识在形成专利保护之前应该予以保密）。如果参与主体没有表示反对，就可以公开出版了。需要注意的是，大体上，产业参与主体对高公开出版强度的做法持保留态度。但是，他们也很清楚，为了能获取卡琳西亚中心的资金资助，他们必须要实现卡琳西亚中心的目标，包括公开出版。

4.3.3　中心内部及其与政府的关系

4.3.3.1　核心成员与创始人

卡琳西亚中心由17个产业伙伴和9个科学技术型伙伴组成。卡琳西亚中心的发起者暨核心成员之一是英飞凌（Infineon）公司，该公司是领域里国际上的领先企业之一。其他的产业核心成员包括李斯特内燃机及测试设备公司（AVL List）、奥镁集团公司（RHI）和贝克曼库尔特公司（Beckman Coulter）。卡琳西亚中心还接纳了一些规模相对较小的地方成员，以示平衡分配。科学领域的核心成员有德国的弗赖堡大学、荷兰的代尔夫特科技大学、奥地利的维也纳工业大学和德国弗劳恩霍夫协会。

4.3.3.2　核心成员的关系演化

和其他案例相似，经过核心成员之间关系的长期演化，卡琳西亚中心形成了自己的特色。这种关系演化是多层次的，既有地区政策层次的，又有科研层次的，如参与主体之间早期的合作项目。要知道，早期参与主体之间合作项目的正式建立并不是一蹴而就的。对于大企业来说，为四年的科研计划制定预算也不是件容易的事，但这又是必须在书面委托书中确定的。对于卡琳西亚中心的管理层来说，在17个成员之间达成共同协议需要做大量的工作，要就具体的权责条款与每一个成员法定行政部门进行协商。

4.3.3.3　有关监管部门的角色

首先，根据股东的组成，区域性监管部门的关系十分清楚。其次，卡琳西亚中心与以奥地利研究促进署为代表的全国监管部门之间的关系，正如机电一体化中心与材料综合中心一样，涉及卡琳西亚中心的选举、监管和评估。

4.3.3.4　中心的历史

起初，卡琳西亚中心是卡琳西亚州和菲拉赫市的一个区域性政策措施。1997年，创建了一个非盈利协会，在智能传感器领域进行研究。该地区真正的研究主题选择是基于奥地利研究中心的一项研究报告。由于英菲尼昂公司在该领域的领导推动作用，区域经济结构对于该协会很适用。协会随后转化成了一家有限责任公司，然后成为了奥地利第一个 K-plus 中心（1998），并得到了奥地利 COMET 计划的前身——奥地利能力中心计划的资金支持。

4.3.4 知识创造和技术扩散

4.3.4.1 创造知识依靠的共同资源投入

到目前为止，在卡琳西亚中心内知识创造的最大投入是人力资源。表 15 展示了 2007 年和 2008 年卡琳西亚中心的人力资源状况。卡琳西亚中心的科技人员具有广泛的学术背景，同时在物理学和电子学方面具有优势。目前，卡琳西亚中心直接雇用研究人员 23 名，他们与来自各个主体的 89 名研究人员根据研究计划共同开展研究工作。研究人员的流动性至关重要，约 80% 的科技人员（非卡琳西亚中心雇员）来自大学。另外，由卡琳西亚中心向各个主体的人员转移在人力资源发展方面具有重要作用，是卡琳西亚中心的一项重要评价标准。

卡琳西亚中心在菲拉赫科技园区租用了约 1900 平方米的研究场地，其中包括一些专业实验室（光学实验室、激光实验室和机械与电子实验室）。2007 年，卡琳西亚中心在基础设施投入达 18 万欧元，2008 年达 15 万欧元。在 COMET 计划为期 4 年的一期计划内，卡琳西亚中心将获得 1400 万欧元的资助，年度预算根据项目计划确定。

表 15 2007、2008 年卡琳西亚中心的人力资本统计（单位：名）

	2007	2008
CTR 雇员	37	34
科研人员	23	23
技术人员	4	3
管理人员（管理、控制等）	10	9
青年科学家人数		
实习生	4	9
博士研究生	3	3
硕士研究生	7	7
CTR 项目工作人员（非 CTR 雇员）	89	89

4.3.4.2 合作成果的管理与扩散

合作成果的管理与扩散由联盟协议和具体项目合同进行规范，比如知识产权和公开发表的规范。卡琳西亚中心在项目计划中初步明确研究活动的预期成果；实际产出结果将由 FFG 在四年后进行评价。在其他情况下,卡琳西亚中心知识创造的成果通过公开发表和专利向区域和奥地利创新系统及国际科学界扩散。表 16 列出了卡琳西亚中心从 2008—2011 年的预期成果,表 17 总结了 2007 年和 2008 年的研究成果。

4.3.5 法律和制度环境

4.3.5.1 与不同领域法律法规的适应性

从卡琳西亚中心管理的角度来看,现行法律没有对卡琳西亚中心的建立和持续运营形成阻碍。奥地利劳工法为大学、企业和卡琳西亚中心之间的人员流动提供了法律保障,并对研究人员的雇佣做了明确的规定。根据税收条例,对非 COMET 计划研究项目,卡琳西亚中心适用奥地利税法中的研究经费免税规定。此规定允许创新企业最多 25% 的研发经费免除税收。

表 16　2008—2011 年卡琳西亚中心预期成果

1. 研究成果	
科学期刊发表文章数(篇)	130
专利许可(件)	20
2. 研究项目	
承担战略项目份额(份)	15%
3. 附加成果	
公司研究强度提升率	37.20%
4. 人力资源	
高级研究人员(名)	48
博士研究生(已毕业)(名)	7
博士研究生(在读)(名)	4
硕士研究生(已毕业)(名)	20
硕士研究生(在读)(名)	8
5. 创新	
产品创新(个)	18
工艺创新(个)	7
6. 经费和预算	
经费比例	15%
获得第三方资助(百万欧元)	6

表 17　2007、2008 年卡琳西亚中心的研究成果

	2007	2008
1. 发表数		
科学期刊(期)	5	15
会议(次)	12	18
图书(册)	1	2
其他(件)	5	1
专利(件)		20
申请数(个)	2	3
授权数(个)	1	4
创新(个)		
产品创新(个)	—	3
工艺创新(个)	—	5
2. 参与科技活动		
展览会(次)	15	17
研讨会(次)	—	2
3. 教育(名)		
博士研究生(已毕业)	1	—
博士研究生(在读)	3	7
硕士研究生(已毕业)	1	4
硕士研究生(在读)	3	3

4.3.5.2 体制条件的作用评价

制度环境为卡琳西亚中心的建立提供了适宜的环境，特别是国家和地区利益的相互作用似乎取得了一种平衡，没有给中心的建设制造障碍。目前的法律如劳工法和税法并没有对卡琳西亚中心的建设提供专门明确的鼓励措施，但是它们与 COMET 计划和具体卓越技术能力中心的目标是一致的。

4.3.6 融资和资金管理

4.3.6.1 资金筹集和成本分享模式

卡琳西亚中心的预算经费主要来自 COMET 计划的资助，占预算总额的 55%。非 COMET 计划资助（占预算总额的 45%）主要包括外部资助（如欧盟项目等，约占 15%）和产业合同研究（约占 20%），及其余的 10% 来自股东。

COMET 为一期（四年）计划提供 1400 万欧元的资助。55% 来自公共资金，包括国家级资助（30%）、省级资助（20%）和大学资助（5%）。大学资助主要以实物形式实现，包括人力资本和实物资本，如仪器设备和材料。另外 45% 来自企业，其中有 60% 是现金。

4.3.6.2 资金的管理和使用方式

卡琳西亚中心按照中心服务规定的公开股份有限公司相关规程进行资金管理，特别是资金的控制和记录。预算安排由卡琳西亚中心管理部门负责制定，并由股东大会和监事会负责监督和控制。

4.4 小结

奥地利 COMET 计划是加强产学研合作创新联盟建设的一种新的组织形式，同时也是奥地利政府在以往支持产学研合作创新政策基础上发展而来的政策支持措施。

（1）从要素组成上看，一是有明确的科学发展目标、技术开发方向和技术产出目标，COMET 的战略定位符合国家发展战略或区域发展重点产业发展的需求；二是中心成员签订一个共同的协议（联盟协议），并在协议的框架下，由参加中心的具有独立法人资格的部分产学研合作伙伴按照 FFG 的要求成立一个具有独立法人的实体，以此为依托开展合作创新活动；三是卓越技术能力中心成员有共同投入、利益共享和风险共担的合作机制。

（2）从组织形态上看，卓越技术能力中心是以合作伙伴之间的共同协议为纽带，在政府 COMET 计划的引导下设立一个独立法人的公司（非营利性质的法人机构），以公司为载体承担和运作政府的 COMET 计划资助，并在中心内部实现资源的开放和共享，形成一种长期的、稳定的产学研合作利益共同体。

（3）从运行机制上看，依托独立法人公司，卓越技术能力中心按照政府资助要求运作，在内部以项目合作形式进行研发活动，并在项目合同对合作知识产权等产出的分配进行详细约定。并对项目进行分类，不同层次的项目具有不同的要求，如战略项目要直接对应卓越技术能力中心的战略目标，所获得的知识产权也是完全由中心所用，成员具有免费使用权。

（4）从主要任务上看，一是联合进行先进技术的研发，实现产业技术创新；二是形成一个合作创新平台，实现合作伙伴之间资源与知识产权的开放与共享，提高创新资源利用效率；三是实现技术转移，加速技术转化，实现创新成果的商业化；四是在联合研发中实现研究生人才的培育，加强人才的交流与流动。

（5）从组建方式上看，卓越技术能力中心的建立都是依托在核心伙伴之间的长期合作关系基础上的，并且都是受到了 COMET 计划的前身 CCP 计划的资助，其中的材料综合中心和卡琳西亚中心都是 CCP 计划中的 K－plus 资助项目。

从机电一体化中心、材料综合中心和卡琳西亚中心三个案例分析可知，政府的资助具有重要意义，在 K2 中心上政府的资助占 55％，并且对经费的使用以及卓越技术能力中心对设定目标的完成进行监督和评估。这对于卓越技术能力中心的发展具有重要的意义。

① 组建目标和组织形态。奥地利是一个发达的中欧小国，在部分领域上的技术优势比较明显。因而，在 COMET 的战略目标制定上，体现出奥地利在技术上以欧洲市场为根本的考虑，具有较高的国际视野，多将科学目标定位为某一领域的全球领先者，并将技术创新目标也定位在相应的国际领先水平上。在组织形式上，由于 FFG 在对卓越技术能力中心的前期评估中强烈建议采取独立法人实体的形式，三个中心分别依据各自情况，建立了非营利性质的有限责任公司、公共股份有限公司以及股份有限公司领导下的非营利性合资机构。

② 治理结构与权责关系。由于成立了具有独立法人资格的公司，卓越技术能力中心的管理上具备了一般公司的规范化管理手段。作为公司，股东大会具有最高的决策权，并在股东大会的领导下建立了监事会代表股东大会管理中心。监事会下辖中心管理层，负责中心的一般事物，如项目的建议、选择与监督管理，协调相关的科技咨询委员会，

指导各个领域部门的工作。具体项目采取项目组组长负责制。中心成员之间的合作有明确分类，按战略项目、多公司项目和单公司项目进行。尽管有比较完整的协调机制，但不同主体的不同动机之间的协调还是很困难的，是合作中较为突出的一个矛盾。但值得注意的是，三个中心都强调了在科研成果应用阶段的合作有力地促进了不同主体之间的协调一致，并加深了相互间的合作信任。

③ 政府的重要支持作用。COMET 的发展离不开奥地利政府的大力支持。一方面，COMET 基金是卓越技术能力中心发展的主要资金来源；另一方面，在卓越技术能力中心合作伙伴关系的建立上，政府也发挥了重要的作用。机电一体化中心的发展得益于上奥地利州对机电一体化领域发展的支持，材料综合中心的发展得益于早期能力中心计划（CCP） K－plus 中心项目的支持，卡琳西亚中心的发展不仅得益于 CCP 的 K－plus 中心项目支持，其本身就是基于卡琳西亚州和菲拉赫市的一个区域性政策举措所建立的非营利性协会。此外，由于是受政府资助，各中心都有一个独立法人实地向政府负责，接受政府的工作年报和评估要求。这些都有力地促进了卓越技术能力中心发展朝着成立时所确定的目标进行，特别是政府对公开发表的要求，也促进了企业与大学在发表上的协调一致。

④ 以项目合同细化约定知识产权。三个卓越技术能力中心都强调人力资源的投入是合作的最重要投入。而合作成果的管理和扩散由联盟协议和具体项目合同进行规范，比如知识产权和公开发表的规范。不同的项目对合作成果有不同的要求。战略项目的成果要实现能力中心的战略目标，研发成果归中心所有，参与战略研究的合作伙伴皆有权使用研发成果（MPPE）或经过授权获得该知识（CTR），出版不受任何限制（ACCM）。对于授予了专利产权的研发成果，参与合作伙伴有权获得项目合同项下业务领域方面的无限期的付费非专营许可证，并可独家转让给附属企业（MPPE）。对于多公司项目或单公司项目，具体的合作投入和成果分配都需要在项目合同中具体约定，参与项目研发的合作伙伴皆有权使用研发成果，而公开发表或出版等事宜需要征得其他所有的合作伙伴特别是企业伙伴的同意。至于生成的专利产权等需要在项目合同预先商定使用和开发权的类型和程度以及申请方式。此外，COMET 的 K2 计划对资助项目有明确的发表或出版要求，对 COMET 的公开发表或出版起到了一定的促进作用。

⑤ 法律法规适应性。三个卓越技术能力中心案例的建立和管理与奥地利的现行法律法规环境是相符合的。如在雇员方面，中心都与就业法兼容。大学的参与也符合大学法

对大学在科学研究成果的转化与应用上的要求。奥地利劳工法也为大学、企业和能力中心之间的人员流动也提供了法律保护。但是，由于 COMET 是一个新的形式，在税法（税收条例）中关于 R&D 经费的 25% 减免问题，对卓越技术能力中心的适用上存在问题，如何统计没有具体说明。而且，在劳工法和税法上也缺乏具体的支持中心建设的专门明确的鼓励措施（CTR）。

⑥ 融资与资金管理。对于 K2 中心，绝大部分的经费来自于 COMET 基金，如机电一体化中心的近 100%，材料综合中心所在的 MCL 经费预算的 92%。而 K1 能力中心的支持力度相对较低，但也达到了 CTR 预算经费总额的 55%。在 COMET 基金中，来自政府的公共资金（包含地方政府资金）占 50%，大学的资助占 5%，其他的 45% 来自企业。由于能力中心的独立法人形式，对于资金的管理比较规范，由股东大会或监事会负责监督和管理。资金主要用于能力中心的研究项目，其中财政资金只可用于完成研究项目。

5

中奥案例比较分析

在这章中，我们要探讨选定的中国产业技术创新战略联盟案例和奥地利 COMET 案例的对比分析。比较分析揭示出很多显著的差异点，同时也展示出两种政策项目之间的共同点。值得强调的是，我们从对比分析中获得结论，这些结论让我们更为深入地了解了中奥两国促进科学界和产业界合作的政策项目，并且为中奥两国科学技术政策的制定提供重要的启示。下面，我们将先探讨中方产业技术创新战略联盟案例和奥方 COMET 案例之间的共同点，随后归纳出主要的差异点。

5.1 共同点

产业技术创新战略联盟项目和 COMET 项目均是中奥两国中央政府支持建立产学研合作联盟最突出的政策典范。两个项目均是在近年来新推出的，其中产业技术创新战略联盟试点工作推出时间是 2006 年，COMET 项目则是 2007 年。在此之前，两国政府都非常关注创新联盟和体制结构在促进产学研合作创新中的重要作用。因此，相对于早期的项目，目前这些的政府战略性指导和支持明显更富于独创性。无论战略联盟的选择还是能力中心的遴选竞争都很激烈。两个项目的基本目标有着一些相似的特点：

- 确定创新体系下产业界和科学界两方面之间缺失的创新连接环节。
- 支持在专业型或通用型技术领域建立科学界和产业界合作创新平台。
- 平台的目的在于从科技、经济两个方面以及组织模式上提出明确的战略方向。
- 创造和管理知识产权是其至关重要的一点。
- 就运行机制而言，无论是产业技术创新战略联盟，还是 COMET，最关键的要素是在产业技术创新战略联盟或 COMET 内参与方的合作都是在专门针对联盟或中心的合作协议约束下进行的。

在联盟或中心研究计划运行机制方面，我们发现下列共同点：

- 产业技术创新战略联盟和 COMET 的管理结构显示出一些共同特点，例如科学技术咨询委员会、项目执行和研发管理方面均有具体机构负责。
- 无论是产业技术创新战略联盟，还是 COMET，均通过具体项目实施研究计划，从而实现其战略目标。项目领导负责项目实施。
- 产业技术创新战略联盟和 COMET 均有核心成员单位/组织，这些核心单位/组织依法负责组织、管理和协调各合作伙伴的之间合作和冲突。

在产业技术创新联盟或 COMET 的关键目标方面，我们归纳出了下列共同点：

- 依据通用技术领域的具体要求,实施共性技术研发。
- 鼓励知识交流和相互学习,从而促进参与各方之间隐性知识的转移。
- 在具体技术和科学领域,将所有参与方的研发资源整合在一起,特别在大学和企业间。
- 鼓励加强研究人员在参加各方之间流动,尤其要着重鼓励研究人员在大学和企业之间的流动。
- 在产业技术创新联盟和 COMET 内对年轻研究人员进行具体技术领域的教育和培训。

产业技术创新联盟和 COMET 的这些共同特点在鼓励知识传播的政策性目标背景下,不仅对于产业技术创新联盟和中心各个参与方,而且对于从产业技术创新联盟或 COMET 到创新系统和经济的各方面均具有十分重要的意义。

在联盟和 COMET 建立方面,这些案例参与各方之前的合作均发挥了巨大的作用。一个产业技术创新联盟或 COMET 建立时,通常情况下,核心参与方早已通过其他方式相互间开展了成功的前期合作。在产业技术创新战略联盟和 COMET 内,非常重要的一点就是筹集必要的资金,通过共同投入资金的方式建立联盟或中心。二者的一个显著的共同点是政府支持在建立产业技术创新战略联盟和 COMET 方面发挥着非常关键的作用。

产业技术创新战略联盟和 COMET 的另一个共同点是它们遇到同样问题,即产业技术创新联盟和 COMET 的参与方具有不同的理念和动机。这些理念和动机的合理性可以归纳为下列几点:

- 在很大程度上,影响理念融合的问题与企业和研究机构参与产业技术创新战略联盟和 COMET 的动机不同有关。
- 企业通常希望寻求针对具体技术问题的具体解决方案,而大学的目的是希望提高其在科学界的声誉。
- 通常情况下,企业更为注重新成果的保密,而大学则希望尽早公布新成果。
- 对于产业技术创新战略联盟和卓越技术能力中心而言,在正式成立之前,达成联合协议和管理结构在克服理念差异方面发挥着重要的作用。

就产业技术创新战略联盟和 COMET 的知识产权和出版制度而言,协议及具体项目合同在其中发挥着核心作用。分别负责产业技术创新战略联盟和 COMET 的中奥两国政府权威机构明确地表示,在产业技术创新战略联盟协议中阐明了知识产权(IPRs)的具体规定,并且由参与方签字,是形成产业技术创新战略联盟和COMET公共投入资金的必要前提条件。

两国均意识到,像产业技术创新战略联盟和COMET这样的政策项目需要税收、研发促进、基础设施和财政等方面法律法规制度的创新支持。目前,中奥两国建立的产业技术创新战略联盟或COMET均符合国家法律法规并且得到现有法律法规和现行政策的支持。然而,在两国的税法方面仍存在一些规定不够清晰的问题,特别是产业技术创新战略联盟或COMET项目中针对研发费用的税收减免政策需要具体化和进一步的改进。这是双方成员单位都关注的一个重要问题。

5.2 差异点

在探讨产业技术创新战略联盟和COMET项目的差异时,依据案例实证分析报告得出的结果,充分证明了两个项目不同层面之间存在着差异点,从整体政策设计到项目设计层面,从产业技术创新战略联盟或COMET层面到联盟或中心参与者层面。

就整体政策设计而言,主要的差异点如下:

• 产业技术创新战略联盟的秘书处是非法人的(甚至是非实体结构的),仅通过秘书处实现产业技术创新战略联盟的组织管理和创新目标,当然政府亦不要求其是独立法人。但COMET是在产学研合作创新联盟契约的背景下,形成法人实体来操作运行,实现联盟成员的创新目标。而奥地利政府机构(如FFG)积极建议将卓越技术能力中心——一个类似联盟秘书处的机构组建为法人公司。❶

• 奥地利的政策持续向卓越技术能力中心提供公共资金,而中国政府则有选择地向产业技术创新战略联盟方面提供战略性指导和竞争性公共资金。迄今为止,所有战略性联盟都没有得到中国政府连续提供的资金。

• 目前,产业技术创新战略联盟的目的是在经济政策和更为广泛的社会大背景下,重点致力于国家关注的优先领域。因此,在中国的政策背景下,需要遵循科技、经济和

---

❶ 这与FFG制定的要求存在着紧密联系,因此,当中心以法人公司的形式出现,并依据合同履行责任时,对公共资金的审计和监控就会更加容易。另外,奥地利法制体系中非营利公司的存在是其重要的先决条件。这就意味着有些公司不以追逐最高利润为经营目的,而是通过公司治理,利用高效率获得收益。这些公司既可以享受税收激励政策,又可以清晰地记录各种资金往来。正是因为这个原因,在中国产业技术创新战略联盟的发展中也出现了几个将联盟秘书处建成独立法人资格的单位的情况,但这都是联盟依据发展需要而自主决策的。

基础设施紧密结合的政策。

在项目组织层面，通过对比分析这些根据调研分析得出的结果，可以发现差异点主要与国际化、产业技术创新战略联盟或 COMET 选择机制和评估规程有关。主要的差异点如下：

• COMET 项目明显体现出国际化定位，关注国际一流的技术水平，允许甚至鼓励将重要国际机构引入卓越技术能力中心，特别是在欧洲范围选择合作伙伴。❶ 目前，产业技术创新战略联盟的合作伙伴仅限于国内，特别关注中国国内的先进技术领域。

• 在中方案例中，产业技术创新战略联盟项目直接受提供该项目的国家部委监管。然而，COMET 计划是独立运行管理的。

• 卓越技术能力中心遵循 FFG 制定的系统具体的评估程序，该规程的依据是一系列明确界定的评估指标。FFG 对 COMET 的系统评估体系包括预先评估、中期评估和最终评估。评估结果与其能否持续获得资助关系密切。至今为止，产业技术创新战略联盟只有初选评估，没有综合系统的评估。也就是说，尚未建立针对联盟的系统评估和有效监测体系。到目前为止，产业技术创新战略联盟试点只有初选评估，还没有综合系统的评估体系。

• 这导致在选择机制方面，COMET 和产业技术创新战略联盟存在差异点。产业技术创新战略联盟试点选择与《中国中长期科学和技术发展规划纲要（2006－2020 年）》概括的优先领域有着密切联系的，然而，COMET 选择机制在很大程度上受到科技成果是否公认卓越的影响，而科技成果是否卓越是由国际合作伙伴通过严格的审查过程完成的。

• COMET 是独立的社会主体，有助于他们聘用全职管理人员和研究人员，从而保证科研项目工作的顺利开展。产业技术创新战略联盟的秘书处是专门的执行机构，但不是独立的社会主体，聘用全职人员较为困难，其员工有的是领导小组聘用的，有的是产业技术创新战略联盟成员聘用的，有的则是由具备法人资格的秘书处聘用。这影响了项目研究人员队伍的稳定性。

• 联盟和中心的资金结构差异很大。与产业技术创新战略联盟相比，卓越技术能力中心的公共资金在总资金中所占比例很高，总资金中 55％的资金来自公共投入。而产业技术创新战略联盟的公共资金所占比例相对较低，因此资金很大程度上要依赖联盟成员

---

❶ 这虽然与奥地利国家市场比较小具有密切的关系，但是其国际化的做法仍然是一个比较突出的特点，这也保证了其卓越技术能力中心开展研发与创新活动在国际范围内的卓越性。

自行筹集。另外，产业技术创新战略联盟为数很少的公共资金直接拨给联盟中的具体项目承担单位，而不是由联盟集中划拨，影响了联盟的领导作用。这种情况的一个突出例子就是钢铁可循环流程技术创新战略联盟的曹妃甸项目。

5.3 小结

我们采用表格的形式，将卓越技术能力中心和产业技术创新战略联盟的共同点和差异点归纳在一起。表18总结出中奥双方已取得的主要成果以及存在的不足。对比分析的结果加深了我们对于产业技术创新战略联盟和卓越技术能力中心的了解，为中奥两国制定科技政策提供了重要的启示。

表 18 产业技术创新战略联盟和 COMET 已取得的主要成果以及存在的不足

类别		中国产业技术创新战略联盟	奥地利 COMET
整体政策环境	已设立的方法	• 2006年推出，在此之前，政府非常关注体制改革在产学研合作中的重要作用 • 由此产生大量的政府战略指导和支持 • 与早期的项目相比，具有明显的新颖性 • 目标定位于国家经济、科技和社会问题 • 依据十一项国家优先领域确定主题定位[1]	• 2007年推出，在此之前，政府非常关注体制结构在科学界和产业界合作中的重要作用 • 由此产生大量的政府战略指导和支持 • 与早期的项目相比，具有明显的新颖性 • 采用自下而上的方法，由申请方自行筹划主题 • 解决创新体系中的结构缺陷
项目设计	范围	• 建立具体的产学研合作平台 • 国家在经济政策方面需要优先处理的问题 • 重点放在国内先进技术领域	• 建立具体的科学界和产业界合作平台 • 卓越的国际科技成果
项目设计	选择机制	• 通过竞争加以选择的过程 • 与11个国家优先领域有关 • 国家在经济和基础设施政策方面需要优先处理的问题	• 通过竞争加以选择的过程 • 关注卓越科技成果的应用 • 以国际同行的评审为依据
项目设计	评估	• 评估规程只有初选评估，系统评估规程尚未制订	• 系统的预先、中期和最终评估 • 以一系列评估指标为依据 • 评估结果影响获取政府资助

续表

	类别	中国产业技术创新战略联盟	奥地利 COMET
联盟和中心层面	战略目标	• 联盟应具有清晰的科技目标和战略定位 • 在具体领域，特别是大学和企业合作领域，将各相关参与方的研发资源整合在一起 • 为国内具体经济部门提供解决方案 • 鼓励合作伙伴之间的知识交流和相互学习 • 鼓励加强研究人员的流动性	• 中心应具有清晰的科学目标和战略定位 • 在具体领域，特别是大学和企业合作领域，将各相关参与方的研发资源整合在一起 • 按国际水准开展研发活动 • 鼓励合作伙伴之间的知识交流和相互学习 • 鼓励加强研究人员的流动性
	组织形式	• 依据契约协议组建联盟	• 依据奥地利现行的卓越技术能力中心计划
	组织治理	• 理事会发挥着至关重要的作用 • 秘书处通常在理事会的领导之下负责管理工作 • 具体负责科技咨询的机构 • 因理念不同而产生的问题主要与参加联盟的动机不同有关	• 依据奥地利公司法设立法定的公司要素 • 中心聘用管理人员 • 具体负责科技咨询的机构 • 因理念不同而产生的问题主要与参加联盟的动机不同有关
	参与方	• 企业、大学和科研机构 • 参与各方之前的合作行为发挥着巨大的作用 • 管理层的核心单位至关重要	• 产业界、大学和科研组织 • 参与各方之前的合作行为发挥着巨大的作用 • 管理层的核心单位至关重要
	权利和制度	• 联盟协议是基础	• 联盟协议是基础
	知识产权	• 将规范联盟内部成果使用协议 • 在一个项目参与成员之间划分权利	• 中心可以持有专利权 • 针对不同类型的项目有不同的 IPR 规定：战略项目，成果归中心所有，但是每个合作伙伴可以通过获得授权许可，使用成果；多公司项目，成果归具体主题领域的公司所有
	出版物	• 项目各参与方考虑出版物战略	• 战略项目成果对出版物没有限制 • 通常情况下，企业成员有机会拒绝成果出版
	知识资源	• 人力资本和研究人员流动性是核心 • 教育和培训年轻的研究人员	• 人力资本和研究人员流动性是核心 • 教育和培训年轻的研究人员
	资金投入	• 成员提供的资金份额高于公共资金份额 • 联盟中的具体项目采用公共资金投入	• 55%公共资金，45%来自成员 • 作为法人公司，中心可以申请自其他来源的资金，例如欧洲框架项目计划
	法律	• 联盟的设立符合国家法律 • 税法方面相关规定不明确	• 中心的设立符合国家法律 • 税法方面仍存在一些含混不清的情况

注1：中国《国家中长期科学和技术发展规划纲要（2006～2020 年）》概括出 11 个优先领域。

6

总结与展望

目前的研究是在中奥产学研合作政策项目上加以说明,研究重点是依据这一方针比较中奥政策方案。中方在实际工作中研究产业技术创新战略联盟项目合作组织模式,奥方在实际工作中研究卓越技术能力中心项目合作组织模式,将这两种模式进行比较。依据案例实证分析取得的结果,确定奥中两种组织模式之间的主要共同点和差异点。这也为奥中两国政策制定提供了重要的启示。本章将总结项目的研究成果并概括对奥中政策的分析结论。

6.1 研究成果

此次研究从科学和政策的角度获得以下重要成果或共同认知。

（1）产业技术创新战略联盟和卓越技术能力中心均是科学界和产业界制度化的合作组织模式。

（2）均适合在中奥两国创新体系下的具体条件中推进技术创新。

（3）产业技术创新战略联盟和卓越技术能力中心的经验显示,制度创新有助于提高科学界和产业界合作项目的效率和效益。

（4）需要有政府的持续资助和/或公共或私立资金的支持,确保联盟或中心的创新目标和可持续发展的实现。

（5）实现有效的科学界和产业界合作,需要在知识产权管理问题上认真考虑各参与方的实际利益。

（6）联盟和中心均是产学研合作的创新型组织模式。联盟和中心的持续发展,需要借鉴以往的经验教训。

（7）为实现联盟或中心的可持续发展,需要采用系统的评估和监督。

（8）良好规范的国际比较研究有助于实际工作中的决策制定。

研究发现,产业技术创新战略联盟和卓越技术能力中心适合科学界和产业界合作组织模式,从而取得了如下一般性研究成果：

（1）推进人力资源开发,满足产业界需求。

（2）鼓励和放宽企业、大学和研究机构之间的研究人员流动。

（3）鼓励参与联盟或中心的各方之间加强知识流动和相互学习。

（4）鼓励面向国家创新体系的知识扩散。

（5）考虑和解决产业界对技术和创新政策的需求。

(6) 将相关的基础设施政策和研究技术创新政策结合起来。

除了这些研究成果之外，实证分析得出的结论让中奥两国政策制定者获得了不同的启示。随后，我们将探讨对中方政策的分析结论，然后分析探讨奥方的政策给我们带来的启示。

6.2 对中方政策的结论分析

根据实证分析得出的结果，针对中方政策的制订与实施，我们建议应深入考虑下列几点：

(1) 对产业技术创新战略联盟的战略定位和发展进行系统考虑，特别要明确支持产业技术创新战略联盟的公共模式。其重要性如下。

① 确保产业技术创新战略联盟活动符合合同规定的中方政策制定者确定的战略目标。

② 与奥地利卓越技术能力中心项目类似，通过确定不同的"联盟类别"组织实施产业技术创新战略联盟项目，以便对不同的联盟项目实施不同的支持和评估规程。

③ 联盟的组织模式应是多种多样的。奥地利的做法是联盟合作网络中的成员依据不同的需求进行协商，确定哪种模式最适合。在这种情况下，联盟成员可以选择组建法人公司形式的秘书处或研发中心，这就是奥地利卓越技术能力中心的做法。

(2) 应鼓励产业技术创新战略联盟加强秘书处的地位。在这种情况下，联盟就可以聘用全职工作人员。奥地利卓越技术能力中心就采取了这样的方式。就产业技术创新战略联盟未来发展而言，联盟应设立专门的管理和运营机构，聘用全职工作人员负责日常事务、项目管理、协调各合作方以及向有关政府权威部门报告。通过上述方式，联盟管理层的能力和办事效率可以得到显著提高。

(3) 针对评估、监督和项目深入协调，应设立更为系统的产业技术创新战略联盟项目管理方法：进一步发挥政府在开发产业技术创新战略联盟项目方面的积极作用。然而，就具体管理职责而言，奥地利由 FFG 负责的卓越技术能力中心监督和管理更为系统和全面。例如，FFG 要求中心汇报进展情况。如果中心无法实现预计目标或者遇到其他问题，FFG 有权暂停次年资助，甚至完全终止资助。产业技术创新战略联盟可以借鉴这种方法，因为通过这种方法，不仅可以确保公共资金的合理利用，而且可以促使联盟紧密关注已经公布的战略目标。这种方法包括更为系统的项目管理和更为明确的 IPR 和出版物规定。就财政资助而言，根据奥地利的经验，更多的资金（例如项目预算的 50%）应投入基础性项目。

（4）在财务管理和产权管理方面，提高联盟秘书处的作用（控制权）。在产业技术创新战略联盟，公共资金直接划拨给具体项目的承担单位；然而在卓越技术能力中心，公共资金直接划拨给中心，再由中心划拨给参与各方。在卓越技术能力中心，这样做可以确保顺利实施研发项目，分享相关知识产出。因此，就产业技术创新战略联盟今后发展而言，联盟秘书处应在获得授权的情况下，控制项目资金的划拨并监督其使用情况。这将推进联盟的集中研发工作，确保研发项目进度，促进联盟中人员和知识交流，而且改进知识和技术成果的分享和扩散。

（5）鼓励联盟研发工作的地理集中。值得一提的是，设立卓越技术能力中心的要求之一就是组建法人公司，在一个具体的地点开展活动，通常是在同一幢建筑中。通过这种方式，在面对面接触过程中，可以促进隐性知识交流和扩散，促进人员流动，加强相互学习，并且提高研发效率。因此，就产业技术创新战略联盟今后发展而言，依据实际情况，在可行的情况下，应将研发工作集中于一地进行。

（6）实施系统科学的联盟评估。卓越技术能力中心依据一系列明确的指标接受系统和深入的评估。值得一提的是，中期评估直接影响到次年能否获得政府资助。评估标准因中心类别和目标定位的不同而有所变化。产业技术创新战略联盟应采用这样的方式，引进定义明确的系统评估体系，这样才能够有效监督和控制联盟运行和工作进展。根据奥地利的卓越技术能力中心经验，通过联盟和政府间资助协议和定期提供联盟知识产权报告，这种做法才可以实现。

（7）就中期发展工作而言，产业技术创新战略联盟应考虑拟定国际合作计划。在联合研发方面，产业技术创新战略联盟可以参考卓越技术能力中心的经验，促进与国际科学界的交流。

（8）在联盟长期主题定位方面，通过自下而上的方法，让主题定位由市场需求决定。这种方法更为灵活，而且更贴近产业界的创新需求。

6.3 对奥方政策的结论分析

依据实证分析得出的结果，针对奥方政策的制订与实施，我们建议应深入探讨下列几点：

（1）与奥地利的政策相比，产业技术创新战略联盟的技术产业结合政策具有非常明显的特点。在案例分析中最突出的例子是钢铁可循环流程技术创新战略联盟下的"曹妃甸"项目。"曹妃甸"是一家大型钢厂。该厂开展了新金属和钢技术研究。"曹妃甸"钢厂位于河北省,是第一家采用脱盐技术的钢厂。该厂采用循环模式设计,是高品质板材和带材的专业生产基地。"曹妃甸"钢厂的资金主要来自中国其他大型钢厂,且这些钢厂是钢铁可循环流程技术创新战略联盟研发活动的平台。这一模式也适用于奥地利政策环境,尤其是基础设施政策和技术政策相结合的情况,可以推进公共基础设施项目研发工作。

（2）在一些情况下,进行主题定位时,比自下而上的方法更为合适的是以使命为导向的自上而下的方法,通过这种方法来确定优先主题。中方的一些案例中采用了这种方法,这种方法也同样适用于奥地利。对于流动性或能源等经济和/或社会问题,可以在这些领域设立卓越技术能力中心,采用这种方法来解决这些问题。

（3）卓越技术能力中心灵活的组织形式是值得期待的。应将行政管理工作转让给第三方,将更多资源集中在研发和管理的核心工作上。

（4）必须重新评估是否在申请设立卓越技术能力中心方面花费了太多的精力,妨碍潜在的重要合作伙伴参与申请。在实证分析中注意到了这方面的迹象。似乎产业技术创新战略联盟的申请规程所需努力相对较低,当然这主要与已经确立优先主题和无需关注国际上科学研究成果是否卓越有关。然而,我们期待今后COMET的申请要求和规程更为方便,更少耗精力。

（5）应考虑通过对产业技术创新战略联盟参与方免税,在更大范围内对研究活动实行间接鼓励措施,另外,针对现行税法的规定和卓越技术能力中心作为非营利公司的定位,必须去除一些含混不清的规定。

（6）由于目前卓越技术能力中心的明确目标瞄准科学国际上的卓越科学水平,因此下一步不仅是参与其中,还要成为在国际研究界具体主题领域的核心力量。这将成为今后项目的明确目标。

6.4 研究展望

产学研合作组织模式分析对于政策制定者来讲是至关重要的。基于政策框架和产学研合作个例两个层面,合作研究项目比较了中国产业技术创新战略联盟和奥地利（COMET）规范产学研合作的政策框架,得到了科学的而又具有政策意义的重要结论。值得注意的是，合作研究项目的一个重要产出是中国和奥地利的研究团队，即中国科学技术发展战略研究院（CASTED）和奥地利技术研究院，能够有效地进行研讨，使彼此能够更好地理解对方的研究成果，并最终形成共同的合作研究结论。

合作研究项目的主要结论可概括如下：第一，经验分析揭示了一些一般性结论，产业技术创新战略联盟和 COMET 是产学研合作组织的制度化模式，都适应各自所在国的创新系统所形成的支持技术创新的独特环境。这表明，来自政府和或公共或私人部门的连续的资金支持是保证创新目标实现和联盟或中心持续发展的必要条件。第二，研究系统地分析了中国和奥地利政策手段的相似性和差异性。在宏观政策设计上，两者都明显地导向建立支持持续的产学研合作的支撑平台。能力中心明确要求研究的国际领先水准，并运行国际伙伴加入，而但产业技术创新战略联盟现阶段则仅限于国内合作伙伴。在微观层面，奥地利的能力中心组建了独立法人的公司，而中国产业技术创新战略联盟则是基于合作协议建立一个协调性的秘书处。这使联盟和能力在内部和外部治理结构上形成了不同的机制。

在目前研究结论的基础上，形成了未来共同研究的重要观点。以下事项将会得到优先考虑：

（1）作为未来分析的先决条件，产业技术创新战略联盟和/或 COMET 对中国和奥地利（欧洲）创新体系的有效性和影响，可能是一个适宜的分析起点——知识生产，包括外溢效应，与经济生产率之间的关系。在欧洲，这方面的分析表明了在特定产业领域知识生产对生产率的积极效应（Scherngell，Fischer and Reismann，2008）。此类分析为理解知识扩散机制和制定产业技术创新战略联盟的相关政策提供了重要参考。

（2）对产业技术创新战略联盟和/或 COMET 的效率的评价至关重要。这包括构造监督和估价联盟/中心的恰当的指标，利用网络分析技术研究内外部合作与协调的效率，最后将经验模型概念化，估计产业技术创新战略联盟和 COMET 对创新体系的创新绩效的影响。

（3）建立一个前瞻性研究平台，这是对科技与产业部门合作以证据为基础进行政策设计的另一个贡献。

参 考 文 献

[1] ACCM. 奥地利机电一体化能力中心设立和运行协议. 奥地利：ACCM, 2008.
[2] Asheim B. T., Gertler M. 创新地理学：区域创新体系. Fagerberg, 2005.
[3] FFG. COMET 能力中心卓越技术项目文件. Wien, FFG, 2008.
[4] FFG. COMET 新能力中心项目评估概念. Wien, FFG, 2008.
[5] Lundvall B. – Å. 国家创新系统：建构创新和交互学习的理论. 英国伦敦：Pinter 出版社, 1992.
[6] Metcalfe S. 技术政策的经济基础：均衡和演变角度, 创新和技术变革经济学手册. 牛津（英国）/剑桥（美国）：Blackwell 出版社, 1995.
[7] MPPE. COMET "材料、工艺和产品工程" K2 中心合作协议. 2008.
[8] Nelson R.（eds.）. 牛津创新手册. 牛津郡：牛津大学出版社, 2005：291-317.
[9] OECD. 研究和创新中的公私合营：奥地利经验评估. 巴黎：经合组织, 2004.
[10] Schartinger D., Rammer C., Fischer M. M., Fröhlich J.：奥地利大学和产业界的知识交流：部门模式和决定因素. 研究政策, 2002, 31：303-328.
[11] Scherngell T., Horvat M., Kubeczko K. Schartinger, D. Fröhlich, J.：奥地利产学研合作组织模式：案例研究报告. AIT—F&PD 报告 0194, 2009, 13.
[12] 邱晓燕, 张赤东. 产业技术创新战略联盟的性质、分类与政府支持. 科技进步与对策, 2011, 28（9）：59-64.
[13] 邱晓燕, 赵捷, 张杰军. 科技成果转让收益分享中的政策改进. 科学学研究, 2011, 29（9）：1318-1322.
[14] 钢铁可循环流程技术创新战略联盟：钢铁可循环流程技术创新战略联盟协议. 2007.
[15] 李新男. 把构建产业技术创新链作为联盟重点任务. 中国科技产业化, 2010, 11：36.
[16] 李新男. 创新"产学研结合"组织模式, 构建产业技术创新战略联盟. 中国软科学, 2007（5）：9-13.
[17] 李新男. 推动产业技术创新战略联盟构建提升国家自主创新能力. 中国科技产业化, 2009, 12：21-23.
[18] 联邦政府. 2009 年奥地利研究技术报告：面向议会的奥地利联邦资助研究、技术和创新的联邦政府报告. 2009.
[19] 农业装备产业技术创新战略联盟：农业装备产业技术创新战略联盟协议. 2007.

[20] 新一代煤（能源）化工产业技术创新战略联盟：新一代煤（能源）化工产业技术创新战略联盟协议. 2007.
[21] 张赤东，郑垂勇. 官产学研结合——科技创新之路. 经济论坛. 2006，(9)：60-61.
[22] 张赤东. 奥地利卓越技术能力中心计划管理经验及启示. 科技进步与对策，2012，29（12）：16-19.
[23] 张杰军，张赤东. 中外科技合作研发机构管理中的问题和建议. 科技管理研究，2010，4：20-23.
[24] 赵捷，张杰军，汤世国，邱晓燕. 科技成果转化中的技术入股问题. 科学学研究，2011，29（10）：1485-1489.
[25] 中奥产学研合作组织模式比较研究项目组. 中国奥地利产学研合作组织模式比较研究. 中国科技论坛，2011，(8)：146-149.

Organizational Models of Cooperation between Enterprises, Universities and R&D Institutions in China and Austria:

A Comparative Analysis Based on ITISA and COMET

Work Report of
a Joint Research Project Funded by
the Chinese Ministry of Science and Technology (MOST) and the Austrian Federal Ministry for Transport Innovation and Technology (BMVIT)

(starting January 1st, 2009)

Project Principals/项目负责人

China/中国
Li Xinnan (Policy&Regulation Departmen, MOST), Yao Weike (International Cooperation Department, MOST), Ye Jianzhong (Chinese Embassy in Austrria)

Austria/奥地利
Ingolf Schädler (BMVIT)

Study Team Leaders/研究组负责人

China/中国
Zhang Jiejun (China Academy of Science & Technology for Development), Su Jing (Policy & Regulation Department, MOST), Xing Jijun (International Cooperation Department, MOST), Zhang Chidong (CASTED)

Austria/奥地利
Josef Fröhlich (Foresight & Policy Development Departmet, Austrian Institute of Technology/F&PD, AIT), Klaus Kubeczko (F&PD, AIT), Thomas Scherngell (F&PD, AIT), Manfred Horvat (Vienna University of Technology, BMVIT)

Study Team Members/项目组成员

China/中国
Guo Tiecheng (CASTED), Tang Fuqiang (MOST), Dong Guilan (CASTED), Zhao Jie (CASTED), Di xiaoyan (CASTED), Ma Chi (CASTED), Liu Dong (CASTED), Wang Qingyuan (CASTED), Jiang Shan (CATSED), Fang Xianfa (Chinese Academy of Agricultural Mechanization Science, CAAMS), Wu Haihua (CAAMS), Han Wei (China Iron&Steel Rearch Ihstitute Group, CISRI), Yue Wenliang (CISRI), Li Xiaoli (CISRI), Liu Jiaqiang (China National Chemical Engineering Group Corporation, CNCEC), Ma Shuna (CNCEC), Yang Hua (TD-SCDMA Industry Alliance, TDIS), Zhou Xueyan (TDIS), Wu Ling (China Solid State Lighting Alliance, CSSLA), Ruan Jun (CSSLA), Wang Ersheng (CSSLA), Hao Jianqun (CSSLA), Wang Jinyong (Changfeng Open Standards Platform Software Alliance)

Austria/奥地利
Alexander Unkart (BMVIT), Ruper Pichler (BMVIT), Gottfried Göritzer (BMVIT), Richard Schanner (Integrated Research in Materials, Processing and Product Engineering/MPPE), Reinhold Ebner (MPPE), Gerald Schatz (Austrian Center of Competence in Mechatronics/ACCM), Rudolf Scheidl (ACCM), Werner Scherf (Carinthian Tech Research AG/CTR), Simon Grasser (CTR), Otto Starzer (Forschungsförderungsgesellschaft/FFG), Theresia Vogel-Lahner (FFG)

Organizational Models of Cooperation between Enterprises, Universities and R&D Institutions in China and Austria:

A Comparative Analysis Based on ITISA and COMET

Table of Contents

1 **Introduction** ····· 1
1.1 Objective and Significance of the Research ····· 2
1.2 Empirical Framework ····· 3

2 **Policy Initiatives to Support Science-industry Collaborations in China and Austria** ····· 6
2.1 Policy Programmes in China ····· 6
2.2 Policy Initiatives in Austria ····· 20

3 **Cases of Industrial Technology Innovation Strategic Alliance (ITISA)** ····· 32
3.1 The Technology Innovation Promotion Alliance for Agricultural Machinery Industry (TIPAAMI) ····· 32
3.2 The Industry Technology Innovation Strategic Alliances for New-Generation Coal (Energy) Chemicals (ITISANCC) ····· 48
3.3 The Strategic Alliances for Recycling Steel Processes Technology Innovation (SARSPTI) ····· 60
3.4 Summary of Chinese ITISA Cases ····· 67

4 **Cases of Competence Centers of Excellent Technologies (COMET)** ····· 70
4.1 The Austrian Centre of Competence of Mechatronics (ACCM) ····· 70

4.2　The Centre on Integrated Research in Materials, Processing and Product Engineering (MPPE) ································· 84
4.3　The Carinthian Tech Research Centre for Advanced Sensor Technologies (CTR) ··· 97
4.4　Summary of Austrian COMET Cases ································· 107

5　Comparative Analysis of Chinese and Austrian cases ········ 111
5.1　Similarities ··· 111
5.2　Differences ··· 114
5.3　Summary of the Comparative Analysis ································ 117

6　Conclusions and Outlook ··· 120
6.1　General Findings ··· 120
6.2　Conclusions Regarding Chinese Policies ····························· 122
6.3　Conclusions Regarding Austrian Policies ···························· 124
6.4　Summary and Future Research Agenda ································ 125

7　References ··· 128

Appendix: List of Interviews ·· 130

1 Introduction

Today it is widely recognized that collaborative activities between the science and the industry sectors are crucial for the innovation capacity, and thus, for the economic competitiveness of firms, regions and countries. Various theoretical and empirical contributions in the economics of innovation literature emphasize the important role of knowledge flows and interactions between public research and the enterprise sectors (see, for instance, Schartinger et al. 2002). This is also reflected in the systems of innovation approach (see, for instance, Lundvall 1992 among many others), pointing to the importance of efficient interactions among all actors of the innovation system, in particular among firms, universities, public research organizations and technology policy for successful innovation. The systemic perspective is characterized by its focus on institutions (formal and informal) and networks of actors which shape the direction and rate of learning and innovation at different aggregate levels in the innovation system (see *Asheim and Gertler 2005*, among others)❶.

In this context, the stimulation and creation of collaborative research activities between firms, universities and research organisations became an essential element of recent technology and innovation policy initiatives. Various countries have established policy programmes to promote science-industry cooperation. Prominent early examples are *VLSI (Very-large-scale Integration) of Japan* in 1976, the ESPRIT (European Strategic Programme in Information Technology) launched in 1982, the *Alvey Programme in Information Technology in the UK between 1983 and 1988*, *the European RTD Framework Programmes* started in 1984, the

---

❶ The systems approach implies that public intervention can act upon the relationships of the system with its components, coherence and possible dysfunctions at different and/or territorial levels. In this context, complexity and self-organisation in a non-linear innovation process are to be taken into account. There are often deep tensions in the policy systems which tend to render public interventions less effective, i. e. competing rationales, different views and understanding of innovation policies, different imperatives for different policy areas or fragmentation and segmentation of public organisations and responsibilities. Thus, modernized public policy interventions rely on flexible decentralised management practices, adaptive learning, participatory coordination mechanisms and flexibility. A high degree of self-organisation under a broader strategic objective from the top is typical. Policy instruments, taking into account these characteristics, might include foresight activities.

Semiconductor R&D *Division of Korea in 1986*, SEMATECH (*Semiconductor Manufacturing Technology*) *of the United States* formed in 1987, JESSI (*Joint European Submicron Silicon Initiative*) established in 1988 in EUREKA, the US Advanced Technology Programme launched in 1991 or the *"Faraday Partnership Program"* of Britain.

Both Austrian and Chinese technology policies were following this trend in the recent past. While the Austrian government already established formalized policy programmes supporting science-industry cooperation-in particular the *Austrian Competence Center Programme* (CCP) later developed into the *Competence Centers of Excellent Technologies* (COMET) *programme in* the mid 1990s, Chinese technology policy has established concrete initiatives in this direction over the past five years, which resulted in the launch of the *Industry Technology Innovation Strategic Alliances* (ITISA) in 2007. Chinese government gradually issued a series of polices to support ITISA.

The Austrian policy measures, adopted as new programme-based support activities, had the objective to encourage bottom-up cooperation among enterprises, universities and scientific research institutions. It is worth noting that the Austrian programmes were referred to as innovative and influential policy initiatives for stimulating science-industry cooperation with the background of the systems of innovation approach by OECD (2004).

The Chinese ITISA programme is an active effort to inaugurate the new form of organization for science-industry cooperation and innovation and seeks to promote the establishment of continuous and stable cooperation relationship among all sides of science and industry at the strategic level around the industry technology innovation chain. In contrast to the Austrian programme it is clearly focused on national strategic needs, and in this context strongly related to the *Outline for National Mid and Long Term Science and Technology Development Plan* (2006-2020) (Hereinafter referred to as "plan outline") and the 11 thematic priorities outlined there.

1.1 Objective and Significance of the Research

The objective of this project is to investigate organisational models for cooperation between enterprises, universities and research institutions in China and Austria, based on the principle of public private partnership (PPP). The focus is on the comparison of Chinese and Austrian policy initiatives and organizational models for science-industry cooperation. By this, the objectives of the study are to identify similarities and dissimilarities between Chinese and Austrian models for science industry cooperation, and to derive implications from such comparative analysis in a Chinese and Austrian policy context.

The project draws on empirical case studies. These case studies focus on concrete cases of science-industry cooperation in China and Austria and shift attention on the operational mechanisms, the corporate governance structures and the legal framework of the selected cases of science-industry cooperation (see, Scherngell et al. 2010). The Chinese cases are part of the *Industry Technology Innovation Strategic Alliances* (ITISA) Programme established by the Ministry of Science and Technology (MOST), including *the Technology Innovation Promotion Alliance for Agricultural Machinery Industry* (TIPAAMI), *the Industry Technology Innovation Strategic Alliances for New Generation Coal (Energy) and Chemicals* (ITISANCC), and the *Strategic Alliances for Recycling Steel Processes Technology Innovation* (SARSPTI). The Austrian cases involve the Austrian Centre of Competence of Mechatronics (ACCM), the Centre on Integrated Research in Materials, Processing and Product Engineering (MPPE), and the Carinthian Tech Research Centre for Advanced Sensor Technologies (CTR). These are part of the *Austrian Programme on Competence Centers for Excellent Technologies* (COMET) established by the Federal Ministry of Transport, Innovation and Technology (BMVIT) which is currently the biggest policy initiative to support cooperation between science and industry in Austria.

The significance of this research project is underlined by recent scientific literature focusing on science-industry relations. Various theoretical and empirical studies point to the importance of analyzing concrete examples of science-industry cooperation induced by public policy programmes in order to enhance our understanding on the mechanisms of cooperative R&D between the science and the industry sector. Thus, the empirical analysis of selected Chinese ITISA cases and Austrian COMET cases is of great scientific and strategic significance for promoting the development of science-industry cooperation and the policies for such cooperation.

1.2 Empirical Framework

The analytical framework used puts special emphasis on corporate governance structures and responsibilities, internal and external relationships as well as knowledge generation and diffusion processes. The empirical analysis is carried out via face-to-face interviews and by accumulating and analyzing material provided by the selected cases and other institutions. The analysis of the cases serves as a basis for the comparative analysis of Chinese and Austrian organizational models for science-industry cooperation. In what follows we will briefly reflect

on the main components of the analytical framework that have been analysed:
   i) Goals and Organisational Forms
   • Strategic Goal of the Programme
   – Deficits addressed
   – Derivation of goals addressed and methods applied in the programme
   • Strategic Goals of the Selected Cases
   • Legal Organisational Forms of the Selected Cases
   ii) Corporate Governance Structures, Responsibilities, Rights and Codes of Conduct
   • Governance Structure and Internal Management
   • Exploration of the Most Serious Problems that Impede Interaction, Integration or Translation of Different Rationalities
   – Profit, market shares vs. academic eminence
   – Short term thinking vs. long-term cumulative knowledge generation
   – Exclusion of competitors vs. disclosure of knowledge
   • Which Governance Structures and Rules Are Used to Integrate the Different Rationalities Within one Centre/Alliance?
     • The Organisation of Collaboration on the Different Levels
     • The organisation of the Operational Plan, Selection of Tasks/Projects
     • Characteristics of R&D Management, Controlling and Marketing
     • Analysis of Structures, Rights and Rules (as for instance the issue of Intellectual Property Rights), Codes of Conduct, Flows of Information, Which Are Particularly Conducive to Stimulate the Creation of New Knowledge or, Ultimately, Innovation.
     • Identification of Characteristic Sectoral, Disciplinary, Size-related or Regional Differences
   iii) Analysis of Relationships: Scientific Community, Relevant Governments and the Firm Sector
   • Identification of Core Actors, Initiators
   • Evolution of Their Relationships, Identification of the Influence of Their Relationships on the Development of Centres/Alliances
   • Investigation of the Role of Related Government Bodies
   • The History of the Centre/Alliance
   – Course of Critical Events in the Establishment of the Centre/Alliance (time dimension)
   – Identification of Barriers in the Course of Events

iv) Knowledge Generation, Technology Diffusion
- Identification of Joint Resources for Knowledge Production
– Human Resources
– Machinery, Equipment
– Funding
- Identification of Management and Diffusion of Collaboration Outputs
– Joint Products
– Joint Processes
– Joint Patents
– Joint Publications
– Joint Organisation of Scientific Conferences, Symposia, etc.
– Joint Supervision of Students
– Exchange and Diffusion of Human Resources

v) Institutional Conditions: Laws and Regulations
- Compatibility With Present Laws and Regulations in Different Fields (Such as Society, Economy, Science and Technology, etc.). For the Austrian Case, This Includes:
– Law of University Organisation
– Law of Public Research Institutions
– Employment Law
– Regulations of Financing Universities and Departments
– European Union Competition Law
– Tax law
- Assessment of Their Effects and (In)Appropriateness

vi) Financing and Administration of Funds
- Investigation of Different Models of Financing and Cost Sharing in the Selected Cases
- Ways of Managing and Using Financial Resources

2 Policy Initiatives to Support Science-industry Collaborations in China and Austria

This section discusses the evolution of policies in China and Austria that are intended to address the problem of missing links in the innovation systems referring to missing interactions between science and industry sectors. Before we describe the establishment of ITISA, in the *subsection* 2.1 that follows we reflect in four parts in regard to the evolution of Chinese policy programmes, and with emphasis on the formation and development of ITISA, the key measure to promote science industry cooperation by Chinese government in recent years. Then, in *subsection* 2.2 we will discuss the establishment of PPP programme based support for science industry cooperation since the 1990s and introduces the main features of COMET, the most important programme based support for science industry cooperation in Austria.

2.1 Policy Programmes in China

Science industry cooperation is an important part of technology innovation system. The initiatives of policies on promoting science industry cooperation shows a deeper understanding about innovation system, especially about development in theory in regard to national innovation system.

In the past 30 years, with more and more practice, policies and regulations in connection with enterprises, universities and R&D institutes cooperation were adjusted constantly in China.

This subsection divides the evolution of science industry cooperation policies into two parts. The first part reviews macro policies on advancing the cooperation between enterprises, universities and R&D institutes in China. The second part gives an introduction to some policies specifically for ITISA.

2.1.1 Macro Policies to Promote the Cooperation between Enterprises, Universities and R&D Institutes

i. The stage of promoting the cooperation between enterprises, universities and R&D institutes via reform (1985~1992)

In 1978, a resolution on carrying out economic restructuring was adopted on the Third Session of the Eleventh Central Committee of the Party. Accordingly, a reform of science and technology system was also carried out. In 1985, the reform of science and technology system entered into a new phase marked by *the Decision of the Central Committee of the Communist Party of China on Science and Technology System Reform*. It is expressly indicated in such decision that, the appropriation system shall be reformed to change the relations of dependence of R&D institutes on administrative authorities, thereby making them serve economic development and transform their scientific and technical achievements on their own initiatives; the technical market shall be opened to recognize scientific and technical achievements as commodities in terms of policies and laws, thereby to establish a mechanism of assignment for value based on the law of value. The government has, in succession, issued *the Patent Law of the People's Republic of China*, *the Technical Contract Law of the People's Republic of China* and corresponding implementation regulations, providing basic rules for various technical transactions such as technical development, technical transfer, consultancy and service has restructured scientific research organizations, changed the status of separation of research institutes from enterprises, disconnection between research, design, education and production, division of the research for national defence and that, for civilian purpose segments and regions; has made great efforts to enhance the technical absorption and development capability and the intermediate link where the technological achievements are transformed into capacity, was promoted the cooperation and alliance between research institutes, design institutes, universities and enterprises and has enabled the reasonable disposition in depth of the scientific and technical force in all respects.

In the process of selecting modes for enterprises, universities and R&D institutes combination during this period, it is particularly stressed that R&D institutes should enter enterprises or the two should closely combine with each other. In 1986, it was indicated in *Several Rules of the State Council on Further Promoting Science and Technology System Reform* that, most technical development-based R&D institute, especially those engaged in product development, should gradually enter enterprises or business conglomerates or closely combine with them and the fund for R&D should be provided by enterprises or business conglomerates from their sales step by step. In 1998, it was indicated in *the Decisions of the State Council* on *Several Issues Arising from Deepening Science and Technology System Reform* that, R&D institutes and enterprises may contract for, lease, participate in shares of and merge each other, may establish joint venture, enter enterprises or business conglomerates or develop into scientific research-based enterprises etc.

To advance the transformation of technological achievements and enhance the cooperation between enterprises, universities and R&D institutes, the government has formulated a range of technological programs, concentrating its efforts on solving major technological problems arising from national economy and social development and enhancing the intermediate link where technological achievements are transformed into production to advance the transformation of technological achievements into productivity as soon as possible, thereby enable technologies to contribute to economic development.

ii. The stage of exploring new forms of enterprises, universities and R&D institutes combination in the context of market economy system (1992-1999)

In 1992, it was expressly proposed at the Fourteenth Congress of the Communist Party that the establishment of socialist market economy system should be the objective of the economic restructuring in China. Thereafter, the concern about enterprises, universities and R&D institutes cooperation changed from technological achievements transformation to how to form an effective enterprises, universities and R&D institutes cooperation mechanism. In 1992, the former State Economic and Trade Commission, the Ministry of Education and Chinese Academy of Sciences jointly implemented the "Enterprises, Universities and R&D Institutes Joint Development Project", which is a major step to promote enterprises, universities and R&D institutes combination at the national level.

It was indicated in *the Outline of Mid and Long-term Science Technology Development Programme* issued by the State Council in 1992 that lateral economic alliance between enterprises, enterprises and development institutes and universities should be advanced by multiple means and establishment of business conglomerate combining technology development, production, sales and service through combination of scientific research and production, with large and medium-sized enterprises as the backbone and quality commodities of famous brands as the flagship should be encouraged. Special support should be given to the business conglomerates which were sciences-and-technologies-oriented or internationally competitive.

It was proposed in *the Law of the Peoples Republic of China on Science and Technology Progress* issued in 1993 that, a mechanism which effectively combines science and technologies and economy should be established, enterprises to establish and improve technology development institutes and unite and cooperate with R&D institutes and universities to enhance their R&D, pilot program and industrial demonstration capacity. The state encourages and guides R&D institutes engaged in technology development to develop technological achievements or jointly with enterprises and institutes and to effect an economy combining technology, industry and trade or technology, agriculture and trade. It is the first time in China to propose the alliance and cooperation among enterprises, universities and R&D institutes in the form of a law.

In 1994, State Science and Technology Commission and National Economic System Restructuring Commission proposed in *the Key Points for Adapting to Development of Socialist Market Economy and Deepening Science and Technology System* (GuoKeFaZheng No. [1994]29) continued to encourage R&D institutes to explore and practice an economy combining technology, industry and trade or technology, agriculture and trade, with an aim to developing scientific and technological industry. The government fostered these institutes in terms of new products, intermediate test product and technical income; encouraged R&D institutes to conduct technical development jointly with enterprises; encouraged qualified R&D institutes to directly enter large or medium-sized enterprises or business conglomerates and become their technical development departments or centers. In the same year, the State Science and Technology Commission, National Economic System Restructuring Commission and National Education Commission jointly issued *Opinions on Development of Technological Industry by Universities*, for the purpose of regulating the development of technological industry of universities and leading it to a healthy and orderly path.

It was expressly proposed in *the Decision of the Central Committee of the Communist Party of China on Acceleration of Science and Technology Progress* in 1995 that cooperation between enterprises, universities and R&D institutes should be further promoted and the scientific and technical force of R&D institutes and universities were encouraged to enter enterprises or business conglomerates by multiple means and participate in their technical innovation and development. Medium and large-sized enterprises should generally establish and complete technical development institutes and cooperate with R&D institutes and universities through various means to greatly enhance their technical development capacity, thereby gradually becoming the mainstay in technical development. It was indicated in the *Decisions of the State Council on Deepening Scientific and Technological System Reform* during the Ninth Five-Year Plan period that, during the ninth Five-Year Plan period, a scientific and technological system which fits in with the socialist market economy system and the law of development of science and technology themselves to form a mechanism closely combining scientific research, development, production and market, establish an enterprise-based technical development system combining enterprises, universities and R&D institutes, a scientific and technological service system led by R&D institutes and universities and socialized technological service system, thus to improve the contribution of technology in national economy. Large and medium sized enterprises and business conglomerates should, oriented to the needs of market, gradually establish various forms of technical development institutes such as alliance with R&D institutes and universities.

The Law of the PRC on Promoting the Transformation of Scientific and Technological Achievements promulgated by China in 1996 (Order 68 of the President of the People's Republic of China) stipulates that the State encourages R&D institutes, universities and other institutes to join efforts with manufacturers for the transformation of scientific and technological achievements. In addition, it stipulates that of the funds the government allocates to scientific and technological undertakings, to investment in fixed assets and to technological updating, a certain proportion must be used for transforming scientific and technological achievements. The State encourages establishment of funds or risk funds for transformation of scientific and technological achievements, such funds shall be raised by the State, local authorities, enterprises, institutes and other organizations and individuals and shall be used to aid transformation of such scientific and technological achievements as need substantial investment, involve considerable risks and promise high yields and to accelerate the application of major scientific and technological achievements in industrial production.

To coordinate with the implementation of *the Law of the PRC on Promoting the Transformation of Scientific and Technological Achievements*, the State Council published *Several Rules on Promoting the Transformation of Scientific and Technological Achievements* in 1999, which stipulates that where high and new technology achievements are used as investment into limited liability companies or non-corporation enterprises for shares, unless otherwise agreed, the evaluation may be up to 35% of the registered capital of such companies or enterprises; R&D institutes and universities which transform functionary technological achievements shall give awards to people who make such technological achievements and who make great contribution in the transformation of such achievements. The income of R&D institutes and universities is exempt from business tax. Income of R&D institutes and universities from technical service such as technological achievements assignment, technical training, technical consultancy and technical contract is temporarily exempt from income tax.

It is also expressly stipulated in the Interim *Regulations of the Ministry of Science and Technology and the Ministry of Finance on the Technical Innovation Fund for Science and Technology-oriented Small and Middle-sized Enterprises* (Guobanfa [1997]47) published in 1999 that priority shall be given to support of joint innovation of enterprises, universities and R&D institutes and to various high-tech and high value-added projects which are provided with independent intellectual property, can offer a great many employment opportunities, save energy and reduce consumption, are helpful to environment protection and can earn foreign exchange.

In this stage, as China has established the objective of socialist market economy system reform, the building of the technical innovation system corresponding thereto and advancement of policies combining enterprises, universities and R&D institutes were still under exploration.

iii. The stage of exploring new enterprises, universities and R&D institutes cooperation mechanism (1999-2006)

In 1999, the Central Committee of the Communist Party of China and the State Council published the *Decision on Strengthening Technological Innovation, Developing High Technology and Realize Industrialization*. The Decision requires that our country proactively advance supporting reform of scientific and technological system, educational system and economic system to eliminate the disconnection of science and technology, education and economy completely. It also requires large and middle-sized enterprises to enhance cooperation with universities and R&D institutes. In the principle of complementing each other and sharing benefits, a bilateral and multilateral cooperation mechanism shall be established to enhance exchange among scientific and technical personnel of different organizations through holding concurrent post in each other's organizations and training etc. Certain proportion of the R&D fund of enterprises shall be used for enterprises, universities and R&D institutes cooperation. The decision also expressly stipulates that, support shall be given to development of the scientific and technological zone of universities to foster a group of knowledge and intelligence intensive enterprises and business conglomerates which have advantages in market competition to enable more close cooperation between enterprises, universities and R&D institutes.

The Decision of CPPCC on Several Major Issues Arising from the Reform and Development of State-owned Enterprises published in 1999 requires to form an enterprise-centered technical innovation system, promote the cooperation between enterprises, universities and R&D institutes and encourage R&D institute and universities to join enterprises and business conglomerates to enhance development and promotion of applied technique and increase investment in pilot program, thereby advancing the transformation of technological achievements into real productivity. *The Opinions on Accelerating Implementation of Technical Innovation Project to Form an Enterprise-centered Technical Innovation System* (No. GuoJing-

MaoJishu [2000]60), which was published by the former State Economic and Trade Commission, proposed to strengthen the building of enterprises, universities and R&D institutes joint mechanism, encourage most large-sized state-owned enterprises to establish open, stable cooperation relationship with universities and R&D institutes and carry out various forms of enterprises, universities and R&D institutes combination through achievements assignment, agency development, joint development, joint establishment of technology development institutes and science and technology-based enterprises, thereby to establish an enterprise-based interests and risk sharing enterprises, universities and R&D institutes combination mechanism with wide involvement of universities and R&D institutes. *The State Industrial Technology Development Policy* (No. GuoJingMaoJishu [2002]444) issued in 2002 requires that an enterprise-based risk sharing enterprises, universities and R&D institutes combination mechanism be established. It also requires to establish an enterprises, universities and R&D institutes association of enterprises, universities and R&D institutes to form a market-oriented R&D system and open enterprises, universities and R&D institutes cooperation mechanism.

The Several Opinions on Protection and Management of Intellectual Property in *Connection with Science and Technologies* (No. GuoKeFaZhengFa [2000]569) published by the Ministry of Science and Technology in December 2000 proposed to further enhance cooperation between enterprises, universities and R&D institutes and improve the capacity and actual effect of scientific and technological achievements transformation through reasonable agreement on ownership of intellectual property and share of benefits under technical contracts. It proposed to adjust policies on ownership of the intellectual property in respect of scientific and technological achievements. Any intellectual property in respect of scientific and technological achievements made through implementation of national scientific and technological programme may be owned by the organization which undertakes such programme, unless it is for the purpose of assuring major national interests, national security and social public interests and expressly agreed upon in the contracts by the competent authority for such scientific and technological programme and the undertaker. It is expressly stipulated in *The Several Rules on Management of Intellectual Property in Respect of Research Achievements of Scientific and Technological Research Programme*, which was published in March 2002 (No. GuoBanFa [2002] 30), the scientific and technological achievements of scientific and technological research programme and the intellectual property in respect thereof shall be owned by the undertaker of the scientific and technological research programme awarded by the state (hereinafter referred to as programme undertaker), unless they involve national security, national interests and major social and public interests. The state may, as necessary, reserve the right to use it for free, develop it, make it to be effectively used and benefit from it. In addition, the government may exercise right of involvement under special conditions.

It is stipulated in the *Notice on Tax Policies in Connection with Promoting Transformation of Scientific and Technological Achievements* (No. CaiShui [1999]45) jointly published by the Ministry of Finance and State Administration of Taxation that, the income of R&D institutes from technical transfer shall continue to be exempt from business tax and the income of universities from technical transfer shall be exempt from business tax as of May 1st, 1999; income of R&D institutes and universities from technical service such as technological achievements assignment, technical training, technical consultancy and technical contract is temporarily exempt from income tax; As of Jul. 1st, 1999, the winner of awards, which are given by R&D institutes and universities in form of share or proportion of contribution when transforming functionary technological achievements, shall be temporarily exempt from individual income tax upon obtaining of such share or proportion of contribution, and shall pay individual income tax according to law upon receipt of dividend based on such share or proportion of contribution or income from assignment of such share or proportion of contribution. *The National Science & Technology Awards System* also focuses on application of scientific and technological achievements and incorporates content on promotion of enterprises, universities and R&D institutes combination. *The Regulations on State Science and Technology Prizes* as amended in 2003 stipulates that "the State Highest Science and Technology Prize" shall be granted to scientific and technical workers who have made great breakthroughs at the frontier of contemporary science and technology or who have made remarkable contributions to the development of science and technology and in addition have created great economic or social profits through innovation of science and technology, transformation of scientific and technological achievements, and industrialization of high-tech. The State Scientific and Technological Progress Prize shall be granted to citizens and organizations that have made remarkable contributions to the application and dissemination of advanced scientific and technological achievements and the accomplishment of significant scientific and technological projects, plans and programs.

iv. The stage of promoting the cooperation between enterprises, universities and R&D institutes to national strategy level (2006 up to now)

At the 2006 National Science and Technology Conference, it was proposed to build an innovation-oriented country. *The Decision of the Central Committee of the Communist Party of China and the State Council on Implementing the Scientific and Technological Development Planning Outline and Enhancing Independent Innovation Capacity* proposed to establish an enterprise-based technical innovation system combining enterprises, universities and R&D institutes; make great efforts to promote cooperation between enterprises, universities and R&D institutes; and encourage enterprise to, jointly with R&D institutes and universities, establish technical innovation organizations such as R&D institutes and industrial technology alliance etc. The cooperation between enterprises, universities and R&D institutes is, as an important part of technology innovation system, promoted to an unprecedented strategic level. *The Outline for Mid and Long Term Science and Technology Development Plan* (2006—2020) (hereinafter referred to as "plan outline") pointed out that, the scientific and technological resources can be effectively allocated, the innovative vigor of R&D institutes can be aroused and enterprises can acquire sustained innovation capacity only through the cooperation between enterprises, universities and R&D institutes. While significantly improving the technological innovation capacity of enterprises, a new mechanism combining enterprises, universities and R&D institutes, where R&D institutes and universities proactively serve enterprises according to their requirements for technical innovation, must be established. The supporting policies of the Plan Outline establish a range of preferential policies designed to promote cooperation between enterprises, universities and R&D institutes, including tax incentive and finance support, encouraging enterprises, universities and research institutes to jointly import, absorb and innovate in technologies and establish National Key Laboratory relying on restructured universities and institutes and enterprises. With the convening of National Science and Technology Conference, the promotion of enterprises, universities and R&D institutes combination by the government entered into a new period. In 2006, the Ministry of Science and Technology, State-owned Assets Supervision and Administration Commission and National Federation of Trade Unions jointly implemented a *Technological Innovation Guiding Project* intended to improve the innovation capacity of enterprises and promote cooperation between enterprises, universities and R&D institutes. As a form of cooperation between science and industry, ITISA becomes a key carrier of the National Technological Innovation Program.

2.1.2 Policies to Promote Formation and Development of ITISA

Since 2006, policies to support the formation and development of ITISA have gone through four stages. With the increasing of number of ITISA established and the expanding of their influence, forms of supporting policies become multiple in reality.

i. Exploring the building of four pilot ITISA

In 2006, the Ministry of Science and Technology, the Ministry of Finance, the Ministry of Education, the China Development Bank, the All China Federation of Trade Unions, and the State-owned Assets Supervision and Administration Commission of the State Council set up *the Steering Group for Coordination in Promoting Cooperation between Science and Industry*. The steering group has actively driven and encouraged the setup and development of Industrial Technological Innovation Strategic Alliances in China. The goal of governmental support for setup of strategic industrial alliances between science and industry is: to take the technological innovation needs of the country's strategic industries and regional pillar industries as the orientation, make enterprises as the principal players, encompassing the industrial technological innovation chain, employ market mechanisms to attract resources for innovation, realize effective integration of enterprise, universities and R&D institutes, and jointly make technical breakthroughs for industrial development. Universities, R&D institutes or other organizations can form cooperation organizations for technological innovation through joint development, mutual-complementation and sharing of benefits and risks, based on the respective interests and development needs of each party, to improve the industrial technological innovation capability, after entering legally binding agreements.

On June 22, 2007, with the efforts of the six ministries/commission, the first pioneering batch of four Industrial Technological Innovation Strategic Alliances were set up, including the Strategic Industrial Technological Innovation Alliance of Agricultural Equipment, the Strategic Industrial Technological Innovation Alliance of New Generation Coal (Energy) Chemistry, the Strategic Industrial Technological Innovation Alliance of Recycling Steel Processes, and the Strategic Industrial Technological Innovation Alliance of Coal Development and Utilization. These alliances are willing to operate as pilots which, as a feature of the policy implements in China, refers to experimenting in one or several areas so as to gain experience to verify the feasibility of the policy before the formal launch or implementation of a policy on national scale. With the prerequisite that alliance volunteers for the pilots, ITISA pilot policies which focus on alliance organization model building, carry out the experiments and exploration on six aspects including goals and the organization model, corporate governance structures, rights and responsibilities, alliances and government, knowledge generation and technology diffusion, legal environment and funds management, under macroscopical guidance by the government. This was another significant move of the *"Technological Guidance Program"*, following the development of innovation-oriented pilot enterprises.

ii. Releasing "Guiding Principle" to Encourage ITISA Establishment

In 2008, based on pilots experiences of four ITISA, the Ministry of Science and Technology released *the Guiding Principle to promote the Establishment of Strategic Industrial Technological Innovation* Alliances, which defines the significance, setup principles, setup criteria, facilitation, etc. for strategic industrial technological innovation alliances.

The guiding opinions clearly states that industrial technological innovation strategic alliances are cooperation organizations for technological innovation between enterprises, universities, R&D institutes or other organizations through joint development, mutual-complementation and sharing of benefits and risks, based on the respective interests and development needs of each party, to improve the industrial technological innovation capability, after entering legally binding agreements. The development of Industrial Technological Innovation Strategic Alliances will improve the organization of cooperation between science and industry, keep stable and legally-protected cooperation relationship on the strategic level; benefit integration of resources for industrial technological innovation, attract innovation resources to advantageous enterprises; protect the seamless interfacing between science and industry, facilitate the commercialization of innovation achievements, facilitate technology integration and innovation, and drive the optimization and upgrading of industrial structures. The guiding opinions also noted that, according to *the Contract Law of P. R. C.* , the following criteria should be met when an alliance is to set up:

i. the alliance is to comprise multiple legal persons, including enterprises, universities and R&D institutes;

ii. a legally binding agreement must be entered, and states the goal of technological innovation and work division among the parties of the agreement;

iii. the organizational structure of decision making, consultation and execution must be set up, effective decision-making and execution mechanisms are in place, and the principal party for taking liabilities caused by the alliance must been named;

iv. a complete range of rules on fund management is in place;

v. an interest guarantee mechanism is in place,

vi. open development mechanisms are in place.

Alliances are encouraged to be engaged in 11 preferred fields given in the Plan Outline (2006-2020). , i. e. energy, water and mineral resources, environment agriculture manufacturing, transport, information industry and modern service industry, population and health, urbanization and urban development, public security and National defence.

Alliances are also encouraged to be engaged in new materials, new energy, information industry, electric motor vehicles, biopharmaceutical, energy conservation and environmental protection, marine industry, etc.

iii. Releasing tentative rules regarding the support to development of ITISA

In 2009, the Ministry of Science and Technology released *the Tentative Rules on Support in National Science and Technology Programs for Strategic Industrial Technological Innovation Alliances*, which clearly supports the development of Industrial Technological Innovation Strategic Alliances with national science and technology programs (major dedicated programs, national science and technology support programs, the 863 Program, etc.), provides active support in addition to the input from alliance members, and explores the opportunities of fund appropriation, discounted interest loans, post-subsidies, etc.

In 2009, the Ministry of Science and Technology released *The Rules on Advancing the Setup and Development of Industrial Technological Innovation Strategic Alliances (Tentative) (Abbreviate Rules on Implementation)*, which makes clear requirements on setup and pilot work related to development of alliances, creates favourable policy background for development of alliances, and explores effective measures for supporting setup and development of alliances.

Rules on implementation shows clearly that under government guidance, the alliances joining the pilot make experiments and exploration in building the credit mechanism, responsibility mechanism and interests mechanism for science-industry cooperation, establishing organization model and operation mechanism for undertaking national projects of technology innovation, integrating resources for construction of industrial technology innovation plateform and serving small and medium-sized enterprises. Implementation of endogenous innovation policies of the government gives full play to the guiding and driving force of industrial technological innovation, and provides experience for setup and development of more alliances.

Industrial Technological Innovation Strategic Alliances

In the same year, a group of ITISA applied to MOST for joining the pilot project. After being evaluated by the intermediary organization experts authorized by the six ministries/commission, 52 alliances were selected to join the project. *The Circular on Pilot Work in Selecting the First Batch of Industrial Technological Innovation Strategic Alliances* made public the names of the 52 Industrial Technological Innovation Strategic Alliances. By August 2010, 56 alliances joined the pilot programme all togther, including the first four alliances.

iv. Exploration of Ways and Means to Suport ITISA by National Science and Technology Programme

The government supports the development of ITISA and provides favourable policy conditions for their innovation. Based on the previous input, the national science and technology plans offer priority support for the pilot alliances reviewed and approved by MOST in order to achieve great breakthrough of technology, upgrade the industrial structure and enhance the competitiveness of China. In 2010, After consultation with other ministries, MOST made exploration for a series of ways and means to support the development of ITISA, such as government funding support, interest free loan etc., in *The National Science and Technology Support Programme* and *the National High Technology Research and Development Programme*.

Addenda 2-1: List of 56 ITISA Pilots

1. The Strategic Alliances for Recycling Steel Processes Technology Innovation (SARSPTI)
2. Industry Technology Innovation Strategic Alliances for New-Generation Coal (Energy) Chemicals (IISANCC)
3. Industry Technology Innovation Strategic Alliance for Development and Use of Coal.
4. The Technology Innovation Promotion Alliance for Agricultural Machinery Industry (TIPAAMI)
5. TD Industrial Alliance(TDIA)
6. Industry technology Innovation Strategic Alliance for Digit Control High Precision Machining.
7. Industry Technology Innovation Strategic Alliance for Lightweight Car Manufacturing
8. Industry Technology Innovation Strategic Alliance for Antibiotics Manufacturing
9. Industry Technology Innovation Strategic Alliance for Vitamin Composite
10. Industry Technology Innovation Strategic Alliance for Semi-conductor Illumination
11. Changfeng Software Allaince for Open Standard Platform
12. Industry Technology Innovation Strategic Alliance for Energy-efficient Aluminium Electrolysis
13. Industry Technology Innovation Strategic Alliance for Soybean Processing.
14. WAPI Industry Technology Innovation Strategic Alliance
15. Industry Technology Innovation Strategic Alliance for Advancing 3G Technology.
16. FTTX Industry Technology Innovation Strategic Alliance
17. Industry Technology Innovation Strategic Alliance for Nonferrous Metal W and Hard Alloy.
18. Industry Technology Innovation Strategic Alliance for Chemical Fiber
19. Industry Technology Innovation Strategic Alliance for Storage
20. Industry Technology Innovation Strategic Alliance for Open Source and Basic Software in Common Use.
21. Industry Technology Innovation Strategic Alliance for Poly-si.
22. Industry technology Innovation Strategic Alliance for Farm Chemical
23. Industry Technology Innovation Strategic Alliance for Dyestuff
24. Industry Technology Innovation Strategic Alliance for New-generation Spinning Equipment
25. Industry Technology Innovation Strategic Alliance for Solar Thermal.
26. Industry Technology Innovation Strategic Alliance for New Energy Dynamical System for Business

Car and Construction Machinery.
27. Tea Industry Technology Innovation Strategic Alliance
28. Industry Technology Innovation Strategic Alliance for Hybrid Rice
29. Wood and Bamboo Industry Technology Innovation Strategic Alliance
30. Industry Technology Innovation Strategic Alliance for Orange and Tangerine Processing
31. Industry Technology Innovation Strategic Alliance for Brassica Processing.
32. Industry Technology Innovation Strategic Alliance for Slow Release Fertilizer.
33. Industry Technology Innovation Strategic Alliance for Fine Varieties of Livestock and Poultry
34. Forage Industry Technology Innovation Strategic Alliance.
35. Meat Processing Industry Technology Innovation Strategic Alliance.
36. Industry Technology Innovation Strategic Alliance for Condensed Milk.
37. Industry Technology Innovation Strategic Alliance for Science Instruments in Yangtze River Delta.
38. Industry Technology Innovation Strategic Alliance for Integrated Circuit Industrial Chain.
39. Industry Technology Innovation Strategic Alliance for Processing and Application of Remote Sensing Data.
40. Industry Technology Innovation Strategic Alliance for Small Satellite Remote Sensing System
41. Industry Technology Innovation Strategic Alliance for Air Remote Sensing Data Acquisition and Service.
42. Industry Technology Innovation Strategic Alliance for Electronic Trade
43. Industry Technology Innovation Strategic Alliance for Navigational Fixing Chips and Terminal
44. GPS Industry Technology Innovation Strategic Alliance
45. Industry Technology Innovation Strategic Alliance for Special Biological Resources
46. Industry Technology Innovation Strategic Alliance for Environment Protection of Nonferrous Metals.
47. Industry Technology Innovation Strategic Alliance for Comprehensive Use and Recycling of Metal Resources.
48. Industry Technology Innovation Strategic Alliance for Diagnosis Reagent of Contagious Disease
49. Medical Equipment Industry Technology Innovation Strategic Alliance
50. Industry Technology Innovation Strategic Alliance for Comprehensive Use of Gangue Mine
51. Industry Technology Innovation Strategic Alliance for Coal Bed Gas.
52. Industry Technology Innovation Strategic Alliance for Development and Use of Metallurgy Mine Resources
53. Industry Technology Innovation Strategic Alliance for Bio-gas Development in Cities
54. Recycling Resources Industry Technology Innovation Strategic Alliance
55. Industry Technology Innovation Strategic Alliance for Influenza Vaccine.
56. Industry Technology Innovation Strategic Alliance for Test Reagent and Equipment for Food Security.

2.2 Policy initiatives in Austria

In this section we discuss the evolution of policy programmes to support and shape science-industry cooperation in Austria. Furthermore, we provide a detailed overview on the COMET programme, the most significant Austrian policy initiative in this direction.

2.2.1 Establishment of PPP Programmes in Austria from the Mid 1990s

Science-Industry relations have been identified as one of the major weaknesses of the Austrian innovation system (see OECD 2004) in the early 1990s as reflected by
- a low level of industry funding in university research via research contracts (1998: 1.8% in Austria; 6.4% in the EU),
- no strategic co-operation between science and industry, and
- a short term horizon of R&D management in the industry sector.

This was caused by both supply side and demand side factors, the Austrian patterns of specialization of the industry sector, a lack of critical masses and incentive schemes, and a low mobility of researchers between the science and the industry sectors.

In this context, the implementation of new policy initiatives based on a Public Private Partnership (PPP) approach came to play an important role in the mid 1990s, as for instance highlighted in *The Expert Draft for a Technology Policy Concept of the Austrian Federal Government*(1994/96). This shift was characterized by the establishment of new programme based support actions, clearly targeting the weaknesses of the Austrian innovation system, in particular in the area of R&D co-operations between the science and the industry sectors.

The Austrian technology policy has gradually expanded and diversified its portfolio of instruments over the past two decades. The diversification of instruments can be explained by a shift to a systemic perspective on innovation processes widely reflected in the upcoming systems of innovation perspective in the early 1990s (see, for instance, *Lundvall 1992*, among many others). From this background, technology policies in Austria began to focus more intensively on inter-linkages, interactions and framework conditions in such innovation systems, characterized by the establishment of structural and programme oriented funding.

In what follows, we briefly introduce the Austrian portfolio of instruments: Basically we distinguish between indirect (or tax-incentivised) promotion schemes for R&D, direct promotion schemes for R&D and institutional R&D funding (see *Federal Government 2009*). In the following, we will focus on direct R&D promotion since COMET is one essential initia-

Figure 1 FFG: Subsidy Statistics 2008-General Overview

Area	Programme	Programme line	Projects	Actors	Participants	Total costs	Total funding		Cash value	Commissions
ALR	ASAP		36	48	74	10,816		7,072	7,072	318
			36	48	74	10,816		7,072	7,072	318
BP	BASIS	General funding					Subsidy	91,445		
							Loan	94,247		
			709	575	738	424,458	KKZ	2,866	109,887	
							discounts	540		
							state subsidy	2,074		
							Liability	40,127		
		Headquarters	30	28	31	65,727	Subsidy	20,020	20,020	
		High-tech start-up	25	25	25	11,433	Subsidy	4,856	5,560	
							Loan	3,121		
			764	610	794	501,617		259,296	135,466	
	BRIDGE		96	216	255	30,218		17,767	17,767	
	EUROSTARS		8	11	11	6,309		3,378	3,378	
	Innovation voucher		553	769	1,106	2,760		2,760	2,760	
			1,421	1,498	2,166	540,905		283,201	159,371	
EIP	Procurement financing for science	BMVIT share	11	7	11	100		75	75	
		BMWF share	205	83	205	1,516		1,141	1,141	
			216	90	216	1,616		1,216	1,216	
			216	90	216	1,616		1,216	1,216	
SP	AplusB									65
	brainpower austria									262
	CIR-CE		4	42	42	1,902		862	862	
	COIN	Development	13	36	43	7,523		4,330	4,330	
		Cooperation and networks	13	69	73	5,208		3,125	3,125	
			26	103	116	12,731		7,455	7,455	
	COMET	K projects	7	68	73	27,153		8,728	8,728	25
		K1	11	387	413	187,747		57,241	57,241	
		K2	3	230	241	173,531		57,844	57,844	
		Phasing Out	4	35	35	4,025		1,367	1,367	
			25	645	762	392,456		125,180	125,180	25
	EraSME		6	6	6	2,946		1,429	1,429	
	FEMtech		11	11	11	584		324	324	57
	Forschung macht Schule		254	139	254	893		548	548	
	Josef Ressel Zentren									
	PUST	(FsA, Long Night)	1	6	6	825		288	288	298
	Research Studios Austria		12	16	22	11,615		8,000	8,000	
	wfFORTE	wfFORTE/Laura Bassi Centre								617
			339	878	1,219	423,951		144,085	144,085	1,323
TP	AT:net		54	85	85	21,785		5,143	5,143	100
	ENERGIE DER ZUKUNFT		126	259	397	49,281		29,295	29,295	
	FIT-IT	ES	15	31	39	8,534		5,209	5,209	
		FIT-IT Initiatives	11	19	20	3,429		2,096	2,096	
		SemSys	13	26	35	3,889		2,923	2,923	
		SoC	7	14	23	10,988		5,943	5,943	
		Trust	7	13	16	4,672		2,948	2,948	
		Visual	12	22	27	3,735		2,623	2,623	
			65	114	160	35,248		21,743	21,743	
	GEN-AU	ELSA	3	6	6	1,100		1,100	1,100	
		Pilots	5	5	5	503		435	435	
			8	11	11	1,603		1,535	1,535	
	IEA		24	10	25	1,822		1,822	1,822	81
	IV2S	A3	1	9	9	950		496	496	
		ISB	3	15	15	516		364	364	
		I2	3	7	7	879		430	430	
			7	31	31	2,346		1,290	1,290	
	IV2Splus	A3plus	18	50	66	11,010		5,388	5,388	165
		I2V	23	64	95	9,746		5,163	5,163	
		ways2go	32	67	105	5,892		4,528	4,528	
			73	166	266	26,648		15,079	15,079	165
	KIRAS	PL1 – Networking	2	11	11	357		262	262	85
		PL2 – Coop. R&D projects	3	12	12	2,085		892	892	
		PL4	7	17	18	1,191		1,111	1,111	
			12	37	41	3,632		2,265	2,265	85
	NANO	Steps for further training and education								345
		NANO – Cluster	25	46	74	11,058		8,689	8,689	
		NANO Net	6	10	11	313		229	229	87
		Programme support measures	7	13	13	60		60	60	224
			38	66	98	11,431		8,978	8,978	657
	NAWI	EdZ	10	24	26	1,862		1,105	1,105	194
		FdZ	32	78	88	7,564		4,710	4,710	
		HdZ	21	19	23	2,409		1,430	1,430	
			63	116	137	11,836		7,245	7,245	194
	Neue Energien 2020		31	80	84	12,782		5,713	5,713	
	TAKE OFF		32	64	78	16,793		9,161	9,161	65
			533	905	1,413	195,207		109,267	109,267	1,347
FFG			2,545	2,863	5,088	1,172,495		544,841	421,012	2,989

Source: Federal Government (2009);

Note: ALR denotes Austrian Space Applications Programme ASAP, BP General Programmes, EIP EU Preparatory Funding, SP Structural Programmes, TP Thematic Programmes.

tive of direct R&D promotion in Austria. The distinctive feature of direct funding is that financial support is awarded to applicants as subsidies based on an assessment procedure. Direct funding thus consists of transfers from the public sector to selected applicants (see *Federal Government 2009*). It is inherent to the approach of direct research promotion to establish *foci* that are deliberately content and subject-related and/or actor-related. Thus, it is possible for research projects that are considered to be important and in accordance with defined criteria to be pushed ahead in a very precisely targeted manner, or cooperation may be advanced across the full spectrum of activities between basic research in scientific institutions and applied research in companies via special programmes (see *Federal Government 2009*). It has to be pointed out that the basic funding of universities is denoted as part of institutional funding rather than direct R&D promotion.

Direct research promotion in Austria is organized along a series of programme based initiatives. These programmes managed by agencies promoting science, research, technological development and innovation, namely the Austrian Research Promotion Society (FFG), the Austrian Science Fund (FWF), the Christian Doppler Society (CDG) and the Austria Business Service (AWS). In terms of the share of total funding the FFG manages the largest portfolio of about 400 Mio EUR in the year 2007 (corresponding to 62.5% of total direct R&D promotion in Austria, see *Federal Government 2009*). The FFG focuses on national funding for applied industrial research and manages research projects in the business and science sectors, impulse programmes for the economy and research facilities, and networks fostering cooperation between science and industry. The Austrian Science Fund (FWF) is Austria's central funding organization for basic research with a share of about 35% of total direct R&D promotion in Austria (2007). CDG supports application-oriented research and enables member companies to have a direct access to new knowledge (about 1.5% of total direct research promotion) via joint university-industry research labs established at universities, while AWS is Austria's national promotional bank offering a broad range of company-specific R&D and innovation investment promotion programmes and services (about 4% of total direct research promotion).

Figure 1 provides an overview of the programmes managed by FFG. The Structural Programmes (SP) aim at creating an environment that allows all the actors of the Austrian Innovation System to cooperate effectively and efficiently. The programmes encourage partners from the science and business sectors to cooperate at the highest levels of international research. They also assist regional research facilities in providing technology transfer to small and medium-sized enterprises and they promote the training of research personnel. Further programme lines of the FFG are the General Programmes (BP) where firms receive financial support for their research and development projects, the EU Preparatory Funding (EIP) helping Austrian organizations to participate in cross-border EU research programmes and to network with international partners, the Thematic Programmes (TP) that focus on strategic priorities for Austria's research landscape and thereby promote research activities in promising fields concerning socio-economic and technological needs, and the Austrian Space Applications Programme ASAP (ALR) that is geared towards promoting sustained growth in Austrias aerospace cluster.

2.2.2 The Austrian COMET Programme

The programme COMET (Competence Centres for Excellent Technologies) is administered by the Austrian Research Promotion Agency (FFG) ❶. COMET is part of the structural programme line (see Figure 1) that aims to create an environment allowing actors of the Austrian innovation system to cooperate efficiently (see FFG 2008a). COMET was launched in 2006 and will run until 2017, building on past experiences and lessons learnt from the preceding Austrian Centres of Competence Programme, running from 1998-2007 (OECD 2004). The latter was the most representative and prominent example of policy initiatives in Austria in the 1990s to foster cooperation between firms, universities and research organization❷. Such policy initiatives were constituted as new programme based support actions, clearly targeting the weaknesses of the Austrian innovation system. In particular science-industry relations have been identified as one of the weaknesses of the Austrian innovation system, as reflected by a low level of industry funding in university research via research contracts (1998: 1.8% in Austria; while 6.4% in the EU), no strategic cooperation between science and industry, and a short time horizon of R&D management in the industry sector (see OECD 2004 for further details).

---

❶ COMET is sponsored by the Federal Ministry for Transport, Innovation and Technology (BMVIT) and the Federal Ministry of Economic Affairs and Labour (BMWA) now Federal Ministry for Economic Affairs, Family and Youth (BMWFY). Some Austrian provinces also support COMET with additional funds. The Austrian Research Promotion Agency FFG is responsible for the management of COMET. The FFG was founded on 1 September 2004 (pursuant to the FFG Act on establishing a research promotion agency, Federal Law Gazette I No. 73/2004). The FFG is wholly owned by the Republic of Austria, represented by the Federal Ministry for Transport, Innovation and Technology (BMVIT) and the Federal Ministry of Economics and Labour (BMWA).

❷ In the late 1990s, the implementation of new policy initiatives for the promotion of co-operative R&D between science and industry came to play an important role in Austria, as for instance highlighted in the Expert Draft for a Technology Policy Concept of the Austrian Federal Government (1994/96).

Strategic Goal and Strategic Orientation

Building on experiences and lessons learnt from the Austrian Centres of Competence Programme, COMET puts special emphasis on high-level research activities which operate at the cutting edge and promise high international profile and visibility. The strategic goal of COMET in the short-and-medium-term is to intensify cooperation between science and industry building on the established competence centres of the preceding programme. The competences of the players working at the centres are to be bundled to a greater extent than in the past, with the aim of systematically leveraging content-related synergies. The positive results and experiences of the preceding programme, in particular the development of a new culture of cooperation between science and industry, are to be utilized and strengthened within COMET. By this, COMET is also intended to make a significant contribution to developing human resources in the Austrian innovation system with attractive opportunities for researchers to work in the area of research and technological development. The long-term strategic goal of COMET is to foster international excellence in specific research fields, to expand and to secure technological leadership of Austrian firms, and to strengthen Austria as a research location.

Table 1　　　　Actual COMET K-projects, K1-centres and K2 centres

K2-Centres

 ACCM-Austrian Centre of Competence of Mechatronics, Upper Austria*

 ACIB-Austrian Centre of Industrial Biotechnology, Styria **

 K2-Mobility-K2-Mobility SVT sustainable vehicle technologies, Styria*

 MPPE-Integrated Research in Materials, Processing and Product Engineering, Styria*

 XTribology-Excellence Centre of Tribology, Lower Austria **

K1-Centres

 ACMIT-Austrian Centre for Medical Innovation and Technology, Lower Austria **

 ABC&RENET-Bioenergy 2020+, Styria*

 CCPE-Competence Centre for Pharmaceutical Engineering, Styria*

 CEST-Centre of Excellence in Electrochemical Surface Technology and Materials, Lower Austria*

 CTR-CTR Carinthian Tech Research AG-CC for Advanced Sensor Technologies, Carinthia*

 Pvolaris-evolaris Next Level, Styria*

 ICT-Competence Centre for Information and Communication Technologies, Vienna*

 K1-MET-CC for Excellent Technologies in Adv. Metallurgical Processes, Upper Austria*

 KNOW-Know-Centre Graz, Styria*

ONCOTYROL-Centre for Personalized Cancer Medicine, Tyrol*

PCCL-K1-Competence Centre in Polymer Engineering and Science, Styria**

SBA 2-Secure Business Austria 2, Vienna**

SCCH-Software Competence Centre Hagenberg, Upper Austria*

VRVis-Centre-Visualization, Rendering and Visual Analysis Research Centre, Vienna**

Wood COMET-CC for wood materials and chemicals, Upper Austria*

K-Projects

AAP-Advanced Audio Processing, Styria*

ECV-Embedded Computer Vision, Vienna*

E-motion-e-Motion-Research in ICT for the tourism, sport and leisure industries, Salzburg*

FB-Donauuniversity Krems, Lower Austria**

HFA-TIMBER-Holzforschung Austria, Vienna**

Holz. bau-CC for wood technologies, Styria*

Macro Fun-Bio Engeneering of Macromolecules, Styria*

MPPF-Multifunctional Plug & Play Facade, Styria*

Sports Textiles-Technologiezentrum Ski- und Alpinsport GmbH, Tyrol**

ZPT-FH OÖ Forschungs und Entwicklungs GmbH, Upper Austria**

Source: FFG (2008a); Note: Selected Cases for the Empirical Analysis Highlighted in Bold; * 1st COMET call (2008), ** 2nd COMET call (2009)

COMET involves three programme lines: the relatively small K-Projects aim to foster high-quality research defined jointly by science and industry with a medium-term perspective (Number: approximately 20, Public financing: 40-50%, Project duration: 3-5 years), the K1-Centres are intended to implement medium-to-long-term top-level research with a focus on scientific and technological developments to qualify for future markets (Number: approximately 15, Public financing: 40-55%, Project duration: 7 years), and the K2-Centres that are characterized by outstanding research programmes corresponding to high risks in development and implementation, high international visibility and international networking (Number: maximum 5, Public financing: 45-55%, Project duration: 10 years). All three programme lines are open to all kinds of thematic fields as identified by proposers, but each project/centre must have a clearly defined scientific theme. Further more, it is worth emphasising that in principle, the legal organizational form of a COMET centre is left to the partners. However, it is strongly recommended or almost requested by the FFG to form a limited liability company (LLC) in order to be able to administer the financial flows between all participating actors in a well organized way. The first COMET Call allowed funding for three K2-Centres, eleven K1-Centres and six K-Projects with a total of 125 Mio EUR public funding. Table 1 provides an overview of established K-projects, K1 centres and K2-centres, while Figure 2 highlights their spatial distribution across Austrian provinces.

Figure 2: Geographical distribution of COMET K-projects, K1-centres and K2-centres (2008)

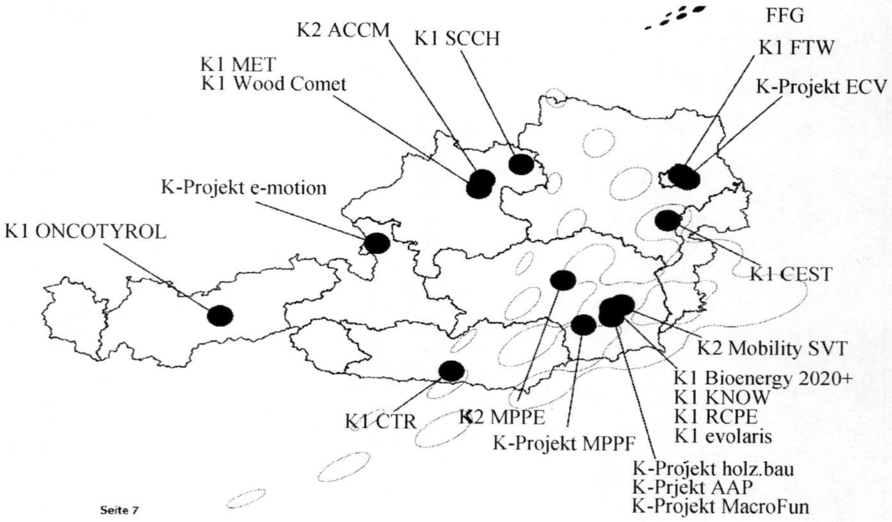

K2 ACCM K1 SCCH FFG
K1 MET K1 FTW
K1 Wood Comet K-Projekt ECV

K-Projekt e-motion

K1 ONCOTYROL

K1 CEST

K2 Mobility SVT
K1 Bioenergy 2020+
K1 KNOW
K1 CTR K2 MPPE K1 RCPE
K-Projekt MPPF K1 evolaris
K-Projekt holz.bau
K-Prjekt AAP
K-Projekt MacroFun

Source: FFG (2008a)

In what follows, we briefly reflect on general aspects concerning the motivation of innovating organizations to participate in COMET (case-specific findings on this issue are given in the respective sections on the selected cases).

For universities, the motivation for participating in COMET and the possible benefits can in general be summarised as follows:
- Bridging the gap between university and industry, and networking with national and international partners.
- Access to financial resources for research.
- Achieving critical mass for ambitious collaborative research activities in mid- and long-term strategic planning perspectives in the frame of a research programme that is jointly defined together with business partners; the joint planning processes en-

sures close linking between university activities and R&D demand of enterprises.
- Joint monitoring and quality assurance of research performance.
- Mid- and long-term orientation of the research programme disburdening the partners of the centres from multiple applications for individual research projects.
- Strengthening the human resource base in the thematic areas of the centres by attracting and employing high-quality researchers and by involving doctoral students; substantial increase of the industry relevance and the number of dissertations and co-authored publications.
- Possibilities for the exploitation and implementation of research results in industry.
- Access to or joint use of research infrastructure.
- Raising the national and international visibility of the participating universities.

The joint mentoring of doctoral theses by researchers from universities and industry is seen especially beneficial in the area of research. Regarding education, there are cases where excellent researchers employed by a COMET centre give also courses at universities and thus enrich their educational programmes. The participation in COMET centres may even induce more far-ranging changes in educational programmes. The sometimes highly interdisciplinary nature of their activities calls for developing a basis of common understanding across different disciplines. For instance, educational programmes at Graz University of Technology have been restructured so that in the first one and a half years a common basis of fundamental courses is provided for all programmes. The interdisciplinary nature of the activities may also stimulate the cooperation between different departments within universities.

In contrast to universities, firms generally participate in COMET to get access to concentrated high-level competences. Overall, it is cheaper and more efficient for firms to accomplish joint R&D and produce the knowledge that they need within one specific platform than to acquire this knowledge via the market. Furthermore, firms can acquire additional funding for already planned and ongoing R&D activities. From a network theory perspective, such firms are able to reduce transaction costs (see Williamson 1975). Other important points involve mutual learning and the integration of codified and even tacit knowledge into their knowledge base.

Of course, the motivation and interests of partners in different COMET centres are different. Therefore, in each case the motivation and interests as well as the expected benefits of partners have to be clearly defined from the outset. In doing so, the different rationalities of the industrial and scientific partners have to be considered and mutually accepted. It is essential for the long-term success and sustainability of COMET centres that win-win situations are ensured.

Selection and Evaluation of COMET Centres

The selection process, i. e. the ex-ante evaluation of K1-centres and K2-centres is based on a two-stage process based (see Figure 3) on clearly defined evaluation criteria. The first stage includes an internal and external evaluation of a short proposal. The external evaluation, coordinated by the Austrian Science Fund (FWF) and the Christian Doppler Research Association (CDG), involves an international peer-review process that evaluates the research programme jointly designed by science and industry, the quality of the consortium, the quality of cooperation, and the international visibility (FFG 2008b). In the closing panel of the first stage, the jury (panel 1 consisting of FFG internal and external experts) decides if the applying consortium should be invited to submit a full application based on the recommendations of the internal and external reviews. Other possible decisions are rejection or recommendation of other programme lines as potential application routes. In the second stage, applicants have to submit a full proposal covering the detailed scientific programme, including goal criteria and the detailed financial budget and commitments of the partners. The full proposal is reviewed by the international jury (panel 2 consisting of FFG internal and external experts) addressing all scientific criteria as well as a detailed examination of the management, and the financial

Figure 3: Ex-ante evaluation of COMET competence centres

Source: FFG (2008a)

Evaluation Process K1/K2-Centres	
LEVEL 1	
Austrian Science Fund (FWF)/Chiristian Doppler Research Association (CDG) External evaluation	Austrian Research Promotion Agency (FFG) Internal evaluation
Recommendation level 1:Panel 1 Invitation to submit full application K1/K2	
LEVEL 2	
Austrian Science Fund (FWF)/Chiristian Doppler Research Association(CDG) External evaluation	Austrian Research Promotion Agency (FFG) Internal evaluation
Hearings with members of the jury and experts with specific thematic expertise	
Funding recommendation level 2: Panel 2 (K2,K1)	
Decision on funding by the Federal Minister	

budget (FFG 2008b). Before the final decision will be taken, hearings are held with the applicants and members of the jury and further experts with scientific and thematic expertise. As a result of the evaluation, panel 2 can recommend funding, reject the proposal or suggest other application routes. The final decision on funding is taken by the Federal Minister.

During the first funding period of established centres (five years), the centre will be evaluated several times on the basis of mid-year reports and further formal and informal contacts with FFG. At the end of the first funding period, the realization and achievement of the objectives outlined in the proposal will be evaluated by a in-depth ex-post evaluation procedure. Usually, the goal criteria include the number of publications in peer-reviewed international journals, the number of international patents (applied and granted), the number of innovations, the share of strategic research projects, the acquisition of additional funding from other scientific funds, the acquisition of additional funding from external industrial contract research, number of dissertations, and the number of new international partners. Further evaluation criteria include the estimation of additionality, i.e. the impact of the centre on the innovative behaviour of participating actors, for instance, by means of higher R&D expenditures or the establishment of a new culture of cooperation. The estimation of additionality will be carried out via a survey of the participating partners (further details are given in FFG 2008b).

The Legal Framework and Institutional Conditions for COMET

The specific rules of the COMET Programme are summarized in the "Programme Document" (FFG 2008a) that presents a substantiation of the *"Richtlinien zur Förderung der wirtschaftlich-technischen Forschung- und Technologieentwicklung"* (*Guidelines for the Promotion of the Commercial and Technological Development of Research and Technology*, "FTE guidelines"), issued by the Federal Minister of Transport, Innovation and Technology and the Federal Minister of Economics and Labour, in accordance with the Federal Minister of Finance. In general, the legal framework in Austria provides a sound basis for the establishment and smooth conduct of COMET centres. Regarding the legal organizational setup, the centres are-in principle-free to choose the appropriate form, such as limited liability company (LLC) or incorporated company. For every possible organizational form the legal basis is given by the Austrian legal system. In general, the FFG as the COMET programme management agency strongly recommends establishing a limited liability company (LLC). Besides the advantages related to liability law the associates enjoy the advantage that the necessarily deposited registered capital can be used for purposes of the company immediately. From the required minimum registered capital of $ 35.000 only $ 17.500 have to be deposited in cash.

Further considerations influencing the choice of the legal form of competence centres are related to tax law. Competence centres have to pay taxes in accordance with their organizational set up. In principle, they have to pay value added tax and corporate tax. When they are organized as a non-profit limited liability company, they enjoy a reduced rate of VAT of 10%. For-profit limited liability companies, in accordance with the tax regulation, they can utilize the so-called "Forschungsfreibetrag"-tax exemption for research-of the Austrian tax law that allows innovating firms to set up their basic R&D expenditures against tax up to 25%. There are, however, limitations and special regulations regarding different forms of research such as industrial contract research. Thus, a more precise regulation might be necessary for specific cases.

Independently of the individual legal form, it is important to note that competence centres are eligible for funding programmes for research and technological development only if they are organized in the form of a legal entity. Therefore, since in most cases COMET centres are companies, they can apply for funding from national and regional programmes for the promotion of science, research, technological development (e. g. offered by the Austrian Science Fund or by the Austrian Research Promotion Agency FFG for applied research) without direct involvement of the partners of the centre and distribute resources according to the internal budget plans. Furthermore, competence centres may also submit proposals to the *7th European Community Framework Programme for Research Technological Development and Demonstration (FP7)*. However, great care has to be applied to avoid double funding from the COMET programme and from non-COMET sources. Therefore, in most cases, in the organizational structures of the centres the "COMET area" is clearly separated from the "non-COMET area".

The Austrian employment law (AngG) is compatible with the different organizational models of competence centres and provides a reasonable framework for the administration of staff. In general, companies own the rights of inventions made by their employees on-the-job ("Diensterfindung") as defined in the *Austrian Patent Law* (PatG). There are cases where employees of universities become partially employed also at a competence centre. In such cases, clear arrangements for the payment of the salary and also for on-the-job inventions and intellectual property issues have to be made.

The Austrian University Law 2002 (UG 2002) lays the ground for the participation of universities in COMET. According to the law, Austrian universities are legal persons of public law (Article 4) following the principles of autonomy and self-governance. The mission, strategies and profile of activities of a university are defined in the development plan and are agreed upon in a performance agreement with the Ministry of Science and Research (BMWF). Universities are supposed to develop their strategies and related activities regarding their education and research missions as well as their third mission. From the university leadership's point of view, it is important that the participation of a university in COMET is in accordance with the objectives and activities defined in the university development plan. It is a very important new aspect of Austrian universities, that under the new law, university staff members-both academic and non-academic are employees of the university, rather than civil servants.

The general objective of the COMET programme to support the implementation of research results is compatible with *Article 3 of the University Law* stating that universities are supposed to support the utilization and implementation of their research results. *Article 10* gives them the right to form LLCs, foundations or associations. Article 106 regulates the procedures regarding inventions and IPR issues. Universities have the right to exploit research results and inventions produced by employees of the university in the course of their research activities. That means that inventions are the property of the university. If the university does not intend to exploit the intellectual property the inventor becomes the owner of the rights. Finally, the activities in a COMET centre especially regarding the cooperation between the university and the business partners have to comply with the legal framework defined by the European Community regarding state aid for R&D and innovation, in particular with Article 3.2.1 entitled research on behalf of undertakings (Contract research or research services). This point concerns the situation in which a project is carried out by a research organization on behalf of an undertaking. The research organization, acting as an agent, renders a service to the undertaking acting as principal in situations where (i) the agent receives payment of an adequate remuneration for its service and (ii) the principal specifies the terms and conditions of this service. Typically, the principal will own the results of the project and carry the risk of failure. When a research organization carries out such a contract, normally there will be no state aid passed to the undertaking through the research organization, if one of the following conditions is fulfilled: (i) the research organization provides its service at market price; or (ii) if there is no market price, it provides its service at a price which reflects its full costs plus a reasonable margin.

3 Cases of Industrial Technology Innovation Strategic Alliance (ITISA)

In this section we will discuss the empirical results of the case studies on the Chinese Industry Technology Innovation Strategic Alliances (ITISA) along the empirical framework presented in *Section 1. 2.* In the next section we will focus on the Technology Innovation Promotion Alliance for Agricultural Machinery Industry (TIPAAMI) before we shift attention to the Industry Technology Innovation Strategic Alliances for New-Generation Coal (Energy) Chemicals (ITISANCC). The last subsection presents the results on the Strategic Alliances for Recycling Steel Processes Technology Innovation (SARSPTI).

3.1 The Technology Innovation Promotion Alliance for Agricultural Machinery Industry (TIPAAMI)

The Technology Innovation Promotion Alliance for Agricultural Machinery Industry was formally established on June 10th, 2007, consisting of 15 organizations including Chinese Academy of Agriculture Mechanization Sciences, Shandong Shifeng (Group) Co., Ltd, Shandong Wuzheng Group Co., Ltd, Futian Liewo International Heavy Industry Group Co., Ltd, Jiangsu Changfa Industrial Holdings Limited. , Tianjin Tractor Manufacturing Corp. , Ltd, Modern Agricultural Equipment Co. , Ltd, China Agricultural University, Zhejiang University, Jiangsu University, Northeast Agricultural University, Heilongjiang Academy of Agriculture Mechanization Sciences, Shandong Academy of Agriculture Mechanization Sciences and Guangdong Academy of Agriculture Mechanization Sciences, of which the Chinese Academy of Agriculture Mechanization Sciences takes the leading role, covering the main technology and key product fields of agriculture equipment. Among those organizations, 8 enterprises are top 10 in the industry, with total capital accounting for 33% of all above-scale enterprises in the industry, production sales volume accounting for 44% of all above-scale enterprises in the industry, and profits accounting for 30% of all above-scale enterprises in the industry. The alliance is aimed to establish such industry technology innovation mechanism with the enterprises as the mainstay, orientated by the market and with integration of enterprises, agricultural colleges and institutes to cluster technology resources. The alliance is committed to conduct strategic research for agriculture equipment development, joint development of common and key technologies via overcoming industry technology difficulties, build up mainstay of industry groups with major product innovation, so as to drive the technology upgrading, support the industry and agriculture.

3.1.1 Goals and Organizational Forms

The Short-Term Goals: firstly, the alliance will conduct research on the generic technology for agricultural equipment, including research of agricultural equipment digital design technology, and research of reliable technology and automatic monitoring technology. Secondly, the alliance will conduct research on the core technology for key products as well as the invention and manufacture of key products, including multifunctional key equipment accommodating to the features of China agriculture, economic agriculture and forestry power machinery, tractor supporting tools. After three to five years of efforts, the Industry Innovation Strategic Alliances for Agricultural Equipment (TIPAAMI) will be built into the core of common technology innovation system in the industry, develop a series of equipment which will obtain the indigenous intellectual property rights and will become influential in the industry so that the gap between the overall technology level in the industry of China and the international advanced level can be narrowed by 10 years.

The Mid-and-Long-Term Goals: (1) integrating resources, establishing an innovation mechanism for enterprises, universities and R&D institutions, and developing a platform for industrial technology innovation; (2) making a breakthrough in the industrial generic technology and addressing the problem of technology supply confronted in the development of the industry; (3) achieving the sharing of resources and promoting technology diffusion and transfer in the industry.

The alliance is organized according to the following principles:

i. All alliance members must sign the alliance agreement, each holding one copy of the agreement. The alliance members are entitled to the same rights and obligations, and are only responsible for the contents in the agreement and legal requirements thereof. Each alliance member do business independently without being bind by deeds, and will not be jointly responsible for liabilities of other members.

ii. Alliance is a kind of organization form of technological innovation for cooperation of enterprises, agricultural colleges and institutes of agriculture equipment, other than an entity. The secretariat is its representative window to the outside. At present, the alliance will step up the cultivation of professional secretariat, and there are full time personnel for relevant job under the support of the alliance chairmen.

The alliance is voluntarily organized by the enterprises, research institutes and colleges committed to the technological progress of agriculture equipment industry and engaging in research, development, production, manufacture and service of relevant technologies and products. It is a network and platform based on contact with no legal status, neither an enterprise nor an organization. The secretariat is its representative to the outside. At present, the secretariat is attached to the chairman unit which is responsible to provide the staff, management and finance accounting.

3.1.2 Corporate Governance Structures, Rights and Responsibilities

The pressing issues that prevent different bodies from getting allied can be summarized as follows:

i) The contradiction of enterprises' pursuit for profit and academic position

Manifestations of their divergence: profit maximization is the constant goal of all enterprises. During cooperation, the enterprise is prone to form monopolistic intellectual property, resulting in monopolistic market. Therefore, when implementing the alliance project, the enterprise will request the participating researchers not to disclose the content of the cooperating research project, and restrain the spread of technologies including knowledge achievements especially key technologies in the form of essay and publications. However, it is contradictive with the pure research goal of researchers in the college, including the goal of academic status, essays and publications. For this contradiction, the cooperation between enterprises and colleges may not be further deepened and continued. As enterprises always entrust colleges to do research on non-core technology, the cooperation will not substantially affect the progress of key and core technologies.

The Focus and Extent of the Divergence: the difference is focused on the distribution of ownership of research findings and intellectual property. On one hand, if the research finding can bring enterprise great economic benefits, the research should deserve certain compensation for the finding. And for the enterprise, facing the market risks, the market prospect of the research finding is hard to expect, and the value identification is confined by the market risks. Due to limited research investment, the enterprise do not expend sufficiently on the research. On the other hand, researchers, especially those in colleges, always pursue the visibility of quantified research findings, mainly embodied by number of issued essays and published works, which are disagreed with by the enterprises.

From the concrete practice of the alliance, divergence exists but has not yet been manifested because the cooperation is still at the early stage.

ii) The contradiction between short-term interests of enterprises and the long-term knowledge accumulation of research institutions

The research for the basic technology and the generic technology complies with the enterprises' needs for long-term interests, but it can not produce any visible short-term interests. So the enterprises do not give it sufficient attention. In the alliance, on one hand, the enterprise is scarcely willing to fund the research institute for technological research of those fields, and is more willing to directly invest in the new product research. On the other hand, the research institute cannot speedily apply the research findings of basic technology and common technology in product research owing to limit of industrial demonstration, which consequently lead to the situation of "technology is available but no products" or "products of low level".

The evaluation of college researchers are more concerned on the research fund, high quality essays, works and patents, etc. What is showed as a whole is the higher pursuit with respect to the research fund, essays, works and patents, with no motivation on industrialization and transformation of research findings. Hence, the college researchers are more inclined to take research programme funded by the government ministries, and show little interest in the programme entrusted by enterprises. So in a long run, the college should give priority to the talent cultivation, especially those needed for various researches and industries. For this practice the enterprises are needed.

iii) The contradiction between enterprises' exclusion of competitors and public research institutions' pursuit of knowledge diffusion

The market share occupied by enterprises in the Alliances and their competition situation: There are 8 enterprises in the alliance, which are all key enterprises in the field, with the scale, output and profits accounting for over 30% of all enterprises in the field. The 8 enterprises have different leading field and products, and each has advantages in single product, but holding no dominant position as a whole. No single enterprise can dominate others. Also, there is competition of same kind of products among the enterprise members.

Enterprises' pursuit of exclusion of competitors and acquisition of competitive advantages: As determined by the features of the agricultural equipment industry, it is hard for a single enterprise to attain the position with absolute advantage in the industry and it can only obtain the competitive advantage in a certain type of product. In general, enterprises in the agriculture equipment industry should work out a way for competition. First, build up the dominant position in the market by self-development; second, take the competitive business into development through merging and restructuring; thirdly, figure out talent training strategy to attract backbone personnel in rivals with favorable remunerations.

In recent years, the agriculture equipment enterprises have sped up the momentum of merging and restructuring. More and larger multinational enterprises swarm into China to procure and merge domestic enterprises, set up production base and seize China market. In addition, China large enterprises also take the means of merging and restructuring to further improve the industry and build up corresponding advantages. As for the alliance itself, the enterprises in the alliance are not eager to eliminate competitors in the alliance, mainly owing to almost the same advantages of enterprises, different equity structures and no severe technological barriers.

The driving force and the pursuit of the diffusion of new knowledge and technology by universities: The college is at the forefront of theory and new technology research, whose pursuit to new knowledge and new technology basically lies in the function positioning. For single researchers, new knowledge and new technology can raise his/her academic position and influence. While for the alliance as a technological innovation platform, it is helpful to spread the new technology and new knowledge, achieve extension and transformation from technologies to products and verify the new technology and knowledge through practice in spite of obtaining the fund.

Corporate Governance Structures

The organization of the alliance comprises of the Executive Council, Experts Technology Committee, the Secretariat and 15 members.

The Executive Council: the executive council is the highest authority of TIPAAMI, which shall be composed of the legal representatives or the authorized deputies of the alliance members, including one director-general, three under-director-generals and twelve members. The council meeting shall convene every six months and the director-general of the council shall be responsible for calling for or presiding over the meeting, which shall convene more in number or in advance or in postponement, if necessary. The council meeting shall be convened only if it is attended by two-thirds or more of the council members, each of whom shall have one vote to decide on matters at the meeting. The matters subject to the examination and confirmation in the council shall be approved and come into force only if they are voted for by two-thirds or more of the council members.

Figure 4: Alliance organization structure

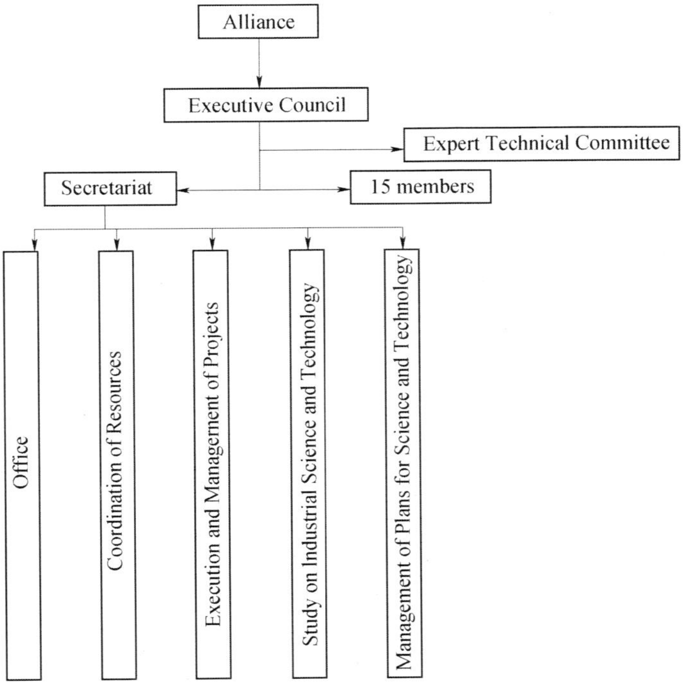

```
                    Alliance
                       │
                       ▼
              Executive Council ──────────► Expert Technical Committee
                  │         │
                  ▼         ▼
           Secretariat ◄── 15 members
                  │
   ┌──────┬───────┼────────┬──────────┬──────────┐
   ▼      ▼       ▼        ▼          ▼          ▼
 Office  Coord.  Execution Study on  Management
         of      and       Industrial of Plans
         Resources Management Science  for Science
                  of Projects and      and
                             Technology Technology
```

Source: The secretariat of Agricultural Machinery Alliance, the same as below unless otherwise separately specified.

The Expert Technology Committee: the expert technology committee is an advisory body of the executive council. It shall provide the council with recommendations for its decision making, participate in or provide consultations or suggestions for the development, cost-benefit analysis, demonstration, evaluation of a project. The committee shall be composed of entrepreneurs or experts in engineering, economics, policy studies or other related fields, including one director, three deputy director and twenty-one committee members, all of whom shall be appointed by the executive council. The committee shall work by convening the expert technology committee meeting, which shall convene regularly or irregularly as required by the committee and shall be attended by two-thirds or more of the members of the committee. The issues subject to the examination and confirmation in the committee shall be approved and take effect only if they are voted for by two-thirds or more of the committee members.

The Secretariat: the secretariat is the standing executive body of the executive council of TIPAAMI, which shall be directed under the leadership of the director-general of the council and shall be responsible for the day-to-day business and the coordination, management of the alliance. The secretariat shall have one secretary-general, three under-secretary-generals, who shall have one full-time office staff, one full-time resources coordinator, one full-time project executive manager, two full-time industry strategic researchers, and one part-time scientific and technological plan manager as their subordinates. The secretariat shall adopt the secretary-general responsibility system, and the secretary-general shall be elected by the executive council and appointed by the director-general of the council. The staff of the secretariat shall be appointed by the secretary-general from the working staff of the unit in which the director-general of the council works.

The Member Units: TIPAAMI has fifteen members, including eight enterprises, four universities and three R&D institutions. The members are governed by agreements, and take the means of equal consultation and open information to establish an open and transparent responsibility relationship with balanced rights and obligations and equitable participation.

Management of Organizations within the Alliance

The resources involved in connection with the operation of TIPAAMI: the alliance is mainly directed by the research products under the impetus of technologies. The participating units join forces in the alliance mainly through means of relevant technology resources, including researchers, laboratory equipment, devices and supporting fund, etc.

The organization and framework in connection with the operation of TIPAAMI: at present, the alliance is organized around project groups, which shall be supervised by the head of the group, who shall have management groups (to coordinate the work of the alliances) and their members (including the leaders and/or experts from different members).

Project Identification and Leadership

The Identification of Projects: according to the technology development requirements in the field and the technological planning of the alliance, the executive council will propose projects which will be guided by the experts technology committee and applied by the unit where the chairman works. Projects in national scientific and technological program and projects of research and development fund should be approved in accordance with the requirements of China national industry policies, China national medium and long term technology development planning outline, technological development requirements in the field and requirements of alliance technology development planning (2008-2015).

Table 2 **Sketch of Project Approval Process**

Project of national plan for science and technology	Publish project development plan by government competent authorities	Application organized by Secretariat of the Alliance	Feasibility debate organized by government competent authorities	Project approval	
Project of research and development funds	Publish project approval by Secretariat of the Alliance	Application organized by member unit	Debate organized by Expert Technology Committee of the Alliance	Project approval	
Project entrusted by member unit	Technology needs of the member unit	Selection of undertaking unit	Project approval	Put on record in Secretariat of the Alliance	

The project evaluation mainly focuses on: research content and goal, relevance to cutting-edge technology, innovation and novelty of the technology, excellent research and development team integrating enterprises, agricultural colleges and institutes, detailed agreements of ownership of the findings and intellectual property, etc.

The Leadership of Projects

The projects shall be led by the executive council and be left in the full charge by the unit in which the director-general of the executive council works and the day-to-day business of the projects shall be managed by the secretariat. The implementation of a specific project shall be guaranteed by signing the agreement or contract by the unit that undertakes the project as required by the secretariat of the alliance. The projects shall adopt the subject system, in which the head in charge of the project shall regularly report to the expert technology committee and the executive council of the alliance according to the project schedule. The expert technology committee shall be responsible for the assessment and supervision of the projects.

Management of R&D Projects

Management in Different R&D Stages: the measures for the management of national scientific and technological projects undertaken by the alliances shall be formulated, implemented, supervised and managed in accordance with the requirements concerning the management of scientific and technological plans. The focus should be the evaluation of project implementation: whether the tasks specified in the project programme are fulfilled; how about the technology level of the findings and spread degree; contributions of the findings to the technology development of the field; whether the objectives in terms of patent, essay, standard and software are accomplished; whether the objectives of talent cultivation and forming innovation team are achieved.

Table 3   Management Mode and Alliance Functions for Different Projects

Project Type	Management	Alliance Functions
Projects in national science and technology plans	The government science and technology department signs the project program with the undertaking unit.	The secretariat of the alliance is responsible for implementation, supervision, examination and acceptance.
Research and development fund projects	The secretariat of the alliance signs the project programme with the undertaking unit.	The secretariat of the alliance is responsible for approval, implementation, supervision, examination and acceptance.
Projects entrusted by members	The owner of the tasks signs contract with the undertaking unit.	The secretariat of the alliance is responsible for filing and dispute negotiation.

Table 4   Implementation of Different Projects

Project Type	Type of Undertaking Unit	Quantity of Undertaking Units	Agreement Pattern
Projects in national science and technology plans	Member, non-member	Undertaken by multiple units	Project Program
Research and development fund projects	Member	Undertaken by multiple units or single unit	Project Program
Projects entrusted by members	Member, non-member	Undertaken by multiple units or single unit	Commission Agreement (Contract)

Table 5   Financing Ratio of Different Projects (%)

Project Type	State Finance	Self-financing		
			Enterprise	Research Institute
Projects in national science and technology plans	33~50	50~67	70~100	0~30
Research and development fund projects	33~50	50~67	70~100	0~30
Projects entrusted by members	90~100	0~10	100	

Source: the Secretariat of Agricultural Machinery Alliance

Combination of R&D Achievements with Follow-up Production

The research and development of the alliance shall be closely related to the demands of the industry and it is determined by the internal needs of the industry. The research and development is determined based on the internal requirements of industry. The research findings, after being figured out are first transformed in the enterprises in the alliance in accordance with the intellectual property agreement and distribution of findings agreement.

Rights, Responsibilities and Codes of Conduct

Each of the participating party shall have equal rights and responsibilities, which are agreed upon through signing the agreements. The members are entitled to: participatingin discussion and voting for main decision, solutions and events for alliance development; putting forward suggestions and opinions and conduct supervision for the alliance; taking priority in project cooperation, share of rights and interest and technology resources, etc; retreating freely from the alliance. The members shall support and abide by the alliance agreement; provide needed support, make accessible and share superior technology research and development conditions; drive research cooperation and information sharing among members; protect alliance intellectual property and know-how.

The basic codes of conduct abided by all the participating parties shall be equality, voluntarily, shared risks and benefits. They are quite accommodative to the research activities of basic and common technologies and less adaptive to the aspects involving industry interest development.

3.1.3 Analysis of Relationships

The government primarily plays a guiding role in the establishment of TIPAAMI. The chairman unit is the major initiator and core body of the alliance.

There is still no LEADER in the alliance. At present, based on common interest requirements, different parties in the alliance form a relationship of cooperation in the process of research and development. The relations between participating parties are those linked by the interests of enterprises, so the development of the alliance is not established upon a stable and solid basis.

Related government departments have played an important role in the establishment of TIPAAMI and acted as the competent authority at the same time. The ideal role of the government is a policy maker and promoter of the innovation policies.

Historical Course

The alliance is established depending on the long-term contributions and dominant position of Chinese Academy of Agricultural Mechanization Sciences in the field. Being a national scientific research institute with over 50 years of history in China agriculture equipment industry, Chinese Academy of Agricultural Mechanization Sciences has played a leading role in driving agriculture mechanization development and agricultural machinery technology since the establishment in the 1950s, and is always the birth land and radiation source of advanced technology in the field. Since opening up to outside world, especially the reform of S&T system, the academy has found a path for sustainable and sound development of technology industry, and has further strengthened the innovation capability and technology leading position.

Table 6　　　　　　　　　　**Historical Course of the Alliance**

Division of Research Led by Government	1956~1984	R&D and Diffusion of Industry Technology Led by Chinese Academy of Agricultural Mechanization Science (CAAMS)
Close Cooperation	1985~1995	Simple Technology Cooperation relying on available technological resources
Close Cooperation	1995~2006	Implementation of projects of national S&T Plan by CAAMS, Long-term strategic cooperation gradually coming into being
Agreement-based CooperAtion of Enterprises, Universities and R&D Institutions	2007	Establishment of IISAAE led by CAAMS

In the 21st century, the agriculture equipment industry is much more expected along with the progress and innovation of international technology. Indigenous innovation and cooperation research is the essential approach for make great progress, and also the important impetus for the agriculture equipment industry to continuously develop and enhance competitiveness and serve for the economic growth of China agriculture and national economic growth. Being a pattern of production, research cooperation, the strategic alliance of agriculture equipment industry technology innovation consists of backbone enterprises, research institutes and colleges in the agriculture equipment industry. Now the agriculture equipment industry technology has developed into a new historical phase featuring wide participation based on guidance and direction of establishment enterprises with core competitiveness.

Establishment Procedure

The alliance is established preliminary investigation and initiation by the preparation leading team, signing of letter of intent and agreement to announcement of establishment, etc.

i. Obtain broad consensus in the preliminary investigation phase. Viewed from the strategic tasks for developing China's modern agriculture and rural progress, the agriculture equipment industry is well prepared for establishing the alliance with relevant policy environment, with the support of government and consent of enterprises.

ii. Complete preparation in the initiation phase. Led by Chinese Academy of Agriculture Mechanization Sciences, the preparation leading team is set up and has drafted *The Proposal of Strategic Alliance for Technology Innovation of Agricultural Equipment Industry*.

iii. Confirm the basic structure and mechanism of the alliance at the phase of signing the letter of intent. In the principle of free will, *The Letter of Intent of Strategic Alliance for Technology Innovation of Agricultural Equipment Industry* is signed by the first batch of initiators of 15 units including 7 key enterprises (group), 4 research institutes and 4 key colleges. The alliance leading team has drafted the *Organization Plan of Strategic Alliance for Technology Innovation of Agricultural Equipment Industry (draft)*, and concluded the *Agreement of Strategic Alliance for Technology Innovation of Agricultural Equipment Industry*.

iv. The alliance enters the actual operation phase after signing the agreement and declaring establishment. On June 10th, 2007, after one year of preparation and approved by relevant departments including the Ministry of Science and Technology, the strategic alliance of agriculture equipment industry technology innovation was formally established as one of the first four alliances.

Table 7　　　　　　　　　　　Establishment Procedure of the Alliance

Guided by governmental policies	2006	Building of National Innovation System for S&T, Implementation of S&T Innovation System
Led by projects of national S&T plan	2006~2007	R&D projects participated by 105 industry enterprises, universities and R&D institutions
Investigation and study of demands and intentions	2007	Identification of 15 initiators in the alliance and goals and orientation of the Alliance
Agreement-signing ceremony	2007	Operation stage of the alliance, scientific research activities performed in cooperation between enterprises, universities and R&D institutions

The alliance is established under the support of government departments and industry associations with wide acknowledgement in the field of agriculture equipment and approval of relevant government departments. Each party has signed agreement out of its will to stipulate the rights and obligations and guarantees for alliance operation. Hence the alliance becomes an important means to link the government with industry, and the industry with research.

Major Events Occurred in the Establishment of the Alliance

"The project for research and production of multi-functional agricultural equipment and facilities", one of the key projects for national science and technology supporting plans, was undertaken by alliance members as the mainstay of the project.

The Alliance Agreements were jointly signed by its members and the alliance entered the stage of substantial operation.

"The workshop for the technological and developmental strategies of modern agriculture and food manufacturing equipment" was held by the alliance to make policy recommendations for the scientific and technological development in the industry.

Strategies for the scientific and technological development was formulated to prescribe the goals, tasks and priorities on the scientific and technological development, pointing a direction for the future progress of the alliance.

The Turning Point

"The project for research and manufacture of large-sized agricultural power and operating equipment", one of the key projects in national science and technology supporting plans, was first undertaken by the alliance under the organization of Ministry of Science and Technology of China. This new way of project conducting laid the foundation for the alliance to play its role in the industry.

Determination of Certain Factors that Impede the Progress of Events

The Impeding Factors: there exist such impeding factors as the coordination of enterprises who are alliance members, the relationships between the unit in which the director-general of the executive council works and the large-scale enterprises in the alliance, the follow-up development of the alliance, the organizational operation and the supporting mechanism of the alliance.

The Means by which the Impeding Factors can be Overcome: the alliance members can overcome the above impeding factors by means of complying with the alliance agreements, performing job division and cooperation, bringing their own strengths to full play, ensuring their own requests to be fully expressed and their benefits being equal to their contributions to the alliance.

The Prediction and Prevention of Possible Impeding Factors: the clarification of the legal status and identity of the alliance will have a tremendous impact on its orientation and role.

3.1.4 Knowledge Generation and Technology Diffusion

Human Resources: the human resources input from the industry can basically meet the demands for the resources in the course of development. The human resources input from universities and R&D institutions relies chiefly on related schools and departments or specialized resources, and there are limited resources input from universities.

Machinery and Research Equipment: the machinery and equipment in the production and pilot program are mainly invested by enterprises. The investment and sharing of scientific research facilities and equipment can only rely on utilizing the facilities and equipment provided by the public laboratories on the national, provincial or ministerial level that are affiliated to universities and research institutions.

Funds: the alliance first raised RMB 30 million Yuan as its R&D funds from its members according to their institutional nature. Among the alliance members, each of the enterprises shall be required to contribute RMB 3.5 million Yuan while each of the R&D institutions to contribute RMB 1 million Yuan, and the universities shall be exempt from such contributions. The external fund-raising shall include the government-allocated scientific research funds, the self-raised funds by the alliance members, and funds from the projects entrusted by the industry or enterprises, donations and the revenues from the transfer of part of technological achievements. At present, the external funds come mainly from government investment in projects.

Management and Diffusion of Cooperation Achievements

New Products Jointly Developed: the distribution of cooperation achievements within the alliance are as follows. The intellectual properties developed with state finance as the leading support should be managed in accordance with the requirements of management of China national science and technology plans.

The intellectual property in the products and process developed with self-financing as the main support and based on the common technology platform of the alliance, should be owned by the alliance member who developed the technology, and should be managed according to the terms and conditions of the agreement.

The Expression of Benefits-Sharing Mechanism and its Practice: the interest sharing mechanism should be agreed in the principle and spirit of "prior stipulation, priority of share, paid transfer and share of gains". And the disputes shall be resolved by the Executive Council of the alliance.

The Management of Allied Patents: the intellectual property is radiated and speed to the joint development members for free, and transferred with favorable terms to other units in the alliance that do no participating in the development, and transferred with charges to other enterprises out of the alliance. The gains thus obtained will be deducted partially for development fund. Under the guidance and support of the government, the research and development of the key generic technology shall be advanced, the industry technological level shall be enhanced and the industrial development shall be accelerated. As a result the modernization of agriculture and the building of new rural areas will be ensured and the prosperity of the national economy will be fostered.

Table 8　　　　　　　　Sharing Mode of Rights in Different Projects

Project type	Ownership	Use right	Share and transfer mode	Mode of gain sharing
Projects in national science and technology plans	Achievements research unit	Achievements research unit	Used by joint research units for free, and transferred to other units with charge.	Take no more than 15% for research fund
Research and development fund projects	Alliance	Achievements research unit	Used by members for free, and transferred to other units with charge.	100 % for research fund
Projects entrusted by members	Client	Client	Used by trustees according to agreements, and the trustee has the complete disposition right.	The alliance does not participate in sharing

Joint Publications: the rights of authorship: the publication of such scientific and technology papers and works shall follow the principle that the person shall have whatever he has developed and shall be entitled to its authorship. Coordination of publication time: the papers or works shall be published as required by the alliance.

The Joint Organization of Scientific Conferences, Workshops and other Activities: the selection of themes:

This type of conferences shall be organized by the alliance in accordance with the scientific and technological plans for the industry or as entrusted by relevant government authorities and the sponsors of the conference shall be determined by the executive council. The cost of the conferences shall be borne by the unit in which the director-general of the executive council works or by the sponsors of the conference. Workshops shall be in accordance with the goals and objectives of the alliance as well as the scientific and technological plans for the industry, proposed to be convened by the unit in which the director-general of the executive council works, attended by the alliance members and other units in the industry may also be invited to attend.

The joint education of talents: at present, the way by which talents are jointly cultivated by the enterprises, universities and R&D institutions in the alliance is joint cultivation and entrusted cultivation. By joint cultivation, students are jointly enrolled by universities and R&D institutions with the former responsible for the teaching of courses and the latter for that of practice. In the way of entrusted cultivation, universities are entrusted to the cultivation of core talents for scientific research by enterprises and R&D institutions.

3.1.5 Legal Environment of the Alliance

The alliance observes related laws and regulations, such as those concerning universities and public research organizations. To fully play the role of the alliance in industry technology innovation, the support of government financial policies is required.

The alliance is keenly concerned with the laws, regulations and policies closely related to the industry and the sector. It is hoped that the legislation procedure from the bottom to the top can be implemented.

At present, the regulations mainly include related regulations promulgated by the Ministry of Science and Technology concerning the establishment of the alliance and the support for the development of the alliance.

The regulations promulgated by the Ministry of Science and Technology are highly targeted and operational, and they can play a very important role in standardizing and supporting the development of the alliance.

3.1.6 Funds Management

The basic fund for alliance management and operation is mainly allocated by government financial support, apportionment of member unit and donations of groups and individuals. At present, the management and operation expense of the alliance is borne by the director-general unit. In view of the alliance development, the cost apportionment is a must, and the alliance is now studying to work out a relevant system and apportionment principle.

The funds shall be guided by the alliance and managed after approval, and used by those who make contributions.

Detailed Implementation Rules: the legal person unit where the secretariat of the alliance is located shall be authorized to open a special account or item to manage the funds of the alliance. The funds shall be managed according to the project plan of the alliance and earmarked to designated projects. An independent system of budget and final accounts shall be adopted and a strict financial management system shall be set up to ensure that the accounting system is not only legitimate, true, accurate and complete, but also is in strict compliance with the financial management system of China. And the accounting system shall also be subject to audit by accounting firm approved by the council and submitted to the council for review. The funds provided by government shall be subject to supervisions as specified by the related national regulations. As to the use of donated or contributed funds, the will of the donators or contributors shall be respected and the related information shall be publicized to an appropriate way. The revenues earned from the transfer of generic technology of the alliance shall be distributed as specified in the agreements.

Financial Supervision and Control: national funds for science and technology research shall be managed in accordance with the related management rules of China. The funds invested or contributed by the alliance members shall be subject to appropriate supervision and management as agreed upon by the members.

3.2　The Industry Technology Innovation Strategic Alliances for New-Generation Coal (Energy) Chemicals (ITISANCC)

3.2.1　Goals and Organizational Form

i. Developing key and generic technology.

Developing technologies for new-generation coal (energy) chemicals industry, which are required in the program for "the clean and efficient development and utilization, liquefaction and multiple-stage allied production of coal", one of the 68 priority areas determined in *the National Mid-term and Long-term Science and Technology Development Plan Outlines* (2006-2020). Oriented to the industrial demand, the alliance shall focus on the research and development of key, generic and market-appealing technologies as well as on their quick transformation into productive force.

ii. Establishing platform for industry innovation resources sharing.

A sophisticated innovation resources sharing platform for the alliance members and the industry can be formed through integration and construction, which will improve the use of innovation resources and endeavor to ensure that the spread of technological achievements will not be impeded.

iii. Constructing a complete industrial innovation chain.

Based on the unit technology the alliance addresses the system integration to form a steady strategic cooperation between public research organizations and the upstream and downstream enterprises in the industry.

iv. Building-up a technology transfer and diffusion mechanism of the alliance.

Building-up and improve various mechanism to accelerate the merchandising exploration of the innovation achievements within the alliance and the industry and facilitate the transfer, promotion integration and utilization of the technology.

v. Forming proper talent exchange and cultivation mechanism.

The platform of the alliance facilitates the jointly cultivation and interactive exchange of the talents between the alliance members, which makes the alliance an important high-level talent cultivation base.

Based on the goals for the establishment of the alliance, the initiator, China National Chemical Engineering Co., Ltd., determines the principles for the selection of Alliance members as follows: their innovation demands shall conform to the national industrial policy; they shall possess the generic or key technologies needed in the industry; they have done certain innovation work; and they shall play some part in setting up the industrial innovation chains.

Invitations were delivered to qualified alliance members and discussions were made with them concerning the organizational plan and the *Alliance Agreement*. The *Alliance Agreements* were signed and the official establishment of the alliance was announced.

The alliance adopts an open mechanism, by means of which new innovation resources and units with advantage technology and capital that are beneficial to the further development of the alliance will be recruited into the alliance.

An abstract and concrete combined organizational structure is adopted. The alliance now is composed by 14 significant R&D institutes and enterprises in the coal chemical industry in China. Executive council and expert committee members discuss and determine major issues, and the standing body and full-time personnel of the secretariat are in charge of daily work. The alliance is a contract-based organization but not a legal person.

3.2.2 Corporate Governance Structures, Rights and Responsibilities

In the mechanism of combination of the production and the research both enterprises and universities and research institutions get their benefits. For the universities and research institutions: firstly, they get a checking-out platform through the provision of original technology so that they can do further research with enterprises to enhance their R&D capability; secondly, it is good for the postgraduate students' cultivation and it is easier for the students to publish papers to pass the school internal administrative assessments; and lastly, universities and research institutions can benefit from the technology transfer, which makes new technology R&D possible. For the enterprises, firstly, they can acquire and make use of advanced technology to improve the competitiveness in the market and get the expected return through offering cutting-edge market demand, the application place, transforming bridges and key equipment; and secondly, it is possible for them to get financial assistance from relevant government departments. On the basis of the foregoing demands, all parties organically allied for common development.

The Pressing Issues that Prevent Different Parties from Getting Allied

The contradiction between enterprises' pursuit for profit and academia's pursuit for academic position: on one hand, enterprises aim at making as much as profit through reducing costs and adopting economically feasible technology solutions. On the other hand the academia emphasize publishing great number of papers home and abroad and declaring large number of patents neglecting the application costs of the technology. The differences between the evaluating criteria and evaluating system from these two groups seriously hinder the efficiency of cooperation and quality of output result.

The contradiction between enterprises' short-term interest and research institutions' long-term knowledge accumulation: the R&D of coal chemical industry needs large-scale input at early stage from the enterprises and the input is of high risk. While the key and generic technology needs research institutions' long-term knowledge accumulation and repeated testing and verification. Differences in both time and earnings are impediments to the cooperative development of some industrial technology.

The contradiction between enterprises' exclusion of competitors and public research institutions' pursuit of knowledge diffusion: generally speaking, enterprises in the alliance have a relationship of upstream and downstream instead of rivalry. They hope the public research institutions put technology achievement into the alliance's platform and can have the priority to master the technology achievement and the privileges of application. On the contrary, the public research institutions are willing to acquire more benefit via expansion of the scope of technology transfer and selection on the basis of multi-party comparison as well as expanding the influence of the technology. Differences in the proliferation of technological achievements between the two have a certain influence to the close cooperation.

The Corporate Governance Structures

According to the *Alliance Agreement*, the Executive Council is the leading and coordinating body of the alliance. Under the leadership of the council, a secretariat is set up, which runs the daily business of the alliance, responsible for the daily running and the coordination and management of projects. Expert technology committee is also founded as the technology advisory body of the alliance.

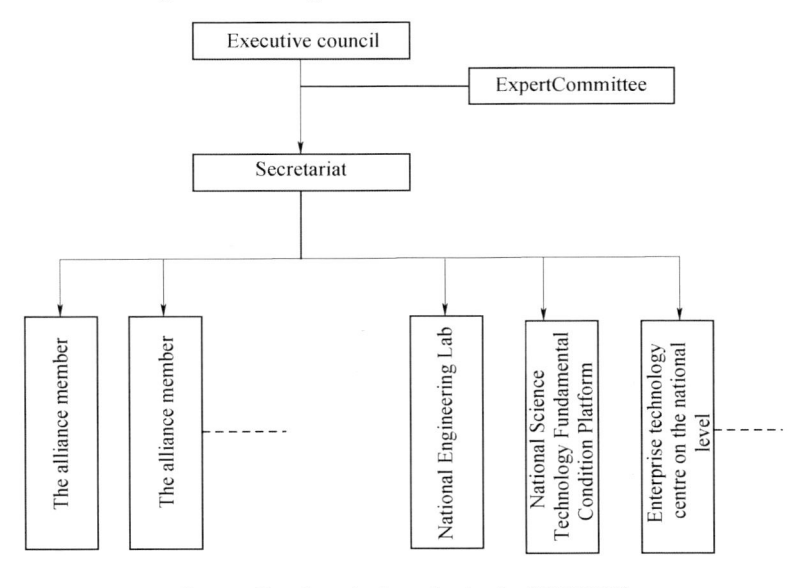

Figure 5 The organizational structure of the alliance

```
                    Executive council
                           |
                           |─────────── ExpertCommittee
                           |
                       Secretariat
                           |
    ┌──────┬──────┬────────┼────────┬──────────┐
    │      │      │        │        │          │
 Alliance Alliance  National  National   Enterprise
 member   member   Engineering Science   technology
                      Lab    Technology  centre on the
                            Fundamental   national level
                            Condition
                            Platform
```

Source: Based on the investigation by ITISANCC

Executive Council is composed of one assigned representative from the alliance member with one president. At present the council consists of 15 members. The term of the council is 3 years. The executive council is responsible to ratify management rules; approve the entry application of alliance members; examine and approve technological development plans; decide the plans for the project determination, implementation, budget and fund allocation as well as acceptance test; determine the raising and use of funds; make plans for the spreading of technology achievements and the distribution of revenues obtained from such achievements; and make decisions on other important matters.

The president shall be selected by the council with a term of 3 years and can be reselected in successive terms. The council takes meetings as its way of decision-making. The Council holds regular meetings each year. An ad hoc meeting can be convened with more than a quarter of the members proposing. Council meeting shall be convened and chaired by the president and implements one-person-one-vote system. Council meeting shall be valid with an attendance of at least two-thirds of the members. The termination, dissolution, separation, merger etc. shall not be valid until all of the members unanimously voted. And other resolutions shall be adopted and take effect by a vote of at least half of the members present at the meeting.

The expert committee consists of one or two experts assigned by each alliance member and well-known influential experts and scholars home and abroad in the industry. Now there are 22 experts in the committee with 1 honorary director, 1 director and 1 deputy director. The expert technology committee provides consultations and suggestions to the council for its decision-making; direct the technology development and work priorities, and instructs the secretariat to make plans for technology development; participate in the cost-benefit analysis, review, implementation, bidding, inspection, check and acceptance test of projects, and provide suggestions and consultations for such participations; and make recommendations on other important decisions.

The secretariat is composed by one person in charge of the R&D from each alliance member and the member unit where the secretariat locates can assign one more person. And there is one secretary-general in the secretariat who is assigned by the member unit where the secretariat locates. It is managed by full-time employees and there are 4 full-time personnel in the secretariat. Under the secretariat, there are 6 departments namely project management department, finance and fund management department, legal affairs department, marketing and promotion department, base management department and information center. The secretariat is obliged to organize the formulation of management rules; organize the making of technology development plans, determine specific development projects; organize related members to sign specific project agreements; supervise and coordinate the implementation of project agreements all through; organize the check and acceptance of project achievements; manage the project determination, ownership of intellectual property rights and spreading of technology achievements; take care of daily office work.

Management of Organizations within the Alliance

China Chemical Engineering Group Company as the president unit is responsible for the daily liaison and organization and assigns full-time personnel to the secretariat. Enterprises in the alliance offer shared office expenses and R&D funds. While the research institutes in the alliance offer research team, laboratory equipment and etc.

The alliance applies project team approach and project engineer responsibility system. The chief engineer in charge of making project general plan, funds arrangement, organizing and coordinating all participants' work in the team and regularly reporting the progress of the project to the secretariat. The president unit authorizes the secretariat to inspect the implementation of the project and complete a report to the council every year.

Project Selection and Leadership

On the basis of the direction of technology development and major work of the alliance proposed by the expert committee, the secretariat draws up technology development plan and in accordance with this plan develop concrete projects and report to the council for approval. The council may authorize the secretariat to determine the undertaker of the project by inviting public bidding in the market-accepted way and it can also determine the undertaker itself according to the evaluation offered by the expert committee. Other alliance member willing to take part in may join in via various ways. In addition, members may voluntarily join together to submit a project application. With the evaluation from the expert committee the secretariat makes its comments and submits the application and suggestion to the council for approval. Now there are 4 industry demonstration (examination) projects under implementation, 3 of which from the secretariat proposal and 1 from the members' proposal.

Project is led by the Council and the president unit takes overall responsibility. The secretariat organizes relevant undertakers to sign a specific project agreement under the framework of the alliance agreement, to clarify the relationship of responsibilities, rights, and interests relations. And this kind of agreement accepts the Secretariat's management, coordination and oversight.

Management of R&D Projects

The alliance shall adopt the important node control management during the implementation of a project. The details are shown in the figure below.

Figure 6 Demonstration of node control in project implementation

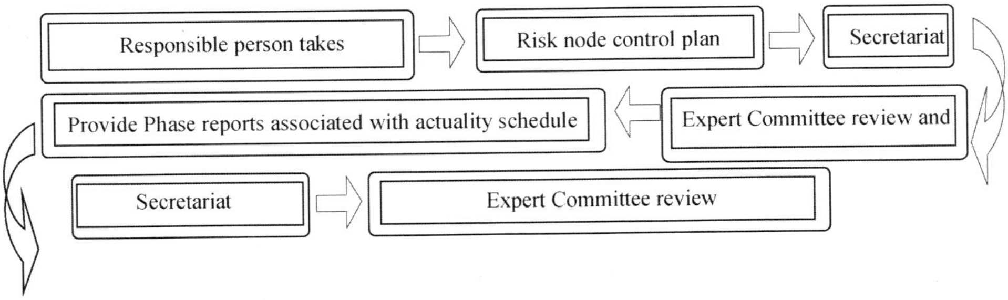

Under the binding force of the Alliance Agreement and Project Agreement, it is ensured that each undertaking party of a project has access to different resources from both inside and outside the industrial technology innovation chain. The participators can improve their innovation capabilities and benefit from the application and spreading of innovation achievements.

With the strict control of node management, the project can be orderly undertaken according to its schedule as defined in the agreement. Its quality can be guaranteed. The combination of R&D achievements with follow-up production: The technology researched and developed by the alliance meets the industrial demands and can be widely promoted. After the success of the industrial trial, the technology can be promoted and diffused in and out of the alliance.

Rights, Responsibilities and Codes of Conduct

According to the Alliance Agreement, the rights and responsibilities of each member are equal. The Project Agreement is to regulate the rights and responsibilities of all participants when it comes to a specific project. The basic rights and obligations of each member are as follow:

The rights of all members includes: voluntarily join in or withdraw from the alliance; elect a representative to serve as the council member; participation in the development of government projects through alliance and alliance's project; acquire alliance's matching funds, relevant national policy and funding support when participating in government projects; acquire alliance's matching funds when participating in government projects; enjoy the right of priority and preferential right when using the alliance's technology achievement.

The obligations of all members includes: obey the provisions of this agreement and the alliance management regulations; not set up obstacles to impede the transfer and promotion of the alliance's technological achievements; protect the intellectual property rights of the alliance from infringement; conserve the alliance's technology secrets; take corresponding technology development tasks, provide appropriate resources and contribute to close cooperation and common development of all parties.

The participators shall conform to the Alliance agreement to closely cooperate with each other and to share risk and interest. According to the Alliance Agreement and specific project agreements, the alliance members cooperate and communicate with each other to build an R&D supporting platform together.

3.2.3 Analysis of Relationships

The alliance is made up of 14 units with great influence in the coal chemical industry including planning authorities, research institutes, manufacturing enterprises, engineering companies and equipment manufacturers, constituting a complete industrial chain. China Chemical Engineering Group initiated the establishment of the alliance and plays a central role for its strong engineering and system integration capability.

Evolution of relations between different parties: Scientific research institutes have different technological advantages. The upstream and downstream enterprises have cooperative relations. Research institutes and enterprises cooperate to do R&D work. So there is no obvious competition among the members and their relationship does not change significantly.

Advantages and disadvantages of the influence by such relations upon the alliance: The member units are quite interested in the promising key technology R&D work. Sometimes, however, it is hard to coordinate the sharing ratio between parties involving in a specific project.

Roles of the Relevant Government Departments

Government has played a positive role in pushing forward the development of the alliance and provided policy support, guidance and coordination for the alliance's development. At the same time part of R&D projects included in the national science and technology programs, and give a certain amount of funding.

History of the Alliance

In June, 2007, promoted by the Ministry of Science and Technology and 5 other ministries, the "Industry Technology Innovation Strategic Alliance for New-generation Coal (energy) Chemical" was officially founded by signing the Alliance Agreement. On the basis of research and analysis of the industrial situation and the capabilities available, the alliance decided five technology innovation fields to address the outstanding problems that hinder the industrial development. The five innovation fields include "the 2nd Generation Coal Gasification Technology", "Clean and Efficient Utilization of Brown Coal", "Production of Alcohol and Ether with Compound Gas", "Further Processing of Methanol" and "Carbon 2 Products".

The alliance served as organizational units and the president unit was responsible for the implementation of the key projects of the national scientific and technological supporting program "coal to olefins". The government-funded money was 12.13 million Yuan, accounting for 6.7% of the total investment.

"Fluidized Bed Methanol to Propylene (FMTP) Industrial Technology Development" got a major breakthrough. With the evaluation by the Evaluation Committee of the China Petroleum and Chemical Industry Association, major technology indicators and the overall technology reached international advanced level.

Relevant government departments signed "Authorization Agreement of Full-time Management of the Alliance Secretariat" with the president unit. The president unit should study and improve the alliance management system, innovate working mechanism and explore the secretariat full-time management model to adapt to the continuous development of the alliance. Relevant government departments funded 300,000 Yuan.

Determination of Certain Factors that Impede the Progress of Events

The issue of legal status:
the alliance cannot assume any obligations and any risk in the undertaking and development of project as an entity, which are undertaken by the president unit, for it is not a legal person. And this has led to unequal rights and obligations of the alliance, which makes it impossible for the alliance to play a real management role.

The issue of evaluation mechanism:
full-time personnel of the alliance are actually the employees of their own units and they are evaluated by the original units, which makes it hard for them to concentrate themselves to the study of the problems in the development of the alliance.

Ways to Overcome These Obstacles

Establish the alliances as an entity. Improve mechanisms like organization mechanism and evaluation mechanism. The so-called entity status is the alliance's legal status.

Prediction and prevention of future barriers

The issue of sustainable development:
The alliance's objective is to develop key and generic technology and the projects are the important starting point. The alliance cannot maintain sustainable and steady development if new technology cannot be developed successively.

3.2.4 Knowledge Generation and Technology Diffusion

Human Resources: Each participating enterprise shall designate full-time management staff, R&D specialists and technicians for certain project according to the project agreement. The related departments of different universities and research institutions that join in a project shall directly assign researchers to the project. Staff from enterprises and R&D institutions will communicate and work together during the whole process of the R&D project.

Machinery And Research Equipment: R&D Institutions will provide laboratories, research center and facilities and equipments. Enterprises will provide pilot plant, industrial demonstration and other machinery equipments.

Funds: The project is financed primarily by investment from the members and is also supported by fund from alliance and government, public fund raising and loan from banks. R&D institutions shall be exempt from such contributions. The reserve fund for technology development comes from a certain part of the benefit from licensing of technologies and the donation from members and other organizations. The reserve for technology development will be used for the expenditure on support matching-up, bonus for relative development staff and other aspects in the actual implementation of the project.

Management and Diffusion of Cooperation Achievements

In *the Alliance Agreement and Management Measures on Intellectual Property Right of Alliance*, there are stipulations on protection for intellectual property right, from patent application, technological confidentiality to punishment and compensation for loss of intellectual property right resulted by breach of the agreement by members. In the contract on the actual project development, the ownership and use of intellectual property right is provided in detail in order to secure the availability of the stipulation on protection for intellectual property right.

Table 9   Existing human and platform resource in the Alliance

Human resources	Experimental platform
4 Academicians from Chinese Academy of Engineering	3 important national laboratories
4 Yangtze Fund Scholars	2 national technological promotion center
5 "973 principal investigators"	2 national technological transfer center
4 national top designers	1 national engineering research center
1 consultation team member of leader group, national coal chemical processing	8 important provincial and ministry level laboratories
	2 national enterprise technological centers
	9 provincial enterprise technological centers

Data source: report compiled by the Alliance members

New Products Jointly Developed

The R&D of the Alliance is mainly for development of new technologies, new process, patents, thesis and professional publications, not for new products.

The management of Allied Patents

i. Intellectual property developed with funds from Chinese government is subject to applicable Chinese laws and regulations.

ii. Intellectual property developed with funds from the alliance is shared by the project participants. The developers still possess the ownership of their previous technologies. The ownership of and the benefit share from newly developed technologies are to be determined by the project participants in compliance with project contract.

iii. The technological achievement, developed by two or more members, can be applied for patent with the consensus by every involving party. Before the involving parties co-apply for patent, they shall follow "Agreement on Patent Co-application and Determination for the Patent Right", determine the fee for patent application, annual patent fee sharing, ranking etc. When one party waives the right for patent application in written confirmation, other parties can apply for patent. The fee for patent application and annual fee are paid by the applicant. After the grant of patent, the party which waived the right for patent application has the right to use the patent technology for free.

iv. The members of the alliance have priority in using technologies at lower cost; the alliance will perform external promotion based on the current market price; any member should not obstruct the promotion; if whoever obstructs the external promotion of technologies, the alliance will compel it for licensing in compliance with applicable regulations.

v. The Alliance can withdraw certain part as reserve fund for technology development; the proportion of benefit sharing will be determined according to the contribution (investment of technologies and capital) of the partners.

Management of the Process or Technologies Jointly Produced

All members shall be obligated to protect the intellectual property right and technical confidentiality. Before the actual implement of a project, all involving parties shall execute agreement or terms on technical confidentiality. The agreement or terms on technical confidentiality shall not conflict with the relative stipulations in the agreement. During technology development process, the project participants should identify the technologies classified as technical know-how (including unpatented technologies). Once recognized, technical know-how should be protected as the technical know-how of all participants.

Joint Publications: The ownership of the relative publications generated from Alliance's R&D is shared by all R&D parties. The ranking will be determined by prior negotiation according to the actual investment and contribution by each party.

Scientific Conferences: This type of conferences shall be organized by the alliance as entrusted by relevant government authorities and the conference shall be organized by the director-general of the executive council.

Workshops: The workshops shall be, in accordance with the goals and objectives of the alliance, proposed to be convened by the unit in which the director-general of the executive council works, attended by the units and individuals in the technology field, who will communicate with the members of the alliance.

The joint education of talents: By organizing diverse conference, it is to improve the communication among talents from enterprises and R&D instructions and cultivate talents. Universities can make use of the R&D project as practice base and culture core technology talents with enterprises.

3.2.5　Legal Environment of the Alliance

The operation of the Alliance is generally compatible with current laws and regulations, such as *Contract Law* and *Anti-monopoly Law*. At present, the regulations mainly include related regulations promulgated by the Ministry of Science and Technology concerning the establishment of the alliance, direct and support the development of the alliance by science and technology. These regulations provide the guideline for the development of the alliance and help determine the objective of the project implementation.

Policies from Ministry of Science Technology are norms and guidelines to the development of the alliance. However, the policies in favor of the alliance conflicts with the current regime for technology innovation supervision. In practice, the old regime is still working thus impairing the effect of the policies in favor of the alliance.

Clarifying the identity and status of the alliance in legal perspective; considering the input the alliance; trying to find ways to develop the alliance gradually into an industry-promoting, non-profit organization with an independent legal person status, which is set up by certain enterprises under the guidance of the government and with the participation of different industrial organizations?

3.2.6　Funds Management

The expense for the daily running and operation includes shared office expense, project fee and reserve fund for technology development. The executive council will determine the amount of annual shared office expense and it will be paid by the enterprises of the alliance.

The project is financed primarily by investment from the members and is also supported by fund from alliance and government, public fund raising and loan from banks. Currently, the alliance has self-raised nearly 700 million of fund and conducts 4 projects. Among those projects, there is one project which obtained 12.13 million Yuan from Chinese government, but it has not been appropriated yet.

The reserve fund for technology development comes from a certain part of the benefit gained from licensing of technologies and donation from members and other organizations.

Principles for financial management: The funds shall be managed with the determination of projects under the guidance of the alliance and whoever provides funds to projects shall be in a leading position to manage the funds. According to the *Agreement of the Alliance*, the alliance has developed *Financial Management Measures*, *Budget Management for Shared*

Office Expense and other funding management rules. The use of fund from Chinese government is subject to the related laws and regulations.

Detailed Implementation Rules: The alliance has carried out independent financial budget and accounting system, opened independent account, used funds for its specified purpose, managed by specified person and implement centralized management for all funds of the alliance.

Financial supervision and control: The R&D project of the alliance shall fully utilize the existing resources (such as experimental equipments, laboratory, installation of pilot plant and existing public constructions), reduce investment; the project expense shall be assessed and appropriated by important node and stage; when the fund from Chinese government is appropriated, the self-raised fund of all partners shall be in place and reserve 5% as the guarantee; the unit which the director-general works can consign an agency which is recognized by the executive council to supervise, review and assess the project.

3.3 The Strategic Alliances for Recycling Steel Processes Technology Innovation (SARSPTI)

3.3.1 Goals and Organizational Forms

Under the framework of WTO agreements, the Industry Innovation Strategic Alliances for Recycling Processes in Iron & Steel Production will continue to explore the development of key technologies, generic technologies and important cutting-edged technologies in the industry.

- The alliance focuses on the development of generic technologies and key technologies in the iron and steel industry. It aims at greatly improving the indigenous innovation capability of the industry and solving the bottleneck problems in resources, energy and environment. The alliance expects to develop new-generation recycling process technology for iron and steel production as well as several generic technologies with indigenous intellectual property rights and being greatly influential in the industry. All these endeavors aim to maintain a healthy development of the iron and steel industry.
- The alliance facilitates the sharing of science and technology resources between key enterprises in the industry, research institutions and universities. It aims to establish a cooperation mechanism based on the value chains of industry technology innova-

tion. It expects to set up a market-oriented multiple-source investment and financing mechanism where enterprises are the main players. Moreover, it also expects to build an efficient mechanism to facilitate the transformation of technology achievements.
- The alliance aims to explore effective ways to improve the indigenous innovation capability of iron and steel industry.

Process and Procedure of its Establishment

In June, 2007, a new type of cooperation organization between enterprises, universities and research institutions — "Strategic Alliances for Recycling Steel Processes Technology Innovation (SARSPTI)" was officially founded by six large-scale steel manufacturing groups, including China Iron & Steel Research Institute Group, Baosteel Group Co. , Angang Steel Company Limited, Wuhan Iron and Steel (Group) Corp. , Shougang Group, Tangshan Iron and Steel Co. , Ltd. , Jigang Group Co. , Ltd. , and three universities with strong research capabilities in iron and steel industry, namely, Beijing University of Science and Technology, Northeast University and Shanghai University. The organizations of the alliance integrate both virtual and entity forms. The alliance is composed of an Executive council, an Expert Technology Committee, a Secretariat and a general office, which is under the guidance and direction of China Iron and Steel Industrial Association. The alliance is not a legal person but an organization based on agreement.

3.3.2 Corporate Governance Structures, Rights and Responsibilities

The pressing issues that impede different parties from getting allied: Enterprises pursue profits in intensive competitions, and thus they tend to make gradual innovation in developing end products and techniques and in reducing costs. China Iron and Steel Research Institute Group focuses on R&D in generic technologies. Universities tend to pursue the advancement and influence of their researches in the world. There are some discrepancies among the three parties.

The Corporate Governance Structures

The responsibilities, rights and interests of each member shall be clarified according to the Alliance agreement. On the basis of voluntary cooperation between initiators, the Alliance agreement is formulated and concluded. And a strategic alliance towards long-term cooperation is finally founded on the basis of signed agreement.

The executive council shall have the responsibilities to: decide the technology development direction and priority projects according to the recommendations of the Expert Technology Committee; coordinate the raising and use of funds, achievement transfers, the plan for revenues distribution and other important decisions made in the alliance. The executive council meets regularly each year to discuss certain matters and make relevant decisions. The executive council of the alliance, composed of heads from major alliance members, shall have one director-general who is elected by the directors of the council.

The expert technology committee shall have the responsibility to: decide the technology development direction and important projects for the alliance; review, supervise, inspect and assess a project; decide the follow-up development plan of a project according to the technology development trend in the industry. The expert technology committee is composed of 18 to 20 experts and leaders in the iron and steel industry, who are appointed by the executive council.

The secretariat shall have the responsibility to run the daily affairs of the council, coordinate and manage projects under the leadership of the council. The secretariat has one secretary-general, five under-secretary-generals, and ten liaison staff. At present, there are three full time staff in the secretariat, who are appointed by the council. The office of the secretariat is located in China Iron & Steel Research Group.

The development of equity entity of the alliance can be promoted by jointly building labs, engineering research centers, joint venture technology companies, etc. At the same time, a platform for industry technology innovation can be established by sharing the science and technology resources among alliance members.

The alliance shall accept any enterprises or institutions that are qualified as independent legal persons and engaged in research, development, manufacture and services of related technologies and products in the iron and steel industry. Such enterprises or institutions shall enjoy the rights and undertake the responsibilities as members of the alliance. The alliance members are independent legal persons, who have no debtor-creditor relations with the alliance.

The alliance members are members of related council. The initial council members are composed of the ten initiating members of the alliance. Any non-allied member who consents to the agreement can propose an application after nominated by the council. Once approved by a resolution of the council, such member can become the council member of the alliance.

Management of Organizations within SARSPTI

The daily liaison and organizing work is in the charge of China Iron & Steel Research Group. The relevant staff in the secretariat is assigned by the member unit and the other full time staff has been in charge of the Group.

The pattern of project group is primarily adopted at present. The leading person is completely responsible for a project. The person maintains the overall direction of a project, organizes experts to decide the overall contents, plans and funds arrangement, coordinates R&D work between different participators and reports regularly to the expert technology committee and the council.

Project Selection and Leadership

The determination of a project shall be discussed and approved by the council after it has been examined by the Expert Technology Committee. A project shall be completely in the charge of a responsible person and shall be subject to the supervision and inspection by China Iron and Steel Industrial Association.

Management of R&D Projects

The responsible person is in charge of the project management. The project shall be subject to the supervision, examination and assessment of the expert technology committee and the supervision and inspection of China Iron and Steel Industrial Association.

New-generation recycling process of iron and steel production is mainly oriented to rectify the inadequacies of the iron and steel industry in China — high energy consumption and heavy pollution. The R&D achievements will be a breakthrough in the clean iron steel production in China. The technology can thus be widely extended. But there exists no practice in the follow-up production yet.

Rights, Responsibilities and Codes of Conduct

The alliance adopts a mechanism in which the research and development are jointly conducted while the cooperation achievements are shared by the participators of the project.

3.3.3 Relations of SARSPTI

There is no leader in the alliance now and China Iron&Steel Research Group (CISRI) plays the role of a bridge.

The iron and steel industry in China is now in the state of full market competition. However, the convergence degree seems very low and the six enterprises in the alliance only cover about 24% of the national total production. The competition between enterprises is very intense. The alliance enterprises compete fiercely in products. However, for the purpose of reducing environmental pollution and energy consumption, they come to cooperate with each other on generic technologies to "save energy, reduce emission, and protect the environment", to achieve encouraged by the Chinese government a goal.

The competition in the market affects the cooperation in the alliance. The relevant parties often engage in long negotiations and it is difficult to reach agreements on cooperation projects.

The relevant government departments play a positive role as a referee and give certain support to the growth of the alliance. The alliance is always ready to have directions from relevant government departments and support from national project. Moreover, the alliance also accepts guidance from China Iron and Steel Industrial Association and undertakes the projects of the association.

3.3.4 Knowledge Generation and Technology Diffusion

Human Resources: The alliance accumulates a R&D team composed of almost 800 personnel from 14 organizations. Each party inputs some human resources. Before R&D in a project is completed, human resources are mainly from China Iron & Steel Research Group and related universities. During industry demonstration and development, human resources depend mainly on enterprises.

Machinery and Research Equipment: Related enterprises invest certain equipment for pilot program experiments.

Funding: Funding is obtained from both national projects funding and self-raising by the alliance.

Management and diffusion of cooperation achievements: The alliance members sign agreements on the intellectual property rights in regard to the technologies jointly developed in the alliance. The agreements shall define the ownership of related intellectual property rights, the plan for revenues distribution at the time when the technology is transferred and applied in production, and the basic principles for sharing intellectual property rights by new members or former members who have withdrawn from the alliance. These definitions will avoid the breach of existing intellectual property rights owned by the alliance and its members.

New products jointly developed: During the industrialization of new products jointly developed, the establishment of an interests-motivating and risk-sharing mechanism will be stressed. The enterprises that undertake the development risks and experiment the use of new technologies will have priority in acquiring the intellectual property rights of the innovation technology.

Management of joint patents

Before an alliance project starts up, the undertaking and organizing organizations jointly sign an agreement on intellectual property rights. In the agreement, the ownership of the intellectual property rights produced in the project and the benefits distribution rules for the revenues from technology extension and application shall be clearly defined in advance. Any organization that undertakes a national project shall promise to follow the principle of sharing related intellectual property rights.

After technology achievements are accomplished, patents can only be applied for on the condition that all the cooperating parties agree on it. Prior to the application of a joint patent, the cooperating parties shall sign *"the Agreement for the Joint Application and Confirmation of Patent Interests"* to clarify the sharing of application fees and annual fees of the patent. The order of applicants shall be arranged in the name list order agreed before. If a party confirms in writing to waive the patent application right, other parties shall still be able to apply and the application fees and related annual fees shall be borne by the applicants.

As to the patented technologies, if the beneficial party tries to use any of them, the beneficial party shall negotiate with the owner of the patented technologies upon problems related to the transfer of patented technologies.

All the parties of the alliance shall take the obligation to protect the intellectual property rights and keep their confidentiality. Before a project of the alliance starts up, a confidentiality agreement for technologies shall be signed, which shall not be in contradiction with related provisions in the Alliance Agreement.

When an alliance member takes the initiative to withdraw from the alliance, the member automatically waives the agreement relationship with the alliance and no longer enjoys the sharing of intellectual property rights owned by the alliance.

Management of Technologies Jointly Produced

As to the generic technologies developed on the basis of governmental funding, including technologies of low pollution, production with high efficiency, energy saving and reduced consumption, they shall be diffused and popularized gratis to the alliance members. Such diffusion and popularization outside the alliance shall be made with change.

As to the featured production technologies and process further developed through the use of the generic technologies of the alliance, the newly formed intellectual property rights shall be diffused and popularized with change to other enterprises. They shall not be monopolized by the undertaking organization as "exclusive" technologies.

As to the patents, technology know-how and non-patent technology achievements produced in the projects of the alliance, the licensing or transfer of such achievement beyond the alliance shall be reviewed by the council and executed in written form. The related revenues acquired will be distributed in the principle agreed upon by parties according to their actual investment and contributions.

Each undertaking party of a project of the alliance can utilize gratis the patents, technology know-how and non-patent technology achievements in its own organization or in the enterprise that owns over 50% of the shares. Each cooperating R&D party shall have the right to use such achievements within its own organization. The said right shall mean the right to apply the technology achievements and products developed in the project to the production, process and equipment of their own organization.

The amendments to the articles related to the management of intellectual property rights shall be proposed by the alliance members, discussed and approved by the council before they become effective.

Joint Publications: The copyrights related to the scientific and technology achievements produced in a project of the alliance are jointly owned by the responsible parties and cooperating parties of the project. Its name list order is arranged through negotiation on the basis of the actual investment and contributions made by the participating parties and the cooperating parties.

3.3.5 Legal Environment of SARSPTI

The Alliance is generally compatible with laws and regulations in effect and conforms to the Chinese Anti-Monopoly Law. Unconformity only occurs in certain provisions concerning the funds management of the Alliance.

3.3.6 Funds Management

The funds of the alliance include fund that keeps the office running and project funding. The office space is provided by the China Iron & Steel Research Academy. The labor expenses of each person in the office shall be borne by the organization he or she affiliated to. The source of the funds mainly includes: national project funding and the funds raised by the members of the alliance themselves.

According to related regulations of China, project funding shall be managed on the subject basis and be spent in the way specified in related contract.

The alliance members that undertake projects shall draw overall budget, process control and total cost verification according to the project plan. The funds of the alliance shall be managed exclusively in a special account opened by a unit that the Secretariat affiliated to. Such funds can be allocated according to related provisions in project contracts. A system of budget and final accounts is applied to such ear-marked fund. The account shall be reported in the form of annual financial reports to the council for reviews and shall be subject to audits by a third party. Examination and acceptance of a project shall be completed in time according to related national management rules or in the way specified in the contract.

By means of transfer and application of generic technologies, a certain proportion can be withdrawn from related revenues and spent to encourage the alliance members to participate in innovations of generic technologies by way of bidding. The proportion and the detailed plan to implement shall be decided upon by the council through consultation.

3.4 Summary of Chinese ITISA Cases

ITISA in China is a new organizational model of cooperation between enterprises, universities and R&D institutions with its focus on governmental leadership, cooperation between the three parties and contractual relationship. There are three key factors: firstly, definite objective for technology development and outcome in compliance with national strategic objectives and requirements for development of local key industries; secondly contract execution in the alliance to provide legal binding force on all core bodies of enterprises, universities and R&D institutions as legal persons; thirdly, all alliance members shall make joint contribution and share benefits and risks. In terms of organizational structure, the alliance is subject to the governmental guidance, fully utilizes market-oriented system, takes new demand and important standards on common technology for industrial or corporate long-term development as the tie, leverages optimal combination of all technology innovation elements and builds up a long-term, reliable and regulated community for cooperation between enterprises, universities and R&D institutions. In regard to operation mechanism, the alliance is not an independent legal person. The contracts explicitly stipulate the obligations, responsibilities, rights and relationship of all members, determine mechanism on investment, decision-making, risk and interest sharing, ownership of intellectual property right and other aspects and ensure the normal operation of the alliance.

With the analysis on TIPPAAMI, ITISANCC and SARSPTI, it is to conclude that these are ITISA under the governmental guidance. They have similarities in terms of organizational structure, goal, and governance structure etc. However, due to different industrial characteristics and participants, there are certain differences among the members with diverse characteristics.

i. The three members have three common objectives: first, develop industrial generic and key technologies; second, construct innovation platform and industrial technology innovation chain to form industrial technology value chain; three, foster technology transfer and diffusion to cultivate industrial technology talents. The three members have similarities in organizational structure. They are all non-corporate organizations under contracts. The loose cooperation has been changed and determined as per the contract in order to form a regulated organizational structure, providing a platform for open cooperation and communication. Such organization can work both separately and jointly not only to leverage the cooperative advantages, but also to fully utilize the activity and resources from each participant. However, it requires high standards for the organizational management and operation.

ii. It is vital for alliance operation and management to establish proper and effective governance structure and appropriately determine the responsibilities, rights and code of conducts. The three practical ITISAs in China each has a contractual organization directed by government and led by enterprise with participation of R&D institutions and universities. The three alliances are highly similar in term of organization. The management for decision-making shall include executive council and expert technology committee. The executive council shall comprise of representatives respectively elected by the alliance members. According to the decision made by the executive council, the secretariat is responsible for the daily operation and management of the alliance.

The backbones for innovative R&D in industrial technology are the alliance members. The members enjoy great flexibility in technology innovation R&D. The organizational structure in the alliance is loose and the secretariat shall not influence the decision making of each member, so the secretariat can only fulfill its limited rights and responsibilities as per the existing contract. With this governance, the responsibility, right and interest of each party are clearly defined, but restriction and supervision system can not work well because of lack of leadership. It leads to unclear common benefit, code of conduct and collective value, thus will surely impair the cooperation among the participators. The general direction, rights and responsibilities are clarified for members with different property.

iii. Governmental function on public management and service put great influence on the governmental support to the alliances. On one hand, the government takes measures to facilitate technology progress and industrial development in order to boost the economic growth and increase the national income. The government helps establish the alliance so as to reach the goals set by the government. On the other hand, the alliance's goal and value is to sufficiently utilize resources, carry out industrial technology innovation and push industrial technology progress, which is in line with governmental strategy. Moreover, the Alliance can not impede market competition. The alliance is not a profit-oriented organization and must gain its own profit in line with the public benefit. The alliance shall try its best to step aside the competitive technology field so as not to be a market competitor. If it does, it will not comply with the governmental goal which aims to increase the economic performance by facilitating market competition.

iv. The key factor in joint research and development is to define rights and obligations of each party in the agreement in terms of intellectual property right, technology diffusion and other aspects. Thus, the alliance is committed to support and encourage application and diffusion of advanced technologies. There is no obvious difference among the three alliances in China in this area. With fulfilling the requests on interests of each party, it can implement paid transfer and share to achieve maximum profit of the intellectual property right. The profit gained will be shared by R&D participators and the alliance's R&D foundation in proportion to their contribution and investment. The diffusion of technologies and achievements will comply with the principle that "the person shall have whatever he has developed and shall be entitled to its authorship; share under cooperation, favor to participants and influence the industry". With clearly defined ownership and rights to use and gain profit, the technology achievement obtained by the alliance shall be diffused or transferred to the industrial enterprises by determining the different conditions for diffusion and transfer according to different sources.

v. The alliance shall comply with the laws and regulations which can ensure it to launch legal business. In terms of law, the alliance is the organizational model between enterprises, universities and R&D institutions. It is the cooperation between different civil subjects under contracts or agreements. It shall be deemed as civil relations, not an organization. Each participant as a legal subject independently involves in business and takes responsibilities, which solves the problem that determines the legal subject of the organization according to laws and regulations.

4 Cases of Competence Centers of Excellent Technologies (COMET)

In this section we will discuss the empirical results of the case studies on the Austrian Competence Centers of Excellent Technologies (COMET) along the empirical framework presented in Section 1.2. In the next section we will focus on the Austrian Centre of Competence of Mechatronics (ACCM), before we shift attention to the Centre on Integrated Research in Materials, Processing and Product Engineering (MPPE). The last subsection presents the results on the Carinthian Tech Research Centre for Advanced Sensor Technologies (CTR).

4.1 The Austrian Centre of Competence of Mechatronics (ACCM)

The Austrian Centre of Competence of Mechatronics (ACCM) is among the biggest joint research centres between science and industry in Austria. The interdisciplinary field of mechatronics combines elements of different research areas including the design of products and manufacturing processes, in particular precision mechanical engineering, electronic control, informatics and systems thinking. The main focus of ACCM is on computational and experimental process simulation, mechanical systems and model-based control, data-based control in complex environments, mechatronic design and actuation systems, sensors and signals as well as radio communication and microwave technology in different industrial fields (see FFG 2008a). Research within these fields should, for instance, lead to the realization of high speed data transfer in sensor networks or highly integrated magnetic bearing systems.

4.1.1 Goals and organizational forms

This section sheds some light on the strategic objectives of ACCM in the context of the funding Programme, the COMET Programme. Furthermore, this section outlines the legal organizational form of the competence centre.

Strategic Goals of ACCM

At present, ACCM is one of the leading research institutions in the field of mechatronics in Europe. Thus, the scientific objective of ACCM is to become a global leader regarding scientific excellence in mechatronics within the coming ten years. This overall strategic objective calls for the realization of the following sub-objectives:

- Bundling of existing national competencies in the field of mechatronics.
- Networking and intensive cooperation with leading international organizations, both from the industry and the scientific sector. The establishment and further development of these networks is essential.
- Establishment of a new culture of cooperation between science and industry, involving the optimization of know-how transfer to the industry sector.
- Alignment of the research in ACCM with strategic interests of industrial branches.
- Generation of trend-setting innovations in the field of mechatronics.
- From a regional policy perspective, the strategic goal of ACCM is to become a key partner in R&D for the local and the Austrian economy, and, thus, to enhance international attractiveness and competitiveness of Austria.
- Enhancement of human resources in mechatronics by attracting excellent researchers and by developing a common strategic research programme on the highest scientific level.
- Stimulation of the education of engineers specialized in mechatronics via educational facilities of ACCM and its partners.
- From a business-administration perspective, the short-term goal is to balance the ACCM budget within the predetermined funds of COMET. The organizational model is intended to secure preservation and further development of ACCM in the long-term.

Legal Organizational Form of ACCM

ACCM Gmbh is a non-profit limited liability company. This form is most appropriate to administer financial flows between the participating partners. It provides an appropriate legal basis for the workflow of ACCM and the relationship to the shareholders and partners. ACCM has the compulsory elements and rights as any limited liability company. The three shareholders of ACCM are the Linz Centre of Mechatronics (LCM) Gmbh, the Vatron Gmbh and the Johannes Kepler University of Linz (JKU). LCM was a former K-Plus centre in the preceding programme of COMET, the Austrian Centres of Competence Programme (see also

Section 2). Vatron is a leading local company in the field of mechatronics, owned by the incorporated companies Voest Alpine and Siemens PLC. JKU is the biggest university of the province Upper Austria with a particular focus on engineering and technology.

4.1.2 Corporate Governance Structures, Rights and Codes of Conduct

This section introduces the internal organization of ACCM and its internal governance structures, including rights of participating partners (such as IPRs) and codes of conduct. Special emphasis is put on the analysis of the R&D management, specification of thematic priorities and the organization of collaboration at different levels of ACCM.

Problems that Impede the Integration or Translation of Different Rationalities

Problems that impede the integration of different rationalities are to a large extent related to different kinds of motivation of industry and scientific partners to participate in ACCM. Basically, the driving motives for firms and research institutions clearly differ due to the underlying rationalities of both types of actors.

The motivation for firms is to draw on concentrated high-level competences of a centre of excellence. In this context, participating firms expect to get all-in-one solutions for specific technological problems of (Interview E). It is assumed to be much cheaper and more efficient for them, to accomplish joint R&D and produce necessary knowledge within one specific platform than to acquire this knowledge via the market from many different suppliers. Apart from the efficiency argument, firms can acquire additional funding in ACCM for these R&D activities by means of the COMET funds. Furthermore, participating firms can integrate codified and even tacit knowledge produced into their own knowledge base. It is also worth emphasising that the connection between basic and applied research makes ACCM quite attractive for such firms (Interview E). A firm partner has one counterpart starting from basic research to the development of concrete innovations in form of new products or processes. This is to a large extent related to the fact, that basic research results from ACCM can be transferred into innovation carried out by the shareholders of ACCM. In the organizational model of ACCM, researchers are employed by LCM, Vatron and JKU. Thus, a solid permanent ACCM staff is leading to the enhancement of interorganizational understanding (Interview E).

Due to their particular rationalities, universities show different motivations than firms. Universities as organizations are interested in increasing their rating concerning different university indicators (Interview E). By this, they are interested in publications and high scientific reputation, including international visibility. In contrast to firms, universities are producers of public goods-confined to keep generated knowledge unpublished. For the case of ACCM, it is attractive for universities to get additional funding for research trainees, in particular in form of funded dissertations and master theses that are easier to realise within a web of international industry and scientific partners. This may yield high-quality dissertations usually leading to high-quality publications. Furthermore, it is attractive for universities to get in contact with new international partners. Networking is crucial, for instance, for future applications of joint research projects using other funding sources.

Governance Structures and Rules to Integrate the Different Rationalities

Figure 7 outlines the internal organizational model of ACCM Gmbh. As a limited liability company, ACCM features the respective compulsory elements. The shareholders are the Linz Centre of Mechatronics (LCM) Gmbh, the Vatron Gmbh and the Johannes Kepler University of Linz (JKU). They are the highest and final authority of ACCM in terms of ownership rights. The shareholders nominate the ACCM centre management, at present represented by one employee of LCM and one employee of Vatron. The centre management is responsible for the realisation of the strategic goals. They jointly head six research areas (Computational and experimental process modelling and simulation, mechanics and model based control, information and control, mechatronic design of machines and components, sensors and signals, wireless technologies) and the core functions of ACCM (controlling, revision, etc.). The centre management consists of two managers who bear the overall responsibility for ACCM, including especially the following tasks (see ACCM 2008):

- Leadership of ACCM and representation to the outside.
- Maintenance of relationships to the funding organization and to the scientific partners.
- Adherence to deadlines, quality and costs in accordance with the project schedules established with the partners.
- Matters of law, personnel, finance and controlling.
- Investments and administrative matters.
- Assurance of planning and on-schedule conducting of the research program. In accordance with the COMET programme, the research program itself will be defined jointly by the partners.
- Budget, costs and financial planning, as well as personnel planning.
- Guidelines and regulations for conducting a project.
- Decisions on new project proposals by partners in cooperation with the area coordinators and with consideration of recommendations of the scientific and technological advisory board.

The six research areas are coordinated by area coordinators, also nominated by the shareholders. Each of the areas consists of key researchers, senior researchers and junior researchers. Key researchers are usually highly skilled with a habilitation degree employed at a university.

The centre management is monitored by the board of supervisors. It is staffed with of two members of each shareholder. In accordance with the the Austrian corporate law, the board of supervisors shall contribute to the successful long-range scientific, technological and economic development of ACCM. The members of the board shall maintain strict secrecy to the outside concerning the negotiations of the board and concerning knowledge about the business affairs gained in their role as members of the board. This nondisclosure obligation remains in force after termination of their board membership. The centre management shall report to the board both at its request and in regular periods concerning the course of business and the situation of ACCM GmbH. In addition, the centre management shall report in written or oral form to the chairman of the board of supervisors or his assistant on important issues, as well as when a recommendation of the scientific and technological advisory board is not met by the management. All matters that the centre management wishes to present to the general assembly must first be handled in the board of supervisors. Resolutions of the board that contradict the recommendations of the scientific and technological advisory board require a two-thirds majority (see ACCM 2008).

Figure 7: ACCM organizational model

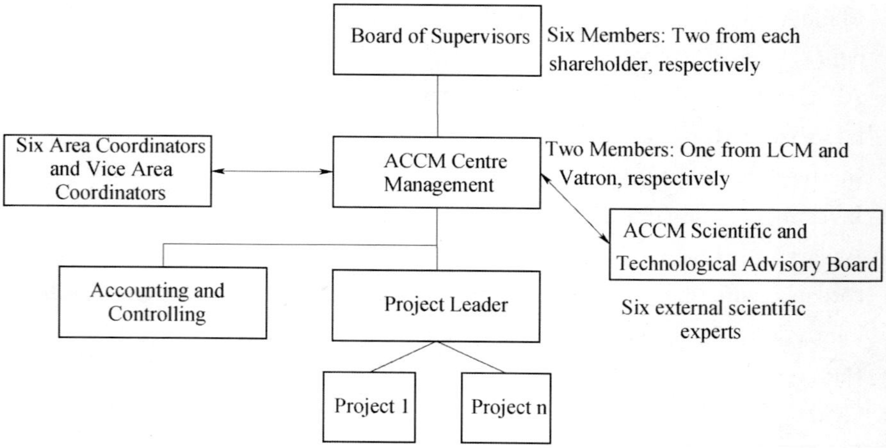

Source: ACCM (2008)

Another essential consulting body of ACCM is the scientific and technological advisory board. It consists of six external experts, three from the industry and the science sector, respectively, and discusses strategic objectives and budget issues of ACCM. The main task is scientific consultancy and support for the ACCM centre management with the goal of fulfilling the evaluation criteria. The composition of the board shall reflect a balance of expertise between science and industry: The members should not simultaneously be members of a partner or founding partner of ACCM GmbH and shall possess documented high scientific or general mechatronic qualifications. Ideally the members shall have well-founded experience in conducting and accompanying evaluation and assessment processes for research projects or in the industrial realization of larger research projects. The member's availability and compatibility with his/her other functions shall be assured. The scientific and technological advisory board is not subordinate to the centre management of ACCM (see ACCM 2008).

Concerning the problem of integrating different rationalities of participating partners in ACCM, one key measure is the equal distribution of members coming from science and industry in all important bodies of ACCM, such as the scientific and technological advisory board. Transparency is very important in this context. However, it has to be noted that barriers between firms, universities and research organizations coming from different rationalities were-according to Interview E-to a large extent removed in the application phase. The application phase was most important for the integration of these different rationalities, and crucial in order to develop trust and a common language between all participating partners (Interview E). In ACCM the application phase was characterized by intensive working groups over a period of three years. Thus, well attuned teams-in particular involving the core actors-were already established before ACCM started in 2008. In general, a culture of cooperation has been developed over the past years due to various joint projects and relations between the core partners.

The Organization of Collaboration on the Different Levels

See also Section 3.2.2. The interrelation of different levels of collaboration in ACCM (i.e. researchers, project leader, key researcher, senior researcher, junior researcher, area manager, centre management) was already planned in the application phase. The complete research programme is organized on the basis of projects that can be categorized into multi-firm projects and strategic projects. Multi-firm projects involve distinct industry projects and an additional strategic or basic research part. Strategic projects are closely related to the overall strategic research orientation of ACCM and produce more generic knowledge than multi-firm projects.

At the project level, a project leader is responsible for the realization of the objectives of a project, and, thus, forms the interface for the organization of collaboration between project partners at this level. At the level of the six research areas, area coordinators are responsible that the strategic goal of the area can be realized by means of the underlying strategic or multi-firm projects. The area coordinators report progress in regular meetings with the ACCM management. They exercise their scientific tasks in the realm of the respective research area in the organizational matrix of ACCM. ACCM management nominates the area coordinators and their deputies on recommendation of the key researchers and project leaders (where the latter are not themselves key researchers) of the respective area. The area coordinators and their deputies together form the platform of area coordinators that advises the management in scientific and technical matters, especially with respect to the research programme. Together with the associated key researchers and project leaders, the Area Coordinators develop measures for achieving the goals in their respective area and coordinate these measures with the management.

The Organization of the Operational plan, Selection of Tasks/Projects

See also Section 3.2.2. and Section 3.2.3. The basic operational plan and the selection of thematic priorities in ACCM were initially outlined in the project proposal. The core partners are crucial in the definition of thematic priorities. Initially ACCM applied for funding of 71 Mio EUR. The granted budget for 2008-2012 equals 57 Mio EUR. Thus, a concrete operational plan, taking into account all projects with respect to needed resources, was established in two discussion rounds for further priority setting with the partners after the notification of acceptance for funding (some initially planned projects had to be removed from the basic operational plan) (Interview E). The detailed operational plan was then established for the period 2008-2012, including a listing of all projects planned, taking into account personnel, workflow, machines, equipment, rooms, etc. IBasically, there is no intent of change in the thematic orientation after the establishment of an operational plan. However, within complex R&D activities changes may always be necessary. Thus, new thematic priorities or new projects can be suggested by the area coordinator and/or by the scientific and technological advisory board. The area coordinator will suggest his/her idea in the regular meetings with the centre management. If the idea is considered as significant, the scientific and technological advisory board will be informed. The board will then give a recommendation to the centre management. The centre management has the final decision and informs the supervisory board.

R&D Management, Controlling and Marketing

See also Section 3.2.4. As mentioned above, ACCM features two types of projects, so-called multi-firm projects and strategic projects. The R&D management involves project controlling and marketing of project results, for instance via publications. Each project is organized by means of a clear project plan, including resources, milestones, budget, etc. A product portfolio management is a crucial governance instrument for the ACCM management, for instance for the planning of resources, and for marketing project results. In the ACCM product portfolio each research project is assigned to a research area and to a specific industrial branch (see Figure 8), i.e. it is based on a connection of the research areas and projects with applications and industrial branches that are potential clients.

Figure 8　Product portfolio management in ACCM
Source: ACCM (2008)

Structure of research												
Projects are organised along scientific disciplines							**Company Partners need a broad mechatronic consortium**					
		Industrial Branches / Applications										
Areas of ACCM	Machine system builders						Vendors of components (sub-systems)					
	Steel making	Tool machines & production plants	Plastics processing	Combustion engines	Agri-cultural machines	Textile machinery	Mobile machines	Integrated measurement and sensor systems	Hydraulic drives and actuation systems	Electrical drives and actuators	Automation Hard- and Software	ICs for communication applications
Comput. & Exper. Process Modelling & Simulation	■	■										
Mechanics and Model Based Control	■											
Information and Control		■										
Mechatronic Design Mach. & Comp.										■		
Sensors and Signals	■											
Wireless Technologies	■											

Rights and Rules, Codes of Conduct and Flow of Information

The ACCM agreement regulates overall responsibilities, such as the entry or exit of partners. For instance, the cancellation period for one partner is six months, cancellation can only be executed at the end of a year. By signing this agreement, rights and rules are obligatory for the partners, i.e. they have to provide the agreed resources-as for instance in form of cash, personnel or infrastructure-according to the agreement.

A crucial issue is the IPR regulation. The ACCM agreement defines the general framework for the granting of rights to ACCM research results for K2 funded projects. A more precise definition of these rights is to be defined in the project specific contracts that shall adhere to the general principles specified in the ACCM agreement (ACCM 2008). The project specific contracts include-apart from IPR regulations-the regulation of financial flows and infrastructure at the project level. The IPR regulation is of crucial importance, in particular in the context of integrating different rationalities of the partners. The ACCM property rules are intended to balance interests of all partners and to secure highest possible transfer of results into practice (Interview E).

The ACCM approach can be summarized as follows (ACCM 2008): In the case of multi-firm projects that consist of industry projects and a basic research part, a firm partner has to specify a concrete thematic area before a project starts for which this firm wants to claim property rights. The field of activity of a partner is defined according to the partner's business areas as listed in the respective cooperation contracts; these business areas are in turn defined by the description of the product and service areas, customers and competitors of a partner. The partner shall list their fields of activity such that they correspond closely to the topic and the desired application of the results of the project (ACCM 2008).

- The ACCM agreement outlines the following rules for firm-specific results of a multi-firm project:
- The respective partner has the right of ownership of the specific results.
- The respective partner has the right of exclusive utilization in his own (defined) field of activity.
- In the case of patentable specific results, patenting is handled by and for the respective partner. Corresponding provisions are to be made in the cooperation contracts. The inventor partners retain the right of noncompetitive utilization.

The agreement outlines the following rules for basic research part results of a multi-firm project:

- ACCM retains the right of ownership of general results.
- Each project partner involved in the production of general results, either by contributing research work or by commissioning, enjoys a nonexclusive right of utilization.
- If such a project partner licenses general results to third parties for purposes other than those enumerated in item, then ACCM shall receive an appropriate share of the net profit (i. e. , after deduction of associated expenses) for such licensing.
- Because of the dissimilarity of the projects, the nature of results, the relevance of rights to the general results for the project partners and the market opportunities for licensing.
- If general results are patentable, then within one month after a patent application at a patent office, all project partners shall be informed of the patent application.

Results of strategic projects are owned by ACCM. Each project partner who is involved in the production of strategic results enjoys the non-exclusive right of utilization of results free of charge. If results are patentable, within one month from application for the patent, all partners of ACCM shall be informed of such application. The partners shall enjoy advance notice of at least three months concerning the patent application and are guaranteed a purchase option over third parties.

Concerning rules for publications, project results of strategic projects can be published without any limitation. In the case of multi-firm projects, planned publications should be discussed in one of the regular meetings with all the project partners (Interview E). Usually, if a project partner objects against a planned publication, a reasonable solution has to be reached. This may for instance lead to alternative ways of publishing, i. e. publishing only preliminary or conceptual results. The following formal rules for publications are given by ACCM (2008):

- The partners to the agreement agree that on the basis of the goals of the K2 program, the partners are urged to attain a high publication quota.
- R&D results of the projects in the research programme can be published principally only with the approval of the respective project partners.
- For intended publications, ACCM or the participating partners shall first obtain the written approval of the project partners affected by the content of the publication. Such affected project partners shall deny approval of the intended publication only for important reasons. Such denial of approval must be justified in written form within four weeks. If there is no reaction within four weeks of notification of intent to publish, then implicit approval is assumed.
- Publications concerning strategic research projects are subject to no restrictions.

4.1.3 Analysis of Relationships

This section describes in some detail the historical background of ACCM and the establishment of relationships between the core actors.

Identification of Core ACCM Actors, Initiators

The ACCM is composed of three shareholders, 42 industry partners, including small and medium sized companies (SMEs), and 36 scientific partners. The core actors are the shareholders, the Linz Centre of Mechatronics (LCM) Gmbh, the Vatron Gmbh and the Johannes Kepler University of Linz (JKU). The JKU acts as the core scientific partner including 14 participating institutes. Others in the scientific sector are the Vienna University of Technology and Tampere University (Finland). The core firm partners-except from LCM and Vatron- are Voest Alpine, Siemens, IH-Tech Sondermaschinenbau und Instandhaltung GmbH, Salvagnini Maschinenbau GmbH und Rosenbauer International AG. These firms are clustered around the industrial sector engineering and electronics.

Evolution of Their Relationships

ACCM shareholders draw on a long established culture of collaboration. The field of mechatronics has been defined as a thematic priority by the province Upper Austria over the past years. JKU started the department of mechatronics in 1990, featuring the first master programme in mechatronics of the world. Thus, during the 1990s, relationships between JKU and local firms (Voest Alpine, Vatron) dealing with mechatronics were established in form of smaller projects or labour mobility between these actors.

The Role of Related Government Bodies

Several policy initiatives of the regional technology policy of Upper Austria addressed the strengthening of the relationships between the actors of the field. In this context, the relationship of ACCM to the local government is well established. In the present case, the role of related government bodies is mainly reflected by the interrelation of ACCM with the FFG that represents the Ministry for Transport, Innovation and Technology (BMVIT) and the Ministry of Economic Affairs and Labour (BMWA)❶. This relationship concerns the selection process (i. e. ex-ante evaluation) on the one hand, and the continuous monitoring and evaluation process of ACCM on the other hand (see Section 2 for a detailed description of the evaluation process).

The History of the Centre/Alliance

Based on relationships that were established since the 1990s, (see also Section 3.3.2) two competence centres were accepted in Upper Austria in the field of mechatronics within the preceding programme of COMET (see Section 2). The industrial K-ind competence centre for mechatronics (IKMA) started in 1999, the K-Plus Linz Centre of Competence in Mechatronics (LCM) in 2001. Both centres led-according to Interview E-to the establishment of a new culture of cooperation and the setup of significant further competencies in the field of mechatronics in the region. Based on the introduction of the mechatronics cluster Upper Austria and the strategy for excellence of the Austrian Council for Research and Technology Development (RFTE) in 2004, LCM, Vatron, IKMA and JKU started initial considerations for further development of mechatronics in Upper Austria, involving a strategic paper for a centre of excellence in the field of mechatroncis in Linz (Upper Austria). With the presentation of the new COMET programme in 2006 by the FFG, it was decided between the core partners to apply for a K2-centre. Following the first competitive call of the COMET programme, ACCM was selected based on the ex-ante evaluation as described in Section 2.3, and was started in 2008.

---

❶ Since the last change in the Austrian government Ministry for Economic Affairs, Family and Youth (BMWFY).

The success story of LCM

The Linz Centre of Mechatronics (LCM) was established in 2001 as one of 17 K-Plus centres in Austria in the preceding progamme of COMET. Nowadays, it is a stand-alone LLC and one of three shareholders of the K2-centre ACCM. It is widely agreed among researchers and policy makers that LCM succeeded as Austria's leading organization in applied mechatronics research. LCM has conducted more than 150 cooperative R&D projects in this field. The spectrum of services incorporates partnerships along the complete innovation chain-from the idea to the finished product, involving six areas of competence (Mechatronic Design and Process-Simulation, Electrical Drives, Hydraulic Drives, Information Analysis and Fault Diagnostics, Multi-Body & Multi-Field Dynamics and Structural Control, Sensors and Communications).

The positive development of LCM was reflected and underpinned by significant contributions to the scientific community in the form of about 500 publications and 100 master and dissertations theses. LCM was the main platform for cooperation in the field of mechatronics in Upper Austria and brought together university researchers and researchers in firms and research organization. Thus, it significantly contributed to the establishment of a pronounced culture of cooperation in the field of mechatronics in Upper Austria. The extraordinary performance of LCM was honoured by a series of innovation awards, such as the Best Business Award 2009, the MEC-Award 2008, the Cross Border Award 2007, the Innovation-Prize of Upper Austria in 2005, 2003 and 2002, the Trauner-Prize in 2003, and the Pegasus in silver in 2002.

4.1.4 Knowledge Generation and Technology Diffusion in ACCM

This section provides an overview of inputs into the knowledge generation process of the ACCM, and presents some figures on the concrete objectives and goal criteria with respect to output.

Joint Resources for Knowledge Production

The most important input for knowledge generation in ACCM is the knowledge incorporated in researchers working on ACCM projects. Table 10 presents an overview of the ACCM human resources for 2008. As mentioned in Section 2.2, researchers working on ACCM projects are not employed at ACCM. The majority of these researchers are employed at the three shareholders, the rest is affiliated with the remaining participating partners (Interview E). Scientific background of ACCM scientific staff has a special emphasis on engineering and mechatronics. At present, about 200 researchers from different partners are working on joint ACCM projects.

The research programme of ACCM requires the use of considerable infrastructure, including rooms, laboratories, machines and equipment. The common location of the ACCM is the new Science Park in Linz, Upper Austria. The main Mechatronic institutes of JKU are located in the same building.

The infrastructure needed and used in the projects is not owned by ACCM, i.e. usually the use of infrastructure is regulated in the consortium agreement and in project specific contracts (see also Section 3.2.6). The financial funding of ACCM within the COMET programme is about 57 Mio EUR for the first funding period of five years. The yearly budget for projects is about 12 Mio EUR.

Management and Diffusion of Collaboration Outputs

The management and diffusion of collaboration outputs is regulated in the consortium agreement and in project specific contracts, for instance, with respect to IPR rules and publications (see Section 3.2.6). An important instrument to manage collaboration outputs is the product portfolio as outlined in Section 3.2.5. The aspired output of ACCM is outlined in the project proposal. As for the other cases, knowledge produced in ACCM diffuses via publications in different publication modes and patents into the regional and Austrian innovation system. Table 11 gives an overview on the planned output of ACCM,

Table 10   Human resources of ACCM

Staff working on ACCM projects	
Total	152
Scientific staff	133
Professor	8
Key researcher	17
Senior scientist	37
Junior Scientist	71
Technical staff	5
Administration (management, controlling, etc.)	14
Number of young scientists	
Trainees	-
Dissertation and Master students	7

Source: ACCM (2008)

Table 11   Planned ACCM outputs for the first funding period

	2008-2012
Research results	
Publications in scientific journals	625*
Patents and licences	40
Research programme	
Share of strategic projects	20%
Additionality	
Increase of research intensity of firm partners	15%
Human resources	
Advanced trainings	27
Dissertations (graduated)	75
Master thesis (graduated)	175
Networking	
Firms	40
Research organizations	40
International partners	32
National partners	48
Costs and budget	
Acquisition of third party funds	2 Mio €

Source: ACCM (2008); *235 of these are planned to be science industry co-publications.

while Table 12 summarizes ACCM outputs for 2008. Note that ACCM has no concrete planned outputs concerning the number of innovations. However, it is noted in the agreement that 90% of firm partners aspire product innovations by participating in ACCM.

4.1.5 Institutional Conditions: Laws and Regulations

This section provides a short overview on the compatibility of institutional conditions with the establishment of ACCM. Information on the general legal framework are outlined in *Section 2.2.2*.

Compatibility with Present Laws and Regulations in Different Fields

Table 12 ACCM knowledge outputs

	2008
Research output	
Publications	159
Patents applied	2
Patents granted	—
Conference participations	22
Education	
Dissertations (graduated)	—
Dissertations (on track)	3
Master theses (graduated)	—
Master theses (on track)	14

Source: ACCM (2008); Note that innovations are not listed here, since they are not formally included in the goal criteria of ACCM. ACCM views innovations as new commercial products. However, ACCM is a non-profit research organization.

In general, the present institutional conditions bear no significant barriers for the establishment and fluent conduct of ACCM❶. However, regarding tax regulation, it is not completely clear to what extent ACCM can utilize the so-called "Forschungsfreibetrag" of the Austrian tax law that allows innovating firms to deduct their basic R&D expenditures from tax liability up to 25%. It is difficult in the ACCM case to distinguish between industrial contract research and basic R&D (Interview E). Thus, a more precise regulation may be conducive.

The Austrian employment law is compatible with the ACCM model and provides a reasonable framework for the administration of staff working for ACCM projects. The contribution of a researcher to ACCM projects is clearly regulated. For instance, a researcher employed at a university may be allocating 30% of his/her working time for ACCM projects, the rest for the university. In this example, 30% of the salary of this researcher would be provided by the ACCM COMET funding. ACCM as a LLC is eligible for funding from national sci-

---

❶ The Austrian University Law 2002 (Federal Law Gazette I Nr. 120/200) lays the ground for the participation of universities in competence centres. Pursuant Article 3 they are supposed to support the utilization and implementation of their research results. Article 10 gives them the right to form LLCs, foundations or associations. Article 106 regulates the procedures regarding inventions and intellectual property issues.

ence and research promotion programmes (e. g. offered by the Austrian Science Fund FWF for basic research or by the Austrian Research Promotion Agency FFG for applied research). Furthermore, ACCM may also submit proposals to the 7th European Community Framework Programme for Research Technological Development and Demonstration (FP7).

Assessment of the Effects of the Institutional Conditions

From the viewpoint of the ACCM management, the institutional conditions provide a suitable environment to establish a competence centre like ACCM. In particular, the interplay between national and regional interests seems to be balanced, not leading to challenging hurdles in the establishment. Present laws and regulations, such as the university law, the employment law or the tax law, provide neither explicit and nor exclusive incentives for establishing a centre like ACCM, but are compatible.

4. 1. 6 Financing and Administration of Funds

This section provides some basic information on the ACCM financing model, and the financial management of ACCM.

Model of Financing and Cost Sharing

The ACCM budget is currently based nearly up to 100% on the COMET funding of 57 Mio EUR per year. 50% (26.5 Mio EUR) are provided by public sources, composed of national funds (30%) and provincial funds (20%). 5% of the total funding are provided by universities. The latter is provided via in-kind contributions, including personnel and physical capital, such as use of equipment and provision of materials. The remaining 45% come from the participating firms, whereas 65% of the firm contributions are provided in cash, 35% in form of in-kind contributions.

Ways of Managing and Using Financial Resources

ACCM uses the compulsory elements of any Limited Liability Company to administer the financial resources, as given by the ACCM central services, in particular controlling and accounting. Budgetary issues are executed by the ACCM management and controlled by the shareholders' meeting and the supervisory board (see *Section 3. 2. 2 and 3. 2. 5* for further details). The financial resources are solely used to accomplish ACCM research projects.

4. 2 The Centre on Integrated Research in Materials, Processing and Product Engineering (MPPE)

MPPE is a COMET K2-Centre focused on Integrated Research in Materials, Processing and Product Engineering. It is the main component of the non-profit joint-venture research institute MCL (Materials Centre Leoben Forschung Gmbh). The centre puts special emphasis on materials development, materials processing, process technology, and innovative use of materials. Materials science, including processing and engineering, is an interdisciplinary research field that particularly investigates the interrelation between the microscopic structure of materials and their macroscopic properties. In this context MPPE supports industry with various diverse materials testing possibilities and carries out numerous R&D projects in close cooperation with partners from science and industry.

4.2.1 Goals and Organizational Forms

This section sheds some light on the strategic objectives of MPPE in the context COMET, and outlines the legal organizational form of the K2-Centre.

Strategic Goals of MPPE

The MPPE is intended to carry out international high-level basic and applied research in the field of materials science and product engineering. In this context, the overall strategic goal is to establish MPPE as an internationally positioned centre of excellence for materials and materials technologies, specializing in complex, multi-disciplinary tasks concerning materials development, materials manufacturing and processing, and applications. Furthermore, MPPE is intended to reach the following strategic goals (Interview D):

- The centre of excellence is to be established as an operative and strategic platform for the cooperation of science and industry in the field of materials science in order to create critical masses in this technology area.
- By this, the MPPE is intended to increase competencies and enhance knowledge production and innovation of the participating partners.
- and to promote the education and training of new researchers and experts in materials science.
- From a regional and national policy point of view, MPPE is intended to promote a sustainable position of the regional and national industry partners in this sector.
- The long-term strategic economic goal is to position MPPE as a stand-alone sustainable research institution after phasing-out of the COMET funding, partly by other funding sources, partly by industrial contract research and product development.

From the perspective of the MCL shareholders that are to a large extent local public research institutions, the strategic goal is to strengthen the region around Leoben as prominent international location for materials science and product engineering (Interview D).

Legal Organizational Form of MPPE

The MPPE K2-centre is a non-profit joint venture under the heading of the MCL Gmbh. It should be noted that MPPE-and thus the COMET funding-is the main budget item of the MCL budget (up to 92%, see also *Section 4.6.1*). MCL Gmbh has the same compulsory elements and rights as any Limited Liability Company. This organizational form has been chosen in order to secure an easy and transparently regulated transfer of financial transactions between MCL and FFG and between MCL and the participating partners. Furthermore, the organizational form as Limited Liability Company offers appropriate legally legitimised boards to control the strategic orientation of MPPE, provides a stable legal security, and serves as appropriate governance instrument for the shareholders. The shareholders of MCL are the University of Leoben, the Joanneum Research GmbH, the municipality of Leoben, the Austrian Academy of Sciences, the Vienna University of Technology and the Graz University of Technology.

4.2.2 Corporate Governance Structures, Rights and Codes of Conduct

This section introduces MPPE's corporate governance structures and its internal structure of organization, including rights of participating partners (such as IPRs) and codes of conduct. Special emphasis is put on the analysis of the R&D management, specification of thematic priorities and the organization of collaboration at different levels of MPPE.

Problems that Impede the Integration or Translation of Different Rationalities

Like in the case of ACCM, problems that impede the integration of different rationalities are to a large extent related to different drivers that motivate firms and research institutions to participate in MPPE. The motivation for firms is to get access to high-level, bundled and highly concentrated research activities. Firms can connect to university institutes via MPPE, for instance, in the context of the search for high-qualified researchers in a very specific field. Thus, networking is one of the most important aspects for firms to participate in MPPE (Interview D). Firm partners have the possibility to get in contact with key actors in this technological area, not only in a formal, but also in an informal way. Furthermore, they are able to screen for new thematic fields, become aware of new technological developments, and get access to strategic research areas since MPPE accomplishes strategic research projects[1]. By this, participating firms can activate new knowledge bases stimulated by interaction with MPPE partners, and integrate this new knowledge into their own knowledge base.

Besides networking and screening, a key motivation for firm participation in MPPE is to reduce costs and risks in the development of product and process innovations by three mechanisms (Interview D): First, costs can be reduced via the cooperation in networks with different scientific and industrial partners. Second, R&D projects that need to be performed by firm partners are partly financed by public funds. Third, medium- and long-term non-core, but potentially relevant R&D activities can be sourced out to MPPE partners.

---

[1] Strategic research projects in COMET are closely related to the overall strategic research orientation of a centre and produce more generic knowledge than multi-firm projects.

In the case of universities, the motivations to participate in MPPE are diverse (Interview D): First, selected universities primarily aim to improve their own scientific and technological knowledge base, their methodological know-how and their scientific infrastructure. Some universities in particular appreciate to get improved access to further methodological knowledge. Second, in other cases universities' motivation lies in the possibility to plan and accomplish strategic research with highly qualified international partners within the MPPE platform. By this, the participating universities aspire to improve the quality of their scientific output. Third, for some universities, the key argument to participate is networking with international partners that may lead to joint research projects funded by additional sources. Fourth, selected universities emphasize the possibility to educate staff and other PhD candidates at an international level, in particular in the context of doctoral dissertations. These dissertations are provided with financial funds from MPPE. Dissertations usually lead to publications that are important for university performance evaluation criteria.

Governance Structures and Rules to Integrate the Different Rationalities

Figure 9 presents the corporate organization model of MPPE under the heading of MCL that is the consortium leader and responsible for the organization and strategic development of MPPE. MCL Gmbh is a non-profit Limited Liability Company. MCL includes a COMET area-for MPPE activities within the COMET programme, and a Non-K area-for activities outside the COMET programme. The COMET area gives the individual partner groups the opportunity to participate in decision-making processes via the COMET board and the COMET programme committee of MCL.

The shareholders of MCL meet in the General Assembly and have to execute the shareholders rights and responsibilities, in particular the nomination of the management. The shareholders are the University of Leoben, the Joanneum Research GmbH, the municipality of Leoben, the Austrian Academy of Sciences, the Vienna University of Technology and the Graz University of Technology. The General Assembly carries out the tasks assigned to it by the Austrian law on limited liability companies. Additional tasks relevant to the COMET Programme include the appointment of members of the supervisory board, and the confirmation of the rules of procedure of the supervisory board (see *MPPE 2008*).

The supervisory board and the General Assembly control the MPPE management that is responsible for the realisation of the MPPE strategic goals and the execution of the research plan. The MPPE management heads three broader company sections: the central functions (including financing, technical administration, controlling, legal department, accounting and public relations), the COMET research section, and the Non-COMET research sections. The management carries out the following tasks (*MPPE 2008*):

- Implementing the research programme, including the development of team competence and stimulation of projects and strategic plans.

- Ensuring the required project portfolio.
- Pre-evaluation of projects.
- Reporting to funding agents based on the reporting regulations.
- Organizational support of the COMET Board and the COMET Programme Committee, e. g. convening a meeting, hand-outs, minutes.
- Applying for subsequent funding periods.

The supervisory board carries out the following relevant tasks in the context of the COMET programme (*MPPE 2008*):

- Examining the strategic plans and concepts of MPPE, the annual research programme, the annual estimate, the annual accounts, the management report and the application of profits, and reporting the results of this examination to the General Assembly.
- Approving the rules of procedure of the COMET board.
- Appointing and dismissing the chairperson of the COMET board.
- Appointing and dismissing the company representatives on the board and in the programme committee based on a recommendation by the MPPE company partners.
- Appointing and dismissing the representatives of the scientific partners on the board and in the programme committee based on a recommendation by the MPPE scientific partners.
- The Styrian provincial government shall be entitled to delegate two members to the supervisory board.

The COMET research section is categorized in seven research areas, each headed by one area manager (Integrated Research in Materials, Processes and Product Engineering; Multi-scale Materials Design, High Precision Processing and Manufacturing; Damage-Mechanisms; Evolution and Modelling; Tool Technology for Advanced Processing; Fatigue-proof Lightweight Design; Design and Reliability of Components with Functional Properties). The non-COMET section (about 8% of the total MCL budget) is related to research funded by other sources and consists of three business areas.

Additional important elements of the MPPE governance structure are the COMET K2-board and the K2 programme committee. In MPPE, the K2-board is the most important decision supporting-body. The main tasks of the COMET board include:

- Advising the supervisory board on strategic issues based on proposals by the MCL management.
- Specifying the framework conditions for multi-firm projects and strategic projects in COMET.
- Recommending the members of the programme committee to be appointed by the su-

Figure 9 MPPE organizational model

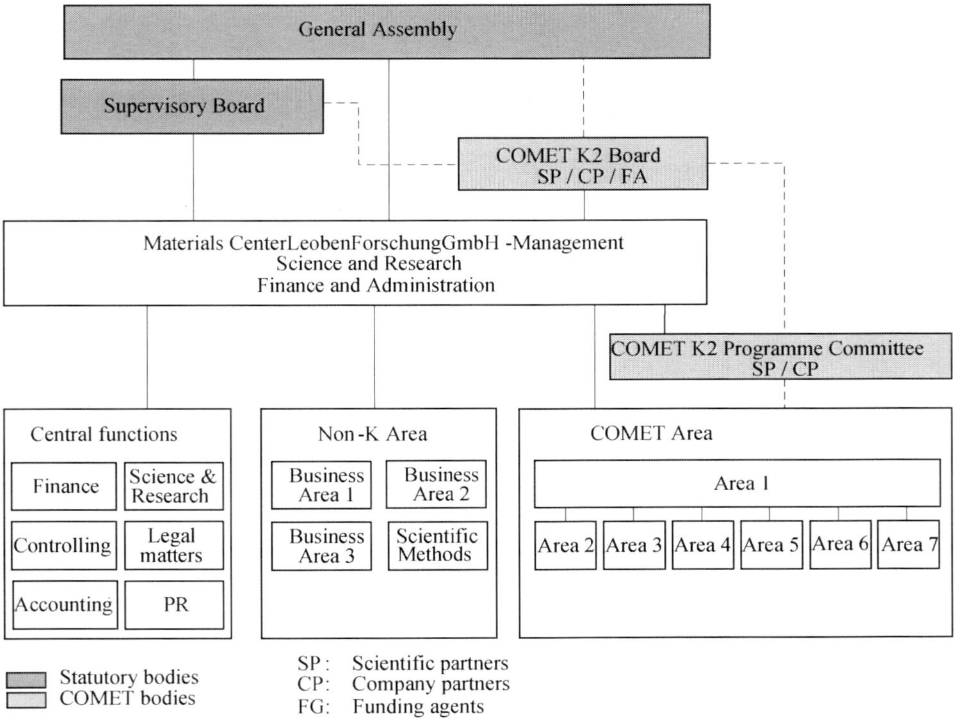

[Organizational chart showing:
- General Assembly (Statutory body) at top
- Supervisory Board (Statutory body) below General Assembly
- COMET K2 Board SP / CP / FA (COMET body) connected to Supervisory Board
- Materials CenterLeobenForschungGmbH - Management, Science and Research, Finance and Administration
- COMET K2 Programme Committee SP / CP (COMET body)
- Three groups below Management:
  - Central functions: Finance, Science & Research, Controlling, Legal matters, Accounting, PR
  - Non-K Area: Business Area 1, Business Area 2, Business Area 3, Scientific Methods
  - COMET Area: Area 1, Area 2, Area 3, Area 4, Area 5, Area 6, Area 7

Legend:
- Statutory bodies
- COMET bodies
- SP: Scientific partners
- CP: Company partners
- FG: Funding agents]

Source: MPPE (2008)

pervisory board based on proposals by the partners.
- Recommending the COMET research programme to the Supervisory Board based on proposals by the MCL Management.
- Deciding on COMET projects based on a proposal by the management and recommendations by the programme committee.
- Monitoring the attainment of scientific objectives based on COMET project reports.
- Carrying out and supporting national and international activities aimed at securing the existence of MCL in the long term.

The COMET board should ideally consist of company partners and scientific partners in equal parts. International partners should also be represented. Representatives of the FFG are non-voting members of the COMET Board.

The programme committee supports the MPPE management in questions related to the research programme and has the character of an advisory panel. It consists of representatives of the seven MPPE research areas and gives recommendations concerning new projects or thematic priorities. The tasks of the programme committee include the evaluation of project proposals and providing recommendations to the board, and the participation in the further development of the research programme. The committee should ideally consist of company partners and scientific partners in equal parts and ensure balanced expertise. By this, the MPPE governance structures differ quite significantly from the ACCM governance structures.

The Organization of Collaboration on the Different Levels

See also *Section 4. 2. 2.* The interrelation between different levels of collaboration in MPPE (i. e. researchers, project leader, key researcher, area manager, management) is defined in the MPPE proposal. The complete MPPE research programme is organized on the basis of projects. Projects can be categorized into strategic projects, multi-firm- and single-firm projects. Strategic projects are broader and more basic research oriented in the context of the general strategic orientation of MPPE, while multi- or single firm projects are often related to concrete applications.

The project leader is responsible for the operative execution, and, thus, needs to organize the collaboration between the project members coming from different MPPE partners. The success and the scientific outcome of a project will be assessed by the area manager and the so-called key researcher of each area. The management and organization of collaboration at the level of the overall research programme is left to the MPPE management.

The Organization of the Operational Plan, Selection of Tasks/Projects

See also Section 4. 2. 2. and *Section 4. 2. 3.* The strategic operational plan and the selection of thematic priorities in MPPE was defined in the project proposal for the first funding period (2008—2012), already at the level of projects (strategic projects and multi-firm projects). This included planning of personnel as well as infrastructure needed for the projects (machines, equipment, laboratories, etc.). By this, also the selection of very concrete thematic fields and tasks of MPPE was defined in the application phase.

After the establishment of MPPE, the selection of tasks and new thematic priorities can be suggested by the programme committee, i. e. area managers or area members can suggest new thematic priorities within this platform. The programme committee decides if the idea will be suggested to the COMET board that can accept or reject the suggested field. The assessment is based on scientific excellence of the new idea and its relevance for the strategic orientation of MPPE.

R&D Management, Controlling and Marketing

See also *Section 4.2.4*. The project leader is responsible for the project management, while the MPPE management is responsible for the overall programme management. Each project is organized by means of a clear project plan, including resources, milestones, budget, etc. The working hours of a researcher on a project are captured automatically in real time. The time plan and budget issues are monitored by the financial controlling unit of MPPE. Marketing of project results and new products and processes is accomplished via newsletters and publications. It is administered by the public relations unit of MPPE.

Rights and Rules, Codes of Conduct and Flow of Information

First, MPPE is regulated via a contractual agreement between MCL and the FFG. It defines the flow of funds from FFG to MCL, and the goods and services of MCL. Second, a consortium agreement, signed by all partners before MPPE has started, is the main document that regulates rights and rules of the partnership, such as the EU rules for funding or the entry and exit of partners, general IPR rules for the different types of projects, and rules for publications. Cancellation of a partner is regulated via a cancellation period. Third, project specific contracts regulate the cooperation in specific projects, including IPR regulations that are considered to be the most important part of these contracts.

As for ACCM, IPR regulations differ between strategic projects and multi-firm projects. General rules are given in the MPPE Agreement, more specific regulations are to be defined in project specific contracts. The general regulation for the outcome of strategic projects is as follows (*MPPE 2008*):

- The use and exploitation of research and development results shall be possible for all partners participating in a strategic project.
- If strategic projects lead to inventions for which industrial property rights are to be obtained, provisions defined in the agreement shall be binding with respect to title and the use and exploitation rights.
- Partners who have participated in a strategic research project (the basis being the project contract) shall, if industrial property rights are granted, be entitled to a paid, non-exclusive license for the business fields defined in the project contract. The license shall be granted for an unlimited period of time without territorial restriction and can be transferred exclusively to affiliated enterprises.
- If MCL or the participating scientific partners waive an application for or the maintenance of industrial property rights, the other scientific partners and company partners participating in the project shall have a corresponding right to take up such industrial

property right for the fields of activity defined in the project contract in return for a payment of an appropriate amount.

The main rules for the outcome of single-firm and multi-firm projects are as follows (MPPE 2008):
- The use and exploitation of research and development results shall be possible for all partners participating in the project.
- In the event that single firm or multi firm projects lead to inventions for which industrial property rights can be obtained, the type and extent of the use and exploitation rights and the filing modalities shall be agreed between the partners in advance in the project contracts.
- With regard to industrial property rights resulting from a single firm or multi firm project, MCL and the scientific partners involved in the project shall be entitled to a non-exclusive transferable license outside the business fields of the company partners as defined in the project contract and a nonexclusive non-transferable license outside the areas of activity of the company partners as defined in the project contract.
- If the company partner(s), the scientific partners or MCL abandon their industrial property rights, they shall be offered free of charge to the partners also involved in the invention. If the latter do not take up the property right, it shall be offered to the other partners involved in the project.

The rules for publications are as follows. Potential publications in multi-firm projects need to be coordinated by consulting all participating project partners. Each project partner must provide a formal approval for a planned publication. A project partner can object against a publication when secrecy is preferred or property rights are affected. Then, the content of the publication needs to be reconsidered or published later. In general, MPPE multi-firm projects should lead to joint publications of all participating partners. Master and dissertation thesis accomplished within projects can be prohibited from publication for one year by a formal objection of a project partner.

4.2.3 Analysis of Relationships

This section describes in some detail the historical background of MPPE and the establishment of relationships between the core actors.

Identification of Core MPPE Actors, Initiators

About 30 firms and 20 research institutions are participating in MPPE. Regarding the scientific context, the University of Leoben is the core partner in MPPE (participating with six different departments) which is also related to the history and the location of the centre in the city of Leoben (province of Styria). The core industry partners are Böhler Uddeholm and Voest Alpine, the two largest Austrian companies specialised in producing steel. These core partners brought in some smaller and medium-sized companies in the MPPE consortium.

Evolution of Their Relationships

The University of Leoben was founded in 1840 with a special focus on mining, metallurgy and materials sciences because of the industrial structure and mining activities in the region. The local industry played an important role to sustain the university at this location (Interview D). Thus, relations between the University of Leoben and the local industry have a long tradition.

Accordingly, the University of Leoben draws on a long-term relationship with the core industry partners of MPPE, both via contract research and in particular via labor mobility (Interview D). Then, the relationship between the shareholders was further institutionalized through the establishment of a, joint K-Plus centre in the preceding programme of COMET, the Austrian Competence Centres Programme. MPPE can be understood as a follow-up of this K-Plus centre established by the core partners.

The Role of Related Government Bodies

The FFG plays a vital role as the agency managing the COMET Programme on behalf of the programme owners the Ministry of Transport, Innovation and Technology (BMVIT) and the Ministry of Economic Affairs, Family and Youth (BMWFY). The FFG is responsible for the ex-ante and ex-post evaluation of MPPE. *Section 2. 2* provides details on the selection and evaluation process. In addition, the local and regional governments played a crucial role in the establishment of the centre. Several regional policy initiatives point to the considerable importance of MPPE as one of the most significant regional drivers for innovation and the regional economy. For all COMET centres, the regional role is an important aspect of their profile.

The History of the Centre/Alliance

See also Section 4. 3. 2. MCL was founded as an association in 1999 in order to foster cooperation between science and industry in materials science in Leoben. It was then transformed into an LLC after the positive ex-ante evaluation of the K-Plus proposal. The ex-post evaluation of the K-Plus centre stimulated the core partners to continue their cooperation, and to apply for a K2 centre in the follow-up programme COMET. The assessment of the existing resources of MCL and its partners, and the already established culture of cooperation between the partners, was the basis for this decision. This was also intensively supported by the local and regional government bodies.

> ### The success story of MCL
>
> MCL was established as association and transformed into a K-Plus centre in the preceding programme of COMET, the Austrian Centres of Competence Pogramme. It is widely agreed among Austrian policy makers that the MCL K-Plus centre could contribute significantly to further sustaining the technological competitiveness in the field of materials science, with a special focus on developing new modeling and simulation techniques. This was reflected and underpinned on the one hand by significant contributions to the scientific community in the form of about 700 publications and 120 master and dissertations theses. On the other hand, the research outcomes of MCL stimulated the introduction of a considerable number product and process innovations in participating firms, in particular materials processing and materials engineering.
>
> MCL successfully accomplished projects with a total volume of 33 Mio EUR. By this, the MCL K-Plus laid basic ground for the successful application for the K2-centre MPPE in COMET, in particular by sustaining and developing further the culture of cooperation between firms, universities and research organizations in the field of materials located in Austria, mainly around Leoben.

4.2.4 Knowledge Generation and Technology Diffusion in MPPE

This section provides a comprehensive overview of inputs into the knowledge generation process of MPPE, and presents some figures on the concrete objectives and target criteria with respect to output.

Joint Resources for Knowledge Production

Similarly as for ACCM, human capital and knowledge of MPPE researchers is the most important input for knowledge generation. Table 13 presents an overview of the MPPE human resources for the year 2008. Scientific background of MPPE scientific staff reflects a special emphasis on engineering and mechatronics. At present, about 125 employees work for MPPE, composed of a-

Table 13　Human resources of MPPE (2008)

MPPE staff	
Total	89
Scientific staff	74
Full time	53
Key researcher	5
Senior scientist	10
Junior Scientist	57
Technical staff	8
Administration(management,controlling,etc.)	7
Number of young scientists	
Trainees	—
Dissertation and Master students	27

Source: MPPE (2008)

bout 90 persons of scientific staff, and 35 persons of administrative staff.

The main location of MPPE is Leoben. The infrastructure includes one office building with laboratories. Further infrastructure needed for the projects (equipment and machines) is usually leased as regulated in project specific contracts. The financial funding of MPPE within the COMET programme is about 53 Mio EUR for the first period of five years.

Management and Diffusion of Collaboration Outputs

The management and diffusion of MPPE collaboration outputs is regulated in the consortium agreement and in project specific contracts. The aspired output of MPPE is outlined in the project proposal; results will be evaluated by the FFG after five years. Knowledge produced in MPPE diffuses intensively via mobility of researchers between MPPE and the partners (Interview D). *Table 14* gives an overview on the aspired output of MPPE, while Table 15 summarizes MPPE outputs for the year 2008.

Table 14 Aspired MPPE Outputs for the First Funding Period

	2008—2012
Research results	
Publications in scientific journals	195
Patents and licences	3
Research programme	
Share of strategic projects	21.7%
Additionality	
Increase of research intensity of firm partners	15%
Human ressources	
Number of key researchers	35
Advanced trainings	105
Dissertations (graduated)	76
Master thesis (graduated)	65
Costs and budget	
Share of overheads	12.5%
Acquisition of third party funds	7 Mio

Source: MPPE (2008)

Table 15 MPPE Knowledge Outputs (2008)

	2008
Publications	
Scientific journals	28
Conference proceedings	30
Books	0
Others	5
Patents	
Applied	0
Granted	0
Participation	
Exhibitions	0
Scientific workshops and conferences	1
Education	
Advanced trainings	33
Dissertations (on track)	42
Master thesis (on track)	11

Source: MPPE (2008)

4.2.5 Institutional Conditions: Laws and Regulations

This section provides a short overview on the compatibility of institutional conditions with the establishment of MPPE. Information on the general legal framework are outlined in Section 2.2.2.

Compatibility with Present Laws and Regulations in Different Fields

According to the MPPE management, the present institutional conditions correspond well with the establishment and handling of MPPE. The objectives of MPPE are compatible with the Austrian legal framework for employment. MPPE staff is normally employed at MCL as regulated by the Austrian employment law. The Austrian employment legislation provides a suitable framework of unpaid leave for university researchers, i. e. they are employed at the MCL for the funding period or the duration of specific projects, but have the right to come back to the university. The tax law is compatible, but provides no specific incentives.

Assessment of the Effects of the Institutional Conditions

As mentioned above, the institutional conditions provide a suitable environment to establish a COMET centre like MPPE. In particular, the Austrian employment law provides a suitable framework to allow for mobility of researchers between MPPE and partners. Other positive or negative effects are not observable (Interview D).

4.2.6 Financing and Administration of Funds

This section provides some basic information on the MPPE financing model, and the financial management of MPPE.

Model of Financing and Cost Sharing

The total budget of MCL is about 57.5 Mio EUR. The budget is currently based up to 92% on the COMET funding of 53 Mio EUR for the first funding period (2008-2012). 8% of the MCL Budget is based on other external funding sources, such as EU Projects and national projects (Bridge Programme), as well as on industrial contract research and income from laboratory services.

The COMET funding of 53 Mio EUR is composed of public resources (50%), including national funds (30%) and provincial funds (20%). Contributions from participating universities (5%) -provided in-kind-are not included in the public funds. The remaining 45% of the resources come from firm partners. About 66% of the contributions of firms are provided in cash, the rest is provided in-kind, including personnel and physical capital, such as equipment and materials. In the MPPE case, it is notable that some firms prefer 100% contribution in cash, while other firms contribute 100% in-kind. However, as a rule set up for COMET, the overall contribution of all company partners can be generated by at maximum 50% in-kind contribution.

Ways of Managing and Using Financial Resources

MPPE uses the same compulsory elements of the management of any Limited Liability Company to administer the financial resources, in particular controlling and accounting. Budgetary issues are executed by the MPPE management and controlled by the shareholders' meeting and the supervisory board (see *Section 4.2.2* and *4.2.5* for further details). The financial resources are mainly used to accomplish MPPE research projects (note that MPPE is a non-profit LLC).

4.3 The Carinthian Tech Research Centre for Advanced Sensor Technologies (CTR)

CTR AG is an industry oriented COMET centre located in Villach (province of Carinthia). The research focus is on intelligent advanced sensor technologies. It is the biggest non-university research institution in the field of intelligent sensors in Austria. The research programme of CTR is disaggregated in three research areas, including optical systems technology, surface acoustic wave (SAW) sensor systems and photonic microsystems technology. Sensor technologies are widely viewed as key technologies for different industries, in particular in electronics when it comes to automating operations, testing and monitoring.

4.3.1 Goals and Organizational Form

This section sheds some light on various strategic objectives of CTR in the context of the funding Programme COMET. Furthermore, this section outlines the legal organizational aspects of the COMET Centre.

Strategic Goals of CTR

Since CTR is, on the one hand, a COMET competence centre, on the other hand a non-university research centre funded by contract research and other non-COMET funding sources, we can identify different strategic goals. From a shareholder point of view, the strategic orientation of CTR is mainly regional, i.e. the shareholder aim to establish CTR as regional engine for innovation, bringing together local firms and the research strengths of scientific partners, and thus, leading to positive effects for the local economy, in particular for small and medium-sized companies (SMEs) (Interview C). Furthermore, CTR should contribute to foster public awareness for the prominent role of R&D in knowledge-based (regional) economies and societies, via the organization of different events and public conferences. CTR as a K1-centre funded by COMET has the following strategic goals (Interview C):

- Accomplishment of industry-oriented, cooperative R&D in the field of intelligent sensors, at an international level.
- Establishment of CTR core instrument for science-industry relations in the field of intelligent sensors in Austria.
- Development of innovative technologies at the international highest scientific level.

- Validation of excellence by means of high-quality publications in peer-reviewed journals, joint dissertations and master theses.
- In the long-term, CTR persecutes the strategic objective to establish CTR as stand-alone competence centre, that can survive after phasing out of the COMET funding.
- From a business-administration perspective, the short-term goal is to balance the CTR budget within the predetermined funds (COMET and other funding sources). In the long-term, it is intended to be able to realize moderate growth.

Legal Organizational Form of CTR

As noted in *Section 2*, it is left to the participants to choose a legal organizational form. CTR is organized as Public Limited Company (PLC) according to Austrian and international legislation. This organizational form has been used in order to avoid any political influence and control, since CTR has exclusively public shareholders (Entwicklungsagentur Kärnten, the Federation of Austrian Industry Kärnten, the municipality of Villach, the Fraunhofer-Gesellschaft Gmbh). Using the usual and compulsory elements of an incorporated company, political influence can be minimized, in particular via the supervisory board (see also *Section 5.2.2*).

4.3.2 Corporate Governance Structures, Rights and Codes of Conduct

The focus of this section is on the internal organization of CTR and its internal governance structures, including rights of participating partners (such as IPRs) and codes of conduct. It involves the analysis of the R&D management, specification of thematic priorities and the organization of collaboration at different levels of CTR.

Problems that Impede the Integration or Translation of Different Rationalities

In fact, the motivation for firms to participate in CTR clearly differs from the motivation for universities, related-as also observed for the other cases-to different rationalities of both types of actors. In the case of CTR, motivation for firms and universities to join the centre corresponds to a large extent with our observation for the other two case studies. First, firms mainly join CTR to get access to external high-level competencies in different fields of sensor technologies, and to utilize this external knowledge to accomplish specific research projects, sometimes-in particular in the case of smaller partners-in quite particular and narrow defined research fields. By this, firms are able to integrate external knowledge into their own knowledge base and realize concrete innovations that can be implemented successfully (Interview C). Second, firms can acquire additional funding for already planned long-term R&D, i.e. firms accomplish necessary R&D within CTR in cooperation with partners at lower costs than if they would produce the knowledge alone or acquire it solely via the market (Interview C). In addition, they enjoy the benefits of networking.

The main motivation for public scientific partners to participate in CTR can be summarized under the heading of networking. Scientific partners participating in CTR show a high interest to get in touch with other scientific partners and companies that work in similar research areas (Interview C). One benefit in this context seems to be the possibility for future applications of joint research projects using other funding sources than COMET. In this context, scientific partners are aware of the chance to close the gap between basic and applied research (Interview C).

As for the other case studies, it has to be noted that the main difference between university and firm participation lies in their different strategic goals. While firms are mainly interested in concrete innovations, which often requires secrecy until implementation, universities are interested in publications and high scientific reputation, including international visibility. It is important that the objectives and activities of a centre are defined in such a way that there is a balance between the different objectives of the industry and scientific partners in order to create a win-win situation.

Governance Structures and Rules to Integrate the Different Rationalities

Figure 10 outlines the internal organization of CTR AG. As an Public Limited Company (PLC), CTR features the respective compulsory elements. The shareholders are the highest and final authority of CTR. In the annual shareholders' meeting, the overall strategy of CTR is planned and monitored. The shareholders' meeting nominates members of the supervisory board that holds a meeting four times a year and observes the realization of the strategic goals of CTR as reported by the CTR management. The CTR management, including CEO (Chief Executive Officer) and CFO (Chief Financial Officer), is responsible for the execution of the strategic goals of CTR and the implementation of the research programme. They are heading the three research areas of CTR (optical systems technology, SAW sensor systems and photonic microsystems technology), and the CTR central services (controlling and accounting, legal administration and human resource management, marketing and sales, information technologies and quality management).

The research areas are headed by area managers responsible for the execution of the area-a-specific research programme and the assigned research projects. Each area consists of one key researcher assisting the area manager to come up with suggestions for new projects.

The CTR management and the supervisory board are supported by a COMET specific strategy board and a scientific advisory board. The strategy board is composed of experts from industry and science, one member of the supervisory board and officials of the FFG. It controls and discusses strategic objectives and the relationship between the participating partners. The scientific advisory board controls CTR in its scientific orientation and provides recommendations to the supervisory board and the CTR management.

In the context of integrating different rationalities of participating partners, the strategy board is of crucial importance (Interview C). The board is especially designed to balance strategic decisions between scientific partners and public research institutions. However, it has to be noted that barriers between firms, universities and research organizations coming from different rationalities must to a large extent be removed in the application phase already. The application phase is most important for the integration of these different rationalities, and to develop trust and a common language between all participating partners (Interview C).

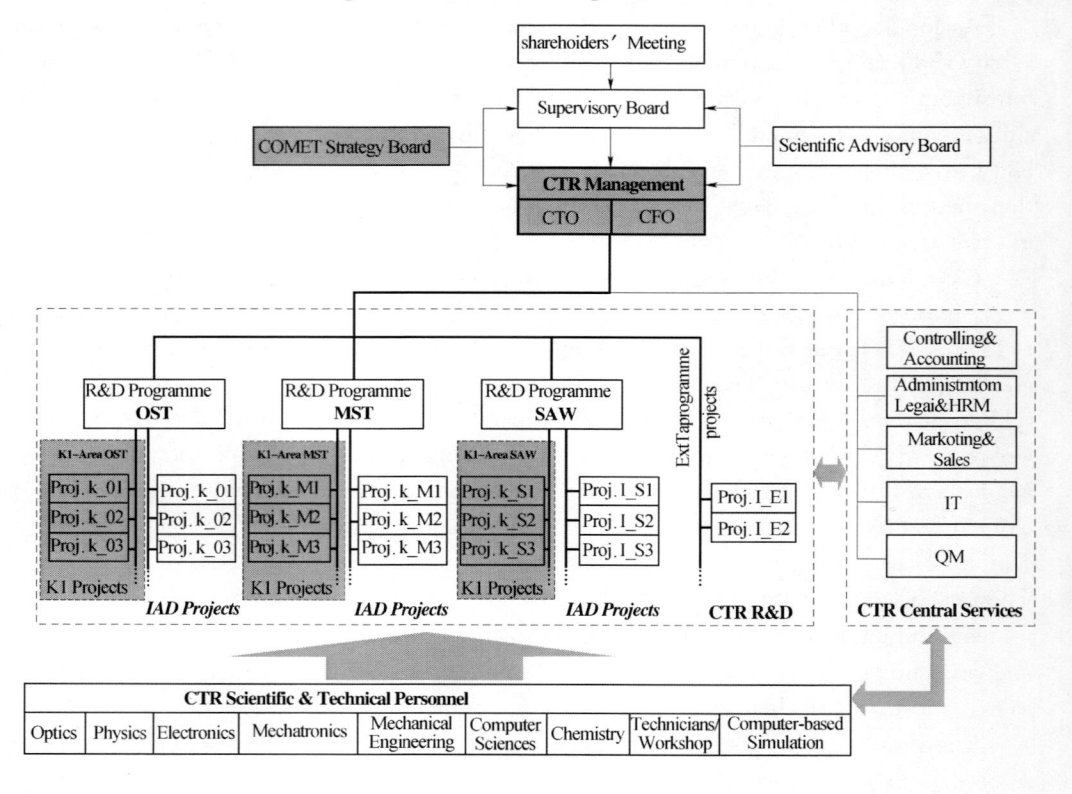

Figure 10   The internal organization CTR

Source: CTR (2008)

The Organization of Collaboration On the Different Levels

See also *Section 5.2.2*. The organization of collaboration on different levels in CTR (i.e. researchers, project leader, key researcher, area manager, CTR management) was planned in the application phase already. The complete research programme is organized on the basis of projects. In the application phase concrete research projects are defined, including resources and personnel. The project leader is responsible for the realization of the objectives of a project. The key researcher controls all projects within one research area and reports to the area manager. The area manager reports the state of the projects to the management and can suggest thematic changes or new projects together with the key researcher.

The Organization of the Operational Plan, Selection of Tasks/Projects

See also *Section 5. 2. 2.* and *Section 5. 2. 3.* The concrete operational plan for CTR is defined in the project proposal. The proposal involves the detailed research plan at the project level, i. e. the selection of tasks and projects was already discussed between all participating partners in the application phase (Interview C). After the establishment of CTR, new thematic priorities or projects, including new partners, can be suggested by the research area manager and the key researcher to the CTR management (bottom-up). The final decision is then accomplished by the supervisory board. Also the strategy board and the scientific advisory board can recommend new projects, thematic priorities or new partners.

CTR conducts strategic projects, multi-firm projects and single firm projects. Strategic projects are broader with respect to their thematic orientation, but clearly target to enhance the core knowledge base of CTR. In general they involve nearly all CTR participants. Multi-firm projects are more specific and involve at least more than two partners, while single firm projects (14 % of all CTR projects) are very specific research projects including only one partner firm.

In the proposal, the detailed CTR research plan was defined for the first project period covering the first four years. For the second period (three years) another proposal has to be submitted. The operational plan includes personnel, infrastructure and materials that are needed for each project, as well as a timetable. The short-term monitoring of the operational plan (personnel and investment) is done yearly by the CTR management and observed by the supervisory board.

R&D Management, Controlling and Marketing

See also *Section 5. 2. 2.* , *Section 5. 2. 3* and *Section 5. 2. 4.* All projects in CTR are conducted under standardized processes, i. e. all projects are conducted in the same way. Each project shows a clear project plan, including resources, milestones, budget, etc. When a project starts, there is a clear plan on hours worked per researcher, all kind of materials needed, etc. The monthly project controlling is done by the CTR management, with respect to content related and budget issues. A project portfolio management is a crucial governance instrument for the CTR management for the planning of the resources.

Rights and Rules, Codes of Conduct and Flow of Information

The CTR proposal, including LOI (letter of interest) and LOC (letter of commitment) for each participating partner, was the basis for the formulation of a consortium agreement. By signing the agreement, rights and rules are obligatory for the partners, i. e. , they have to provide the agreed resources-as for instance in form of cash, personnel or infrastructure-according to the agreement. Also the entry and exit of partners is regulated in the agreement. The formulation of the agreement is crucial, and was quite difficult in the case of CTR due to different interests of participants (Interview C). In addition, project specific contracts regulate the financial flows in a specific project between a partner and the CTR.

Key rules concern the IPR and publication regulations. IPR in CTR are regulated quite similar as in the case of ACCM and MPPE: For multi-firm projects, participating partners have to define a very specific thematic area, for which they are contributing R&D. Project outputs that can be assigned to this specific area belong solely to the respective partner. Project outputs that cannot be assigned to any predefined area is owned by CTR. However, all participating partners in CTR can get access to this knowledge via licensing. The rights for preliminary knowledge of one partner that is contributed to a project stays exclusively in the ownership of this partner. In the case of strategic projects (see *Section 5. 2. 4*), rights for the produced knowledge belong exclusively to CTR, but participating firms can get access to this knowledge via licensing. In general, firms are satisfied with the CTR regulations concerning IPR, because they usually want to concentrate on their specific thematic priority (Interview C). In the case of single-firm projects, the rights for the produced knowledge are exclusively owned by the respective partner.

Concerning rules for publications, each partner of the consortium that wants to publish project results or preliminary project outcomes has to inform the project leader about the planned publication. The project leader informs all participating CTR partners. Partners can oppose against the publication within four weeks, accompanied by a detailed justification for the opposition (for instance, if secrecy is preferred until this new knowledge is patented). If this is not the case, the publication can be realized. It can be noted that, in general, industry partners are skeptical concerning a high publication intensity. However, they are aware that the objectives of CTR, including publications, have to be realized in order to secure funding (Interview C).

4.3.3 Analysis of Relationships

This Section describes in some detail the historical background of CTR and the establishment of relationships between the core actors.

Identification of CTR Core Actors, Initiators

The CTR COMET area is composed of 17 partners from the industry sector, and nine partners from the science sector. Core actor-in particular with respect to the initial establishment of CTR-is Infineon Technologies, one of the leading international firms in the field. Other core actors from industry include AVL List, RHI and Beckman Coulter. Concerning firm size, CTR shows a quite balanced distribution, including smaller regional partners. From the science sector, the core actors are the University of Freiburg (Germany), the University of Technology Delft (Netherlands), the Vienna University of Technology and the Fraunhofer-Gesellschaft (Germany).

Evolution of Their Relationships

CTR is characterized-similar to the other cases-by a long-time evolution of the relationships between the core actors, at different levels, including the regional policy level, but also the scientific level. This involves, for instance, earlier joint projects between participating partners. It has to be noted that the formal establishment was not straight-forward. Even for large firms it is not easy to plan R&D budgets for a period of four years, which, however, has to be done in the Letter of Commitment (LOC). Balancing the consortium agreement between 17 partners was a huge amount of work for the CTR management, since the concrete formulation of the rights and rules had to be discussed with each partner's legal administration.

The Role of Related Government Bodies

First, the relationship is obviously given by the composition of the shareholders, that are regional government bodies (see also *Section 5.2.1*). Second, CTR has the same relation to national government bodies, which is represented by the FFG, as ACCM and MPPE. This concerns the selection process, but also the monitoring and the evaluation of CTR (see also *Section 2.3*).

The History of the Centre/Alliance

Initially, CTR was a regional policy initiative of the province Carinthia and the municipality of Villach. These actors founded a non-profit association in the year 1997 that should carry out research in the field of intelligent sensors. The selection of the actual thematic field in this region was based on a study of the Austrian Research Centres (Interview C). The structure of the regional economy fits quite well (in particular because of the presence of Infineon Technologies that was a leading driver in this context). The association was transferred to an LLC, and then became the first K-Plus centre of Austria (1998), i.e. was funded the Austrian Centres of Competence Programme, the preceding programme of COMET.

4.3.4 Knowledge Generation and Technology Diffusion in CTR

This section provides an overview of inputs into the knowledge generation process of CTR, and presents some figures on the concrete objectives and knowledge outputs.

Joint Resources for Knowledge Production

The by far most substantial input for knowledge generation in CTR is related to human resources. *Table 16* presents the CTR human capital for the years 2007 and 2008. Scientific background of CTR scientific staff is diversified, with a special emphasis on physics and electronics. At present, 23 researchers are directly employed at CTR. They work on projects according to the operational plan together with 89 researchers from participating partners (not employed at CTR). Mobility of researchers plays a crucial role. Most of the scientific staff comes from universities (about 80%) (Interview C). Further, transfer of personnel from CTR to participating firms plays an important role, which is in the context of human resource development an important quality criterion of CTR.

CTR uses rented premises of about 1900 square metres at one location, the Villach Technology Park, including specific laboratories (optical laboratories, laser laboratories, mechatronic and electronic laboratories). The CTR investment in infrastructure in 2007 equals to 180 thousand EUR, to 150 thousand EUR for 2008. The financial funding of CTR within the COMET programme is about 14 Mio EUR for the first funding period of four years. The yearly budget depends on the planned project volumes.

Table 16　　　　　　　　　　　**Human capital of CTR**

Staff employed at CTR*	2007	2008
Total	37	34
Scientific staff	23	23
Technical staff	4	3
Administration (management, controlling, etc.)	10	9
Number of young scientists		
Trainees	4	9
Dissertation students	3	3
Master students	7	7
Staff working on CTR projects (but not employed at CTR)	89	89

Source: CTR (2008)

Management and Diffusion of Collaboration Outputs

The management and diffusion of collaboration outputs is regulated in the consortium agreement and in project specific contracts, for instance, with respect to IPR rules and publications. The aspired output of CTR is outlined in the project proposal; results will be evaluated by the FFG after four years. As for the other cases, knowledge produced in CTR diffuses via publications and patents to the regional and Austrian innovation system and the international scientific community. *Table 17* presents the aspired output (2008-2011), while *Table 18* summarizes outputs for 2007 and 2008.

Table 17   Aspired CTR Outputs for the First Funding Period

	2008—2011
Research results	
Publications in scientific journals	130
Patents and licences	20
Research programme	
Share of strategic projects	15%
Additionality	
Increase of research intensity of firm partners	37.2%
Human resources	
Advanced trainings	48
Dissertations (graduated)	7
Dissertations (on track)	4
Master thesis (graduated)	20
Master thesis (on track)	8
Innovations	
Product innovations	18
Process innovations	7
Costs and budget	
Share of overheads	15%
Acquisition of third party funds	6 Mio EUR

Source: CTR (2008)

Table 18   CTR Knowledge Outputs (2007 and 2008)

	2007	2008
Publications		
Scientific journals	5	15
Conference proceedings	12	18
Books	1	2
Others	5	1
Patents		20
Applied	2	3
Granted	1	4
Innovations		
Product innovations	—	3
Process innovations	—	5
Participation		
Exhibitions	15	17
Scientific workshops and conferences	—	2
Education		
Dissertations (graduated)	1	—
Dissertations (on track)	3	7
Master thesis (graduated)	1	4
Master thesis (on track)	3	3

Source: CTR (2008)

4.3.5 Institutional Conditions: Laws and Regulations

This section provides a short overview on the compatibility of institutional conditions with the establishment of CTR. Information on the general legal framework are outlined in *Section 2.2.2*.

Compatibility with Present Laws and Regulations in Different Fields

From the viewpoint of the CTR management, the present law shows no barriers to the establishment and continuation of CTR. The employment law provides a reasonable framework for personnel transfer between universities, firms and CTR. The employment of the researchers is clearly regulated by the Austrian employment law. Concerning tax regulation, for non-COMET research, CTR can utilize the so-called "Forschungsfreibetrag" -tax exemption for research-of the Austrian tax law that allows innovating firms to upset their R&D

expenditures against tax up to 25% (Interview C).

Assessment of the Effects of the Institutional Conditions

In general, the institutional conditions provide a suitable environment to establish competence centres like CTR. In particular, the interplay between national and regional interests seems to be balanced, not leading to challenging hurdles for the establishment of such centres. The present legislations, such as the employment law or the tax law, provide no explicit and exclusive incentives for establishing a centre like CTR, but are compatible with the objectives of the COMET programme and the specific centre.

4.3.6 Financing and Administration of Funds

This section shortly introduces the CTR financing model, the basic financial management of CTR.

Model of Financing and Cost Sharing

The main component of the CTR budget is given by the COMET funding that shows a share of 55% of the total budget. The so-called non-COMET area (45% of total Budget) is assembled by other external funds (about 15%), such as EU projects, and by industrial contract research (about 20%). The remaining 10% are covered by the basic financial contributions of the (public) shareholders.

The COMET area provides financial funding of 14 Mio EUR for the first funding period (four years). 55% are provided by public sources, composed of national funds (30%) and provincial funds (20%). 5% are contributions from universities. The latter is provided in-kind, including personnel and physical capital, such as equipment and materials. The other 45% come from the participating firms, whereas 60% of the firm contributions are provided in cash.

Ways of Managing and Using Financial Resources

CTR uses the same compulsory elements of a Public Limited Company to administer the financial resources, as given by the CTR central services, in particular controlling and accounting. Budgetary issues are executed by the CTR management and controlled by the shareholders' meeting and the supervisory board (see *Section 5.2.2* and *5.2.5* for further details).

4.4 Summary of Austrian COMET Cases

The program COMET is the most prominent programme to support the cooperation between enterprises, universities and R&D institutions in Austria. It builds on the experiences of the preceding programme, the Austrian Centre of Competencies (CCP) with special support to those research activities which operate at the cutting-edge and which also promise a high international profile.

The empirical results reported in this study show that the Austrian COMET programme provides a suitable framework for the establishment of high-quality science-industry collaboration at an international visible level. The strategic goal of COMET in the short- and medium-term is to intensify cooperation between science and industry building on the established competence centres of the preceding programme. The long-term strategic goal of COMET is to foster international excellence in specific research fields, to expand and to secure technological leadership of Austrian firms, and to strengthen Austria as a research location.

In terms of organizational structure, the COMET partners are connected by a joint agreement. COMET centres are intended to form an independent corporation (non-profit corporate body) in order to ease financial funding and to foster resource sharing inside COMET. This should stimulate the building up of a long-term and stable community for cooperation between enterprises, universities and R&D institutions.

The empirical study on the Austrian cases provides in-depth insight into internal governance structures at different levels of collaboration, ranging from the project level to the programme level. The organizational models of the selected cases show various similarities, as for instance concerning IPR regulations, but also significant differences, as for instance with respect to the legal organizational form and the organization of employment of researchers. The results also clearly show that all selected COMET centres were initiated on the basis of already established, intensive and fruitful cooperation activities of the core partners. The funding of COMET centres is based on public and private funds. 55% are provided by public sources, composed of national funds (30%) and provincial funds (20%). 5% are contributions from universities. In what follows, we briefly reflect on the main similarities and dissimilarities of the Austrian cases, the ACCM, MPPE and CTR

i. Goal and organizational structure: Concerning the strategic goals and organisational structure we observe significant similarities between all three selected cases. However, the larger K2-centres (ACCM and MPPE) lay more emphasis on international visibility and global scientific competitiveness than the smaller K1-centre (CTR), though also CTR has international partners. With respect to the organizational structure, the three centres followed the suggestion of the FFG and formed an independent legal corporation. ACCM and MPPE are non-profit limited liability companies (LLC) while CTR forms a Public Limited Company

(PLC).

ii. Governance structure and rights and responsibilities: The three selected cases show similar but not identical organisational structures. Crucial elements for the governance of the selected cases are the shareholders' meeting, the supervisory board and COMET strategy board. The latter is of particular importance to integrate different rationalities of participating actors. In all cases, the supervisory board controls the COMET management which is responsible for common affairs, such as project setup, selection and supervision. MPPE has in contrast to the other cases one additional body, namely the programme committee that supports the MPPE management in questions related to the research programme and has the character of an advisory panel.

Concerning the project administration in the selected cases, some notable dissimilarities occur. In ACCM all researchers working on ACCM projects are employed by ACCM partners, while in the other two cases a considerable number of researchers is employed directly be the centre. These different strategies may be related to different opportunities for providing incentives for leading researchers to join a COMET centre.

iii. The organisation on the project level is similar for all selected cases: In general we can distinguish between more basic-oriented strategic research projects and more application oriented multi-firm and single firm projects. These classes of projects differ not only with respect to the scientific activity but also with respect to the IPR rules. Results of strategic research projects belong to the centre, while results of multi-firm or single-firm projects usually belong to the participating partners in the project. Note that ACCM has no single firm project. The project itself is subject to the project team leader. Projects are organised along research areas headed by the area manager and consisting of one key researcher.

iv. The composition of funds concerning the COMET centres under consideration is similar. Public support is a significant component of a centres budget. 55% of the budget of the COMET centres is provided by public sources, composed of national funds (30%), provincial funds (20%) and university funds (5%). The latter is provided in-kind, including personnel and physical capital, such as equipment and materials. The other 45% come from the participating firms, whereas 50% of the firm contributions are to be provided in cash. In all three cases about tow third of the firm contributions are provided in cash, the rest is provided in-kind, including personnel and physical capital, such as equipment and materials. In the MPPE case, it is notable that some firms prefer 100% contribution in cash, while other firms contribute 100% in-kind. However, as a rule set up for COMET, the overall contribution of all company partners can be generated by at maximum 50% in-kind contribution.

v. The consortium agreement is the basis of cooperation for all COMET centres under consideration. It regulates overall responsibilities, such as the entry or exit of partners. By signing this agreement, rights and rules are obligatory for the partners, i.e. they have to provide the agreed resources-as for instance in form of cash, personnel or infrastructure-according to the agreement. In general, the main streams of the agreement are similar across the selected cases, as for instance the regulation of IPRs, the governance structures or the organisation of the research plan.

5 Comparative Analysis of Chinese and Austrian Cases

In this section we reflect on the comparative analysis of the selected Chinese ITISA and Austrian COMET cases. The analysis discloses considerable differences, but also some similarities between the policy programmes. It is worth emphasising that the results of the comparative analysis enrich our understanding of both Austrian and Chinese policy programmes to foster science-industry cooperation, and provide significant implication both for the Chinese and Austrian science and technology policy. In the next section we discuss the similarities between the Chinese ITISA and the Austrian COMET cases, before we summarize the main differences. This section serves as a basis for the formulation of policy conclusions and follow-up projects in the final section of this report.

5.1 Similarities

Both programmes, ITISA and COMET, are the most prominent examples for policy initiatives to support and shape cooperation between enterprises, universities and R&D institutions in China and in Austria. Both were introduced recently, ITISA 2006 and COMET 2007, following the attention paid by both governments on the importance of strategic alliances and institutional structures for cooperation between science and industry, leading to substantial governmental strategic guidance and support featuring significant novel properties as compared to earlier programmes. There is a competitive selection process for strategic alliances and competence centres, respectively.

Some basic goals of the two programmes are similar, namely to:
- address the missing link between the science and the industry sector in the innovation system.
- by supporting the formation of platforms for science industry cooperation in a specific thematic or generic technological field.

- The platforms are intended to have a clear strategic orientation in scientific and economic terms, and certain organisational models.
- The creation and management of intellectual property (IP) is crucial.

With regard to operational mechanisms, an essential element of both ITISA and COMET is that the cooperation of participants within an alliance or centre is regulated by an alliance-specific- and centre-specific collaboration agreement, respectively. With regard to operational mechanisms of the research plan of an alliance/Competence centre, we can identify the following similarities.

- Governance structures in ITISA alliances and COMET centres show some similar features, such as specific bodies for scientific advisory and for project administrations and R&D management.
- Both Chinese ITISA alliances and Austrian COMET centres implement their research plans at the level of concrete projects. A project team leader is responsible for the execution of a projects.
- Both ITISA alliances and COMET centres feature core units/organisations who are legally responsible for the organisation and management of cooperation and conflicts between all partners.

Concerning the key objectives of an alliance or centre, we were able to identify few similarities only that can be summarized as follows. Both ITISA alliances and COMET centres

- aim to carry out R&D activities according to concrete needs for generic technologies.
- stimulate knowledge exchange and mutual learning leading to the transfer of tacit knowledge between the participating actors.
- aim to integrate R&D resources of all relevant actors in a specific technological and scientific field of activity, in particular between universities and firms.
- stimulate researcher mobility between participating actors, again with special emphasis on researcher mobility between the university and the industry sector, and.
- educate and train young researchers in the specific technological field of the alliance/centre.

These common characteristics of the alliances/centres are of particular importance in the context of the policy goal to stimulate knowledge spillovers, on the one hand, between the participating actors of an alliance/centre, but on the other hand also from the alliance/centre to the innovation system and the economy as such.

Concerning the establishment of an alliance/centre it is notable that in both cases the earlier cooperative behaviour between the participating partners plays a tremendous role.

When an alliance or centre is established, usually the core partners have been already cooperating with each other in different forms earlier. This is both in ITISA and COMET also of particular importance for raising the necessary additional funds to the public funding in order to establish an alliance or a centre. A further similarity of the two programmes is that governmental funding is crucial for the establishment of an ITISA alliance and a COMET centre, respectively.

Further similarities between ITISA alliances and COMET centres have been identified concerning the problem of different rationalities and motivations for partners to participate in an alliance/centre. They can be summarized as follows.

- Problems that impede the integration of different rationalities are to a large extent related to different drivers that motivate firms and research institutions to participate in an alliance/centre.
- Firms often seek for concrete solutions for specific technological problems, while universities aim to improve their scientific reputation.
- This is also reflected by the fact that usually firms prefer secrecy concerning the publication of new results, while universities prefer publishing new results as early as possible.
- In both ITISA alliances and COMET centres, the pre-establishment phase, the consortium agreement and the governance structure are essential components to overcome these different rationalities.

Concerning IPR and publication rules, for both ITISA and COMET the agreement is of central importance. In both countries, governmental authorities that are in charge of ITISA and COMET, respectively, have explicitly noted that a clear regulation of IPRs outlined in the consortium agreement and signed by all partners is a sine-qua-non condition for establishing public funding for an alliance/centre.

Both countries are aware that policy programmes such as ITISA or COMET require also innovations concerning the legal and regulatory framework, as for instance.

- tax regulation, and
- R&D promotion acts

as well as

- infrastructure policies, and
- general financial support

At present, in both countries, the establishment of an alliance/centre complies with the national laws and regulations and has been fully supported by existing laws and regulations and applicable policies. However, some ambiguities remain concerning tax laws in both countries. Tax reduction or exemption policy towards R&D spending on projects of the alliance/centre needs to be detailed and improved.

5.2　Differences

When it comes to differences between the Chinese ITISA and the Austrian COMET programme, the empirical results of the case study reports provide clear evidence for differences at various levels, ranging from the overall policy design level in a wider technology policy context, the level of programme design to differences on the micro-level, i. e. the level of the alliance/centre and the participating partners in the alliance/centre. Concerning the overall policy design, the main differences are as follows:

- Austrian policy programmes clearly follow a bottom-up approach with respect to the thematic orientation of a centre, i. e. the thematic orientation a centre is proposed by the applying partners, and thus strongly related to the industrial structure of Austria.
- In contrast, the thematic orientation of an ITISA alliance is in most cases to be connected to the eleven thematic priorities mentioned in *the Mid and Long Term Science and Technology Development Plan* (2006—2020) of China. In addition, bottom-up initiatives of alliances are possible and existent.
- An ITISA alliance is not an independent legal person, but organised as an association of partners based on an legal agreement, a COMET centre is strongly encouraged to form a legal company. This is closely associated with the requirements made by the FFG since audit and control of public funds is much easier accomplished when a centre is represented by a legal company and can be held liable for compliance of contracts. Moreover, the existence of non-profit companies in the legal system of Austria is an important precondition. This means that certain tax incentives can be applied to companies which are not set up for the purpose of profit maximisation but to take advantage of the efficiency gains through corporate governance in companies.
- Austrian policy provides continuous public funding for COMET centres, while Chinese government provides strategic guidance and public competitive funds to selected alliances. So far no strategic alliance receives continuous funds from Chinese government.
- By this, ITISA alliances are intended to focus on national priorities in an economic

policy context and with respect to wider societal challenges. Thus, in a Chinese policy context an intensive combination of technology-, economic- and infrastructure policy can be observed.

At the level of the programme, the comparative analysis of the empirical results reveals significant differences mainly related to internationalisation, the selection mechanisms of alliances/centres and the evaluation procedures. The main differences are the following:

- The COMET programme shows a significant international orientation, allowing and even encouraging the consortium to include major international players in a COMET centre.
- In the Chinese case, the ITISA-programme is directly managed by the ministries that are in charge of the programme, while the administration of COMET is transferred to an independent funding agency (FFG).
- While ITISA is at the current stage limited to Chinese partners and lays particular emphasis on domestically advanced technological fields.
- COMET centres are subject to a systematic and detailed evaluation procedure by the FFG based on a clearly defined set of evaluation indicators. For the ITISA alliances no systematic and comprehensive evaluation exists until now.
- This is also related to the fact, that COMET explicitly aims to establish centres reaching scientific excellence in high-tech sectors at an international level.
- While the ITISA alliance are more oriented on national technological, economic and or societal challenges.
- This leads to differences in the selection mechanisms between COMET and ITISA. In ITISA the selection of an alliance is connected to the thematic priorities outlined in the *Mid and Long Term Science and Technology Development Plan (2006—2020) of China*.
- While in COMET the selection mechanism is to a large extent triggered by the validation of the level of scientific excellence in form of strict international peer review processes.

Despite these differences at the overall policy level and the level of programme design, the study identifies numerous important differences at the level of the alliances/centres. In what follows we briefly summarize the most important differences at the alliance/centre level.

- With the organisation of COMET centres as legal companies, they can easily employ full-time staff for the management of a centre and researchers working on projects under the heading of the respective COMET centre. In contrast, ITISA has no spe-

cialized executive branch and is unable to engage full time staff. The staff in the secretariat of an ITISA alliance is either employed by the lead-organization or other member organizations of an ITISA alliance.
- Since COMET centres are usually established as legal companies, the corporate governance structure is very clear featuring the compulsory elements according the EU company laws. The non-corporate body of ITISA alliances allows on the one hand partners to maintain comparatively higher independence in the alliance, but on the other hand may lead to problems with respect to rights and liabilities.
- The composition of the funds for an alliance/centre differs significantly. The share of public funds of total funds for a COMET centre is higher than the share of public funding for ITISA alliances. In COMET centres, up to 55% of total funding comes from public resources that are relatively easy transferred to a COMET centre since it is an independent legal person. For ITISA alliance the share of public funding is considerably lower. Thus, total funding of ITISA alliances is to large extent raised by the members of the alliance. Furthermore, public funds in ITISA are directly appropriated to a specific project within an alliance, and, thus, to specific project participants instead of the alliance for centralized allocation. A prominent example in this context is the Caofeidian project in the SARSPTI alliance that is directly supported by governmental funds.
- There are differences concerning the evaluation of alliances/centres. COMET centres are subject to a very systematic and detailed evaluation procedure by the FFG based on a clearly defined set of evaluation indicators. The systematic assessment system of FFG for COMET consists of pre-assessment, intermediate assessment and terminal assessment. The evaluation of a COMET centre is linked with its ongoing financial support. For the ITISA alliances no systematic and comprehensive evaluation exists until now. Thus, the assessment and effective monitoring of as alliance is yet to be developed and enhanced.
- Significant differences also occur with respect to IPR regulations. This is also strongly related to the fact that COMET centres are usually independent legal companies. While in ITISA alliances the rights for new results are split proportionally between participating partners in a project, in COMET we can identify different IPR rules for different project types. The main difference is that the centre itself is able to hold patents as independent legal company. This is usually the case for strategic projects in COMET centres.

5.3 Summary of the Comparative Analysis

In this section we integrate the similarities and differences between COMET centres and ITISA alliances in compact form. *Table 19* summarizes the main results and comprises the main features of ITISA alliances as compared to COMET centres along the empirical framework. The results of the comparative analysis considerably enrich our understanding of ITISA and COMET, and provide significant implications both for the Chinese and Austrian science and technology policy.

Table 19 Main Dimensions of Comparison between ITISA and COMET

Dimension	China/ITISA	Austria/COMET
Overall policy context		
Establishment approach	• Introduced in 2006 following the attention paid by the government on the importance of institutional structures for cooperation between science and industry • leading to substantial governmental strategic guidance and support • featuring significant novel properties as compared to earlier programmes. • Oriented on national economic and societal challenges • Thematic orientation along the eleven national thematic priorities*	• Introduced in 2007 following the attention paid by the government on the importance of institutional structures for cooperation between science and industry • leading to substantial governmental strategic guidance and support • featuring significant novel properties as compared to earlier programmes • Bottom-up approach, thematically open, self organisation by applicants • Addressing structural deficits of the innovation system
Programme Management	• Ministries	• Agency
Programme design		
Scope	• Formation of concrete platforms for cooperation between science and industry • National priorities in economic policy • Emphasis on domestically advanced technologies	• Formation of concrete platforms for cooperation between science and industry • International scientific excellence

Dimension	China/ITISA	Austria/COMET
Selection mechanism	• Competitive selection process • Related to eleven national thematic priorities and • national priorities in economic- and infrastructure policy	• Competitive selection process • Focus on scientific excellence of the application • Based on an international peer review process
Evaluation	• Loose evaluation procedures	• Systematic ex-ante-, interim-, and ex-post evaluation • based on a set of evaluation indicators
Level of alliances/centres		
Strategic goals	• Alliances should have clear scientific goals and strategic orientation • Integration of R&D resources of all relevant actors in a specific field, in particular between universities and firms • Provide solutions for specific national economic sectors • Stimulation of knowledge exchange and mutual learning among partners • Stimulation of researcher mobility	• Centres should have clear scientific goals and strategic orientation • Integration of R&D resources of all relevant actors in a specific field, in particular between universities and firms • Carry out R&D activities at an international level • Stimulation of knowledge exchange and mutual learning among partners • Stimulation of researcher mobility
Organisational form	• Association based on legal agreements	• Legal company according to the Austrian company law
Corporate governance	• Leading organisation is crucial • Secretariat in charge of the management usually under the heading of the leading organisation • Specific bodies for scientific advice • Problems of different rationalities are related to different drivers that motivate organisations to participate	• Compulsory elements of a legal company according the Austrian company law • Management employed at the centre • Specific bodies for scientific advice • Problems of different rationalities are related to different drivers that motivate organisations to participate
Actors	• Industry, universities and research organisations • Earlier cooperative behaviour between the participating partners plays a tremendous role • Core units for the management of the alliance are crucial	• Industry, universities and research organisations • Earlier cooperative behaviour between the participating partners plays a tremendous role • Core units for the management of the centre are crucial

续表

Dimension	China/ITISA	Austria/COMET
Rights and Rules	• Consortium agreement is essential	• Consortium agreement is essential
IPRs	• Agreement for the usage of results is to be regulated in the alliance • Rights are split between participating members of a project	• Centre can hold patents • Different IPR regulation for different types of projects: strategic projects-the centre owns the results, but each partner has access via licensing; multi-firm projects-results owned by firms for specific thematic areas
Publications	• Publication strategy is to be considered by participating partners of a project	• Results of strategic projects have no limits for publication • Firm partners usually have the opportunity to object against the publication of results
Project management	• Research plans is accomplished at the level of concrete projects • No project classification. Project management is to be enhanced	• Research plans is accomplished at the level of concrete projects • Centres have classification of projects: strategic projects, multi-firm projects and single-firm projects.
Knowledge resources	• Human capital and researcher mobility is of central importance • Education and training of young researchers	• Human capital and labour mobility is of central importance • Education and training of young researchers
Funding	• Higher share of funds provided by members than by the public • Specific projects within the alliance are publicly funded	• 55% public funds, 45% from the members • As legal companies, centres are allowed to apply for additional funding from other sources, such as the European Framework Programmes
Laws	• The establishment of an alliance/centre complies with the national laws • Some ambiguities remain concerning tax laws	• The establishment of an alliance/centre complies with the national laws • Some ambiguities remain concerning tax laws

* Note: The eleven thematic priorities are outlined in the Mid and Long Term Science and Technology Development Plan (2006—2020) of China

6 Conclusions and Outlook

Collaboration between enterprises, universities and R&D institutions is widely considered as one of the most important aspects of the innovation system (see, for instance, *Koschatzky 2002*). Several empirical and theoretical contributions as well as relevant policy briefs argue that the innovation capability of firms, regions and countries is linked with the level and quality of collaboration between scientific institutions and the industry sector. Thus, it is of crucial importance to get a deeper understanding on the mechanisms of such collaborations.

The current study aims to shed some light on policy programmes for cooperation between enterprises, universities and research institutions in China and Austria. The focus of study is to compare Chinese and Austrian policy initiatives in this direction, and to compare real-world organizational models for cooperation, in China as realized by alliances under the heading the Industry Technology Innovation Strategic Alliances (ITISA) programme, in Austria is realized by the Austrian Programme on Competence Centers for Excellent Technologies (COMET). The results of the comparative analysis provide significant implications in a Chinese and Austrian policy context.

In the subsection that follows we focus on the general findings of the empirical analysis that are crucial for the Chinese and the Austrian case, before we elaborate on conclusions in a Chinese and Austrian policy context, respectively. Finally we sum up the main results and highlight some aspects of a future research agenda in the context of the current project.

6.1 General Findings

ITISA and COMET are the most prominent examples of policy initiatives to support the cooperation between enterprises, universities and research organisations in China and Austria, respectively. Both programmes are important publicly supported initiatives for the formation of concrete platforms for science industry cooperation in specific industrial and/or scientific fields. While ITISA is more oriented towards specific national economic and societal challenges, COMET follows a thematically open bottom-up approach and addresses structural deficits of the Austrian innovation systems. However, both programmes aim to integrate and bundle relevant R&D resources of all actors within a cooperative platform.

The project draws on empirical results from a case study approach by investigating organisational models of three ITISA alliances and three COMET centres, respectively. The Chinese ITISA cases analysed include the Technology Innovation Promotion Alliance for Agricultural Machinery Industry (TIPAAMI), the Industry Technology Innovation Strategic Alliances for New-Generation Coal (Energy) and Chemicals (ITISANCC), and the Strategic Alliances for Recycling Steel Processes Technology Innovation (SARSPTI). the Austrian COMET cases are the Austrian Centre of Competence of Mechatronics (ACCM), the Centre on Integrated Research in Materials, Processing and Product Engineering (MPPE), and the Carinthian Tech Research Centre for Advanced Sensor Technologies (CTR).

The analysis produces significant results, both in the context of the actual scientific literature as well as in a Chinese and Austrian policy context. Furthermore, the study produces several general findings that are relevant both for the Chinese and the Austrian case. These can be summarized as follow:

i. Both ITISA alliances and COMET centres are institutionalized models for the organisation of cooperation between science and industry.

ii. and are suitable for supporting technological innovation in the context of the specific conditions of the Chinese and Austrian innovation systems.

iii. The ITISA and COMET experiences show that institutional innovations are necessary to support the efficiency and effectiveness of such programmes for science industry cooperation.

iv. Continuous financial support from government and/or other public or private sources is necessary to ensure the realisation of innovation goals and a sustainable development of alliances/centres.

v. Effective cooperation between science and industry needs careful consideration of the intrinsic interests of each partner in the management of intellectual property.

vi. Alliances/centres are innovative organisational models for the cooperation of universities, firms and research organisations. Continuous development of alliances/centres is necessary to take into account the lessons learnt from previous experiences.

vii. To do so, systematic evaluation and supervision are necessary for a sustainable development of alliances/centres.

viii. Furthermore, the practice of policy development significantly profits from international comparison of good practice between countries.

These general findings may be structured into more detailed sub-findings. The finding that both ITISIA and COMET are suitable models for the organization of cooperation between science and industry is to a large extent related to the capability of such organisational forms.

i. to foster the development of human resources in the context of industrial needs.

ii. to encourage and ease researchers mobility between firms, universities and research organizations.

iii. to stimulate knowledge flows und mutual learning between actors participating in an alliance/centre,

iv. as well as knowledge spillovers to the national innovation system, and,

v. to take into account and address industrial needs in technology and innovation policies.

vi. as well as combining relevant infrastructure policies with RTI-policies.

Besides these overall general findings, the empirical results bear different policy implications for both the Chinese and Austria policy makers. In what follows we reflect on Chinese policy conclusions, before we focus on Austrian implications in a policy context.

6.2 Conclusions Regarding Chinese Policies

Based on the results of the empirical analysis, consideration should be given to the following points in a Chinese policy context:

i. More systematic consideration is to be given to the strategic orientation and development of ITISA, in particular concerning a clearer mode of the public support of ITISA centres. Furthermore, it is of crucial importance to ensure that the activities of ITISA alliance fit with the strategic objectives of the Chinese policy makers. This may be realised by structuring the ITISA programme into different 'alliance categories', such as the Austrian COMET K2-, K1- and K-lines, and formulating different and clear requirements for each programme line. In this context, it may also be considered that ITISA alliances should form an independent legal company, as it is the case for Austrian COMET centres. This may facilitate the supervision and control of the public investment. However, at the current stage the final form of the organisational model should be left to the members of the cooperative network behind the alliance through negotiation according to the needs arising from different issues.

ii. Enable the possibility to establish bodies with full-time personnel for the management and the operation of an alliance: Specialized bodies and full-time personnel have played an important role in the development of COMET centres and have been approved and promoted by the FFG. In the further development of ITISA, the alliance should also be enabled to establish specialized bodies for management and operation, and to employ full-time personnel that should be responsible for routine affairs and project management of the alliance, coordinating participating partners in advancing R&D of projects and promptly reporting to respective governmental authorities. By this, the management capacity and efficiency of the alliances might be improved considerably.

iii. Establish more systematic programme management of ITISA for evaluation, supervision and further programme coordination: Governments have played an active role both in the development of COMET and ITISA. However, in terms of concrete management role, the supervision and management of COMET by FFG is more systematic and comprehensive. For instance, FFG requests a centre to report its progress. If a centre fails to achieve intended objectives or suffers from other problems, FFG has the authority to stop funding for the next year or even suspend the funding at all. Such an approach should also be taken into account for ITISA, as that can not only ensure proper use of public funds, but also urge the alliance to intensively focus on the announced strategic objectives. This may include a more systematic project management as well as clearer IPR and publication regulations. With respect to the extent of financial support, in view of that of the Austrian experience, more funding may be given to basic projects, such as for instance 50% of the project budget.

iv. Strengthen the central role of the alliance in terms of financial management and the management of property rights: In ITISA, public funds are directly allocated to the leader of a specific project, while in COMET public funds are appropriated directly to the centre and then allocated to the partners by the centre. This ensures smooth implementation of R&D projects and sharing of relevant knowledge outputs. Therefore, in further promoting the development of ITISA, alliances should be authorized to control the application for project funds. This should facilitate centralized R&D at the level of alliances, enhance personnel and knowledge exchange within the alliance, and improve sharing and dissemination of knowledge and technical results.

v. Foster geographical centralization of R&D accomplished by the alliance. It is notable that one requirement of the establishment of COMET centres is to form a legal company that operates at a specific physical location, often in one building. This should enhance the exchange of tacit knowledge via face-to-fact contacts, stimulate the transfer of personnel, enhance mutual learning, and improve the efficacy of R&D. Therefore, during the further development of ITISA, geographically centralized R&D should be employed whenever possible and appropriate according to circumstances.

vi. Implement systematic scientific assessment of the alliance: COMET centre are subject to systematic and intensive evaluation according to a well-defined set of indicators. Particularly the intermediate assessment for the purpose of supervising and controlling the centre management has direct impact on the acquisition of governmental funds for the next year. The assessment criteria are different depending on the classification and objective orientation of a centre. ITISA should follow such an approach and introduce a well-defined and systematic assessment and evaluation system to effectively supervise and control the operation and progress of an alliance. This may realised via service level agreements between an alliance and the government, and by requiring regular intellectual property reports of the alliance.

vii. In the medium-term, ITISA should consider following the COMET example and experience with respect to the internationalisation of the programme. When taking into account the internationalisation of science as a whole, scientific excellence can only be achieved at an international level.

viii. In the long-term, it may be appropriate to allow more bottom-up oriented approaches within ITISA with respect to the thematic orientation of alliances.

6.3　Conclusions Regarding Austrian Policies

Based on the results of the empirical analysis, consideration should be given to the following points in an Austrian policy context.

i. The combination of technology- and industrial policy in the context of ITISA is a notable characteristic from the perspective of the Austrian policy arena. The most prominent example of the case studies analysed in this project may be the 'Caofeidian' project within the SARSPTI alliance. 'Caofeidian' is a major steel mill carrying out research on new metal and steel related technologies. Located in the province of Hebei, 'Caofeidian' is the first steel plant with desalination technology, the design of a recycling model, and a professional production base for high-quality plate and strip. Mainly funded by major Chinese steel companies, 'Caofeidian' is used as platform for R&D activities in the context of the SARSPTI alliance. Such a model may be appropriate also in the Austrian policy context, in particular for the combination of infrastructure policy and technology policy in order to stimulate R&D within public infrastructure projects.

ii. The bottom-up approach concerning the thematic orientation could be transcended by allowing in some cases also a mission oriented top-down approach that defines a certain thematic priority. As in the Chinese case, such an approach may be in some cases also appropriate in Austria in order to address certain economic and/or societal challenges, such as mobility or energy, by the establishment of a COMET centre in such a field.

iii. A more flexible organisation of COMET centres should be aspired. It should be made possible to transfer administrative management activities to third parties, in order to release additional resources for core activities in R&D and management.

iv. It has to be re-assessed whether the effort for the application for establishing a COMET centre is too high and prevents potential core partners from applying. Indications in this direction were observed in the empirical analysis. The application procedure for an ITISA alliance seems to require comparatively lower efforts, which is of course also related to the fact that thematic priorities are already given and that scientific excellence at international level is not the focus. However, for COMET, more smooth and not that costly application requirements and procedures should be aspired in the future.

v. A more extensive usage of indirect R&D promotion via tax exemption for participating partners in a COMET centre should be considered. Furthermore, it is necessary to remove remaining ambiguities with respect to the current tax law situation and the position of COMET centres in this context as non-profit companies.

vi. Since a high international level in scientific terms is an explicit goal of the current COMET centres, the next step would be not only to participate, but to become central network nodes in international research networks in specific thematic fields. This may be articulated as an explicit goal in future programmes.

6.4 Summary and Future Research Agenda

The analysis of organisational models for the cooperation between enterprises, universities and research organizations is of crucial importance for policy makers. This project compared Chinese and Austrian policy programmes to design and shape science-industry cooperation, namely the Chinese Industry Technology Innovation Strategic Alliances (ITISA) programme, and the Austrian Programme on Competence Centers for Excellent Technologies (COMET). The comparison-accomplished both at the overall programme level and at the level of individual cases of science-industry cooperation-produced important results in a scientific and a Chinese and Austrian policy context. It is also noteworthy that an important outcome of the project is the fact that the both research teams from China and Austria, namely from the Chinese Academy of Science and Technology for Development (CASTED) and the Foresight & Policy Development Department of the Austrian Institute of Technology (AIT), were able to create effective discussions and joint considerations leading to a much better understanding of the research results from each country, and finally to rather promising and significant joint project results.

The main results of the project may be briefly summarized as follows: First, The empirical analysis reveals some general findings: Both ITISA alliances and COMET centres are institutionalised models for the organisation of cooperation between science and industry, and are suitable for supporting technological innovation in the context of the specific conditions of the Chinese and Austrian innovation systems. It is shown that continuous financial support from government and/or other public or private sources is necessary to ensure the realisation of innovation goals and a sustainable development of alliances/centres. Second, the study systematically highlights similarities and differences between the Chinese and Austrian policy approach: At the overall policy design, both programmes are explicitly oriented towards establishing support platforms for sustainable science-industry cooperation. COMET strongly requires international scientific excellence and allows the integration of international partners while ITISA is at present limited to national partners. At the micro-level, Austrian COMET centres form an independent legal company while Chinese ITISA alliances are established as associations connected by an collaboration agreement. This leads to different mechanisms concerning the internal and external governance structures of an alliance/centre.

Based on the results of the current project, some significant ideas for a future common research agenda come to mind. Priority should be given to the following agenda.

i. As a pre-condition for further analysis of the effectiveness and impact of ITISA and/or COMET for the Chinese and Austrian (European) innovation system, it may be appropriate to analyse-as a starting point-the relationship between knowledge production, involving spill-over effects, and the economic productivity. At the European level, analyses in this direction point to positive productivity effects of knowledge production in certain industries (see, for instance, Scherngell, Fischer and Reismann 2008). Such an analysis may provide important contributions to the understanding of mechanisms of knowledge diffusion and to formulating implications in the context of the ITISA policy.

ii. The assessment of the effectiveness and impact of ITISA and/or COMET centres is of crucial importance. This includes the formulation of appropriate indicators to monitor and evaluate the alliance/centre, an investigation of the effectiveness of internal and external cooperation and coordination mechanisms by using network analysis techniques, and finally the conceptualization of an empirical model to estimate the influence of ITISA and COMET on the innovative performance of the innovation system.

iii. The establishment of a Foresight platform could be an additional contribution to the evidence-based design of policies for the cooperation between the science and the industry sector.

7 References

ACCM (2008): Agreement regarding the establishment and operation of the Austrian Center of Competence in Mechatronics.

Asheim, B. T., Gertler, M. (2005): The Geography of Innovation: Regional Innovation Systems, in Fagerberg, J., Mowery, D., Nelson, R. (eds.), The Oxford Handbook of Innovation. Oxford University Press, Oxford, 2005, 291—317.

FFG (2008a): Program Document for COMET Competence centers for excellent technologies. Wien, FFG.

FFG (2008b): Evaluation concept of the new competence centers program COMET. Wien, FFG.

Federal Government (2009): Austrian Research and Technology Report 2009, Report of the Federal Government to the Parliament, on federally subsidised research, technology and innovation in Austria.

ITISANCC (2007): Strategic Agreement of cooperation within the ITISA for Industry Technology Innovation Strategic Alliance for New-generation Coal (Energy) Chemical.

Lundvall, B.-Å. (ed.) (1992): National Systems of Innovation. Towards a Theory of Innovation and Interactive Learning. Pinter Publishers, London.

Metcalfe, S. (1995): The Economic Foundations of Technology Policy: Equilibrium and Evolutionary Perspectives", in Stoneman P. (ed.), Handbook of the Economics of Innovation and Technological Change, Blackwell Publishers, Oxford (UK)/Cambridge (US).

MPPE (2008): Agreement of cooperation within the COMET K2 Center for "Materials, Processing and Product Engineering".

OECD (2004): Public-Private Partnerships for Research and Innovation: An Evaluation of the Austrian Experience. Paris, OECD.

SARSPTI (2007): Strategic Agreement of cooperation within the ITISA for Strategic Alliances for Recycling Steel Processes Technology Innovation.

Schartinger, D., Rammer, C., Fischer, M. M., Fr. hlich, J. (2002): Knowledge

Interactions between Universities and Industry in Austria: Sectoral Patterns and Determinants. Research Policy 31, 303-328.

Scherngell, T., Horvat, M., Kubeczko, K., Schartinger, D., Fr.hlich, J. (2009): Organisational Models of Cooperation between Enterprises, Universities and R&D Institutions in Austria: A Case study report. AIT-F&PD report 0194, Vol. 13.

TISAAMI (2007): Strategic Agreement of cooperation within the ITISA for Technology Innovation Strategic Alliance for Agricultural Machinery Industry.

Di Xiaoyan, Zhang Chidong (2011): Study on the Nature, Classification and Government Support for Industrial Technology Innovation Strategic Alliance. Science & Technology Progress and Policy (in Chinese), 28 (9):59-64.

Zhang Chidong, Zheng Chuiyong (2006): Cooperation of Government, firms, university and research institutions: A approach of Technology Innovation. Forum on Economy (in Chinese), 9:60-61.

Zhang Chidong (2012): Management Experiences and Revelation of Austrian Competence Centers of Excellent Technologies Program. Science & Technology Progress and Policy (in Chinese), 29 (12):16-19.

The Comparative Research Team (2011): Comparative Research of Industry-education-research Institutions Cooperation Organization Model of China and Australia. Forum on Science and Technology in China (in Chinese), 8:146-149.

Appendix: List of Interviews

Interview A (March 25, 2009)
Austrian Research Promotion Agency:
Otto Starzer (in charge of COMET), Theresia Vogel-Lahner (Head of SP Structural Programmes).

Interview B (March 26, 2009)
Ministry of Transport, Innovation and Technology (BMVIT):
Rupert Pichler (Head of innovation unit), Gottfried G? ritzer (member of innovation unit).

Interview C (March 30 2009)
Carinthian Tech Research Centre (CTR):
Dr Werner Scherf (CEO), DI Simon Granner (CFO).

Interview D (April 1, 2009)
Centre on Integrated Research in Materials, Processing and Product Engineering (MPPE):
Dr. Richard Schanner (general manager).

Interview E (April, 2009)
Austrian Centre of Competence of Mechatronics (ACCM):
DI Gerald Schatz (Centre management), DI Wilhelm Hofmann (Centre Management).

Interview F (November, 2009)
Ministry of Science and Technology, P. R. China (Most):
Xinnan Li (General Director of Department of Policy and Regulations and NIS Office), Jing Su (Head of Department of Policy and Regulations and NIS Office), Fuqiang Tang (In charge of ITISA).

Interview G (November, 2009)
Industry Innovation Strategic Alliances for Agricultural Equipment (IISAAE):
Dr. Xianfa Fang (general manager), Dr. Haihua Wu (Centre Management).

Interview H (November, 2009)
Industry Innovation Strategic Alliances for Recycling Processes in Iron &Steel Produc-